K

DATE DUE

THEY
HAD A
DREAM

Books by J. Alfred Phelps

Breaking Out: On Becoming More Than I Was

*Chappie: America's First Black Four-Star General,
The Life and Times of Daniel James, Jr.*

On Being Black in America

THEY HAD A DREAM

The Story of African-American Astronauts

J. Alfred Phelps

★
PRESIDIO

Published by Presidio Press
505 B San Marin Dr., Suite 300
Novato, CA 94945-1340

Library of Congress Cataloging-in-Publication Data

Phelps, J. Alfred.
    They had a dream: the story of African-American astronauts / by J. Alfred
Phelps.
        p.   cm.
    Includes bibliographical references (p. 275) and index.
    ISBN 0-89141-497-5 :
    1. Afro-American astronauts—United States—Biography. I. Title.
T5789.85. A1P43 1994
629.45'0092'273—dc2O
[B]   93-20956
                                                                 CIP

The poems titled "The Challenger" by Valerie K. Sorosiak, and "Analyzing the
Data (After the Challenger)", by Perie Longo, reprinted by permission of the authors.
    The poems titled "A Pilot's Point," by Danny Gonzalez, and "Gone," by Stacy
Leabhard, both former sixth graders at the Hollister School in Santa Barbara, Calif.,
first appeared in the 1986 anthology *Under the Bridge of Silence*. Reprinted by
permission of California Poets in the Schools (CPITS).
    Excerpts from the hymn "How Great Thou Art"© 1953 by Manna Music, Inc., 35255
Brooten Road, Pacific City, Ore. 97135. International copyright secured. All rights
reserved. Reprinted by permission.
    Material quoted from the videotape of the MIT memorial service for Dr. Roland
E. McNair on 12 February 1986 used by permission of WCVB-TV, 5 TV Place,
Needham Heights, Mass. 02194-2303.
    Photo of Captain Edward J. Dwight Jr. reprinted by permission of the Bettmann
Archives, 902 Broadway, New York, N.Y. 10010.
    All other photos courtesy NASA unless otherwise credited.

Typography by ProImage
Printed in the United States of America

For Shirley

Like a pearl in space—a pearl in the shell of the universe; like an opal taken from the deep mine of the universe. This is Earth, the pearl of creation—its beauty of blues, browns, greens, and white observed by astronauts on their way to the Moon in *Apollo* flights. As Jim Lovell described it: "In the whole universe, wherever we looked, the only bit of color was back on earth. There we could see the royal blue of the seas, the tans and browns of the land, and the white of the clouds."

—Moritz E. Pape, *The Quest of Man,*
in *Canadian Messenger of the Sacred Heart,*
July 1990

CONTENTS

FOREWORD

As the first African-American astronaut, it is a great pleasure for me to recommend this book to all those interested in the history of black Americans in the astronaut program. This book chronicles the successes as well as the failures of those African Americans who have aspired to fly into space. Their commitment and dedication to America's manned space effort serves as an outstanding example for all who wish to participate in mankind's grandest quest.

Spaceflight is one of the most exciting adventures anyone can undertake. The lack of gravity and the panoramic views out the window provide unique capabilities and a broader perspective of our environment for those who routinely work in space. Learning to softly push off walls and ceilings as one travels about the cockpit is both a fun and an exhilarating experience.

As a mission-specialist astronaut who has made four spaceflights, I have participated in a wide variety of extraterrestrial activities. These have included deploying and retrieving satellites, operating the shuttle's robotic arm, and conducting hundreds of experiments in an orbiting space laboratory. All of these efforts have had an immense benefit to all mankind as we learned more and more about America's newest frontier.

I, as well as my fellow African-American astronauts, are very proud to be the subjects of this book and to serve as role models for future generations. We hope that our drive and commitment to excellence will serve as examples for all who want to continue the exploration of space. The lessons learned from our efforts can be applied by all those who set high personal and professional goals in their search for success.

Guion S. Bluford, Jr., Colonel, USAF
Lyndon B. Johnson Space Center
Houston, Texas

ACKNOWLEDGMENTS

The author wishes to thank the following persons who helped with this project:

Colonels Frederick D. Gregory, USAF; Charles F. Bolden, USMC; Guion S. Bluford, USAF; and Bernard A. Harris, M.D., and Mae C. Jemison, M.D., all astronauts at the Lyndon B. Johnson Space Center in Houston, Texas.

Edward J. Dwight, Jr., the first African American selected to become an astronaut, provided many telephone interviews.

Thanks are also due Barbara Schwartz and Lisa Vasquez of the LBJ Space Center for their help in scheduling interviews and securing many NASA photographs, as well as to Joseph D. Atkinson, Ph.D., coauthor of *The Real Stuff,* and a NASA official at the LBJ Space Center, for his valuable insights.

Archivist Lee Saegasser and Curtis M. Graves, Ph.D., deputy for civil affairs at NASA headquarters in Washington, D.C., helped get research for this book on the right track.

John J. Rinkus and Cheryl Gumm at Edwards Air Force Base, California, were a great help, as were Commandant of Midshipmen Capt. Michael J. Haskins, Lt. (jg) Kelly L. Merrell, and Mary Thorese at the United States Naval Academy.

John Payne and Maurer Porter helped me with materials at the John F. Kennedy Library in Boston, and Enos E. Underwood provided advice and support from Arizona State University, as did Myrna Manners at the New York Hospital/Cornell Medical Center.

The staff at the Stanford University News Service Office, Robert DiIorio and Donna Coveney at the Massachusetts Institute of Technology News Office, and James Morgan at the United States Information Agency all responded quickly to my requests for assistance. I am especially grateful to Mrs. Valerie Dyer of Los Angeles, who provided prompt translations of news clippings in French from Madagascar about Colonel Gregory.

Lawrence E. Lamb, M.D., and journalist Roger Mudd clarified issues I found difficult to decipher.

Thanks also to Thomas Sandin, Ph.D., and Donald Edwards, Ph.D., at North Carolina A&T University; Mr. Richard S. Schweiker and Jeanette C. P. Eisenhart at Pennsylvania State University; Marla Otto of the *Philadelphia Inquirer;* Lt. Gen. Thomas Stafford, USAF (Ret.); Brig. Gen. Charles "Chuck" Yeager, USAF (Ret.); Jeanne Moore, secretary to Robert S. McNamara; and Col. John Riley Love, USMC (Ret.).

Mrs. Barbara Lawrence, widow of astronaut-designee Maj. Robert H. Lawrence, Jr., and Mrs. Cheryl McNair, widow of astronaut Ronald E. McNair, Ph.D., killed in the 1986 *Challenger* accident, were both generous with their time and support.

I am also grateful to Donald Gass of the Rohnert Park-Cotati Regional Library in Sonoma County, California, for his unstinting research support; Vonda K. Somerville at Texas Tech University; to Barry L. Spink and Barbara A. Lee at the USAF Historical Research Center, Maxwell Air Force Base, Alabama; and to Emily Rooney of WCVB-TV in Boston.

Poetry teacher and poet Perie Longo (author of *Milking the Earth*) graciously shared her poetry and poems by her students written in the wake of the *Challenger* accident.

Finally, there would not have been an acceptable manuscript without the hard work of Judi Hagle on her word processor in Rohnert Park, California.

These are but a few of the many people who helped me in some way or another along the way. I am sure I have unintentionally missed some. I hope those I did miss will accept my apology and thanks for their contributions toward bringing this project to fruition.

INTRODUCTION

People from as far as four hundred miles away saw the great flash light up the sky like a premature sunrise at 2:32 A.M. on 30 August 1983. Thousands cheered as the space shuttle Challenger roared off its launchpad and rose to taunt space again. Although it was Challenger's eighth trip into the heavens, it was the first night launch of an American space shuttle. The mission was also noteworthy in that the first African-American astronaut, Guion S. Bluford, was on board, breaking the so-called color line in space and making America's shuttle crews more reflective of their nation's melting-pot population.

Two monumental problems faced John F. Kennedy as he began his run for the presidency. One was the gnawing issue of civil rights. Black citizens were pressing harder than ever for some semblance of parity and equality. The other involved a string of Soviet space successes, which began with the launching and orbiting of *Sputnik*, a 180-pound artificial satellite, on 4 October 1957, and several weeks later, *Sputnik 2*, with a nondescript dog named Laika aboard.

Many Americans, and probably Kennedy himself, searched the sky each night, straining to see the glinting orbs gliding by every ninety minutes. Fear gripped the country, and the adrenaline flow it generated translated into wonderment and concern for the nation's ultimate survival. A concerned public demanded action.

If anything, initial American efforts to counter this new communist threat were woefully inadequate, heightening the nation's paranoia. The U.S.'s first attempt to launch its own artificial space satellite ended in spectacular failure when, on 6 December 1957, the *Vanguard* rocket carrying the device exploded four feet off the ground in a gigantic ball of fire.[1]

Finally, on 31 January 1958, with the help of German scientist Wernher von Braun, the *Explorer I* satellite glided into space atop a *Jupiter C* rocket. Later that year three other U.S. satellites were successfully launched.

American dreams of sending a man into space and bringing him back were nothing new. It seemed, however, that those dreams themselves were in constant flux. Who would do it? Who had the responsibility? Assessing these issues was difficult. The United States Air Force, for example, had for years planned for a manned space program of its own. In the wake of the first *Sputnik,* it sought to create its own military space systems. The air force would use aircraft like the X-20 and other experimental space vehicles called "lifting body" ships—wingless craft with hulls shaped for aerodynamic control when coming back into the earth's atmosphere. There was also the dream of a Manned Orbiting Laboratory (MOL)—a space station on which men and women could remain in space and work for indefinite periods.

These were not wild imaginings. The Boeing aircraft corporation tinkered with the first X-20 shuttle craft design and six pilots were chosen to take it into orbit. The air force even envisioned automated aircraft "able to find and destroy a target" and return "to their home stations and land by themselves." This, some in the air force thought, would almost eliminate the need for a pilot, since his only requirement would be to take over in the event the electronic control system failed.[2]

Getting beyond the dream stage was a slow process. Too slow, given the Soviet space successes. For whatever reasons, the air force seemed unable to get its manned space programs off the drawing boards. After the expenditure of millions of dollars on research and development, officials in Washington became convinced that the manned space program should be civilianized.

President Dwight D. Eisenhower personally shot down the air force on 29 July 1958, when he signed an executive order creating the National Aeronautics and Space Administration (NASA). The agency's mandate was to develop a comprehensive program that would clearly establish the United States as the leader in the space race. To prevent dissent in the ranks, Eisenhower further directed the first astronauts be selected from among the 540 military test pilots on active duty. Those selected should hold an adequate security clearance; be under five-feet, eleven-inches tall; and be no older than thirty-nine years of age. They should be graduates of the test pilot school, have at least 1,500 hours of flying time—including jet aircraft experience, and possess a bachelor's degree or its equivalent.[3]

More than a hundred of the 540 serving military test pilots met those criteria. Nothing was mentioned then or later about including minorities in the astronaut program by the Eisenhower administration, however. In the years before the Civil Rights Act of 1964, NASA's management "walked a tightrope between the technical needs of its programs and the social needs of society at large."[4]

Some observers have since speculated that perhaps the promise of fame and glory that came with the title of astronaut led to a conscious decision to exclude minorities and women from the program. This is an idea that can't easily be dismissed, for the fame and glory showered on the first astronauts were tangible—instant celebrity; lucrative contracts with national magazines; speaking tours on the "rubber chicken" circuit. Some astronauts found themselves earning more than $25,000 over their annual military salary. It was good-bye to spartan military housing and hello to custom-designed homes in the suburbs.

According to Tom Wolfe in *The Right Stuff*, it was "a free lunch from one side of America to the other." And in 1959, the fact that all seven *Mercury* astronauts were white had nothing to do with their selection, for "the premise was that you could either do the job or you couldn't. There were no other variables."

That may have been the line in NASA's upper echelons during the late 1950s, but when John Kennedy made his run for the White House, facts were uncovered that served only to heighten awareness that the first astronauts were all "white officers . . . and all Protestant," from "small town America," and "typical of career military officers . . . from 'native' or 'old settler' stock."[5]

This status quo selection process came under careful scrutiny as Kennedy contemplated the presidency, for he knew he would need the black vote to win the election. How to get it was a problem he could not solve alone. Seeking solutions, Kennedy stopped to pick up Harris Wofford, the black campaign advisor on civil rights, one early August morning. As the two men drove into Washington in Kennedy's red convertible, Kennedy attacked the problem head on.

"Now," he snapped, glancing at Wofford, "in five minutes, tick off the ten things that a president ought to do to clean up this goddamn civil rights mess!"

Wofford supposedly responded that cautious movement on the civil rights legislative front and maximum executive energy were needed in order to strike an appropriate balance. The former would quell fears among white voters, especially in the South, while the latter would appeal to African American and other minority voters looking for symbolic cues that progress was being made.

Wofford's advice appears to have had a significant impact on Candidate Kennedy. Until then, the Kennedys had been only "abstractly in favor of equal opportunity, and it took presidential politics to involve them with the movement."[6]

Almost immediately, Kennedy began involving blacks in his campaign, insisting that unlike in previous elections African Americans would not simply be a "minorities section working only the Negro vote," but that blacks would play a vital part in the campaign. Democratic party efforts to secure the black vote would be integrated.[7]

Four black congressmen—William L. Dawson, Charles C. Diggs, Robert N. C. Nix, and Adam Clayton Powell—were asked to head a drive to register a million new African-American voters. Research showed that the proportion of blacks registered to vote was considerably lower than that of whites in practically every state and district—North or South.

Starting in 1958, the Democratic National Committee brought outstanding black and white leaders together for advice and counsel concerning civil rights. Census tracts were carefully considered and verified to ensure a sharp increase in blacks exercising their franchise. Field men spread out across the nation. A publicist was hired to spread timely stories "about our candidate and his speeches to the more than 110 Negro daily and weekly publications . . . radio stations and other media beamed to the Negro market."[8]

By mid-March 1960, positive results were evident. On 1 August 1960, *Jet* magazine's lead story was headlined, "How Negro Vote Can Decide the 1960 Election." John Kennedy was lauded as the first "presidential contender [to go] out of the way to woo a Negro"—Adam Clayton Powell, whose capture of Harlem's strategic vote could help deliver victory. Calling Kennedy "a shrewd, calculating political general

[who] realized the importance of the Negro vote in the fall election," the article laid out the probable outcomes of Kennedy's efforts:

> Experts agree the U.S. Negro voter this fall could elect the next U.S. President. . . . In six major states, where the balloting will be close, Negroes cast almost 1 million votes (N.Y., Penn., Ohio, Calif., Mich., and Ill.), representing 181 electoral votes. Enough—if garnered in a single package—[for] the big victory. . . . With these . . . the Negro bloc now had become more important than the Solid South.[9]

Once elected, Kennedy met with several influential black leaders, including Dr. Martin Luther King. According to Edward Dwight, the first black-astronaut selectee, Whitney Young came up with the idea that African Americans needed to become more involved in the country's increasingly rapid technological growth. It would not be easy, however, in view of the miserable black enrollments in top-flight state schools like Michigan and Purdue and engineering schools like MIT, Harvard, and Cal Tech. Young also noted, according to Dwight, that the service academies were a prime alternative, for "all Kennedy had to do was get enough senators to appoint these kids and we've got a deal!"

But what, Kennedy wanted to know, could serve as an inspiration and catalyst to "get black youngsters interested in the academies and these fields of endeavor?" Again, says Dwight, Whitney Young had the answer: "Why don't you create a black astronaut?"[10]

Kennedy and Young were not the only Americans thinking along these lines. Edward R. Murrow, the famed World War II broadcaster, CBS news commentator, and director of the United States Information Agency (USIA), found himself thinking similar thoughts. Not only would it improve America's image internationally, it was simply the right thing to do. Although a native southerner himself, Murrow had long chafed over the treatment of African Americans. The idea of a black astronaut intrigued him. On 21 September 1961, Murrow sent a letter to James E. Webb, NASA's administrator. After the customary salutation, Murrow got straight to the point: "Why don't we put the first non-white man in space? If you boys were to enroll and train a qualified Negro and then fly him in whatever vehicle is available, we could retell our whole space effort to the whole nonwhite world, which is most of it."[11]

Webb reportedly was not overjoyed. On 18 October he formally replied that, while he understood the value of Murrow's suggestion, NASA received many such promptings, "including interest [in] the selection and flight of a woman." Furthermore, Webb continued, the seven astronauts already in training were adequate for present needs. Teams had already been selected for the next space ventures, and existing timetables made it difficult for him to see "how they could adopt Murrow's suggestion." Although Webb claimed to understand that adding a black astronaut candidate would "gain in a propaganda way around the world," he believed that he "could not encourage the idea because it was inconsistent with the Agency's policies."[12]

Murrow, incensed by the way African diplomats were being treated in Washington, did not let the matter rest. He made his position on race relations in the United States clear in a speech to the National Press Club. Murrow complained that African diplomats found it nearly impossible to live in the nation's capital. "Landlords will not rent to them, schools refuse their children, stores will not let them try on clothes, [and] beaches bar their families," Murrow said. "We could not pin this one on the communists if U.S.-African relations are damaged. We do it ourselves in our own capital!"[13]

Continuing to press NASA on the issue of black astronauts, Murrow elicited this response from Webb in December 1961: "Candidates must be qualified test pilots, and, sorry, there aren't any blacks among the astronauts."

Murrow, unwilling to accept Webb's answer, wrote a memorandum to the president on 28 April 1962. In it, he complained that

If this "qualification" was indeed essential—which there seemed reason to doubt—hadn't they better start training Negro test pilots? The first colored man to enter outer space will, in the eyes of the world, be the first [man] ever to have done so. I see no reason why our efforts in outer space should reflect with such fidelity the discrimination that exists on this minor planet.[14]

Kennedy learned during meetings with minority leaders and from other sources that, although segregation and discrimination had been

outlawed in the armed forces by President Harry S Truman more than
a decade before, there was ample evidence minority discrimination
persisted in the military services. The president, stung by the revela-
tions, resolved to initiate steps to eliminate these sources of "hardship
and embarrassment" for servicemen and women. Taking his cue from
the president, Murrow began enforcing equal opportunity standards
in the USIA.

President Kennedy wielded a double-edged sword. On the one hand,
he had intelligently mobilized the black vote in order to ensure his
election. On the other, he now pressed further, attempting to ensure
equality for blacks in the military. It seemed providential for blacks
aspiring to enter the space program, as the armed forces were the prime
source of astronauts.

On 24 June 1962, Kennedy appointed an advisory committee to study
equal opportunity policies in the military services. The committee was
charged with ensuring that "any remaining vestiges of discrimination
in the armed forces on the basis of race, creed or national origin" were
eliminated.

Among those chosen to serve on the committee were Gerhard A.
Gesell, Dean Joseph O'Meara of Notre Dame University, Nathaniel
Calley, Abe Fortas, Benjamin Muse, John Sengstacke, and Whitney
Young.

While the committee's members set out to gather information, the
president pressed on with the idea of selecting an African American
for the space program.

"The White House," wrote Charles L. Sanders in the June 1965 issue
of *Ebony,* "called the Department of Defense to ask if the Air Force
has 'any Negroes in the new aerospace research pilots course at Edwards
Air Force Base.'" The answer, Sanders asserted, was "No," but "the call
was like the king's wish: it set off a search for a Negro pilot who had
the right amount of flying time, the right academic background and one
who could meet all the other stringent requirements."[15]

The odds are that President Kennedy did not know the extent of
the maelstrom he had unleashed. "There were people out there [who
thought] Kennedy didn't understand that he wasn't the king of the world
versus president of the United States. When you appoint a king, then
all your minions follow in lock step. [But] you can be president and
there can be things going on [during] your watch and you don't know

how the system operates. You're doing all the gracious things on the surface, passing all the edicts, all those laws, and at the end of the whole process you find out these people have taken your directions and, for their own benefit, [gone off] in their direction."[16]

Kennedy's edict stuck, nevertheless. There would be a black astronaut. And while some of the "minions" marched in lock step, there were many others in high places who did not.

Thus began the saga of African Americans in the astronaut program. Its start would be considered by many as grossly inauspicious. But perhaps that has been the nature of the American experience throughout the twentieth century. The first black to sally forth into the American mainstream always seemed to catch hell. It was no different in the astronaut program. The difference was that many of the first black astronaut-selectees were warriors, fighter and bomber pilots who were trained to fly combat missions in Korea or had participated in air combat in Vietnam while that war still raged. Therein lies a story of minority ascension against the odds and into space itself.

J. Alfred Phelps
Galt, California

Edward J. Dwight, Jr.

CHAPTER 1

PUSHING THE ENVELOPE

The single-engine P-39 fighter veered from its formation in the sky above Kansas City, Kansas, careening and spinning crazily out of control. Down and down and down it spun, turning end over end before crashing sickeningly less than a mile from the Fairfax Bridge spanning the Missouri River. Flames erupted from the twisted wreckage and smoke billowed. The pilot remained motionless in the fiery cockpit.

Ten-year-old Edward Joseph Dwight, Jr., and his friends had been wading barefoot in the shallows under the bridge fishing for crawdads. They occasionally glanced up as the sleek fighters roared and swooped across the sky, but they dropped everything and watched in horrified fascination when the troubled P-39 faltered and plunged earthward in its awful death dance.

The boys ran breathlessly toward the burning plane. As they approached the wreckage, the intense heat set off live ammunition, scattering them like tenpins. Some lay prone, watching wide-eyed as the searing flames burned the body in the cockpit to a crisp. Edward Dwight stood transfixed for a moment and thought prophetically, "I don't know, but I'll betcha the pilot must have made a mistake of some kind—and if *I'm* ever a pilot, I won't let that happen to me!"[1]

Because the Dwight family lived a mere mile from the Kansas City airport, which became a bustling U.S. Army Air Forces installation during World War II, the base itself became the source of many an adventure for Eddie—as the junior Dwight was known—and his cousins and friends. They frequently made the short trek to the long, wide fence surrounding the field, where they watched the goings on and talked about the differences in the appearance of the various aircraft types.

When the war ended, the Fairfax base again became a civilian municipal airport. The boys did odd jobs around the planes and hangars, hoping to parlay a ride in exchange for their services. Perseverance finally paid off when a pilot offered to take Eddie up in a two-seater Piper Cub. The ride scared him a bit. "Landing," he later recalled, "was the best part!"[2]

Fishing for crawdads and cadging airplane rides was fun, but there were other, more important things to do; Eddie's mother and father saw to that. Devout Catholics, they taught their children the value of honesty, hard work, thrift, and the proper use of one's time.

Eddie and his sisters—Mary Louise, Elizabeth, Rita, and a fourth who later became Sister Martin Mary of the Sisters of Charity in Leavenworth, Kansas—couldn't, for example, stay out until all hours the way some of their playmates could. There was also the familial link to the church. Eddie became an altar boy at age six and attended mass every day while in grammar school. During the summer he got up at the crack of dawn a couple of times a week to go birdwatching with Father Terence Rhodes, assistant pastor of Kansas City's Our Lady of Perpetual Help Church.[3]

By his own admission, Dwight's parents shaped his life more than he realized at the time. "They taught me more by example than I could have picked up anywhere," he observed.[4] Young Eddie, always thinking about his future, realized the value of the lessons to be learned from their fine examples—and from the homework his parents insisted he complete before doing anything else.

Dwight's grandfather, Lobe, came from the little town of Dawson, Georgia, a few miles north of Albany in the southern part of the state. The enterprising Lobe acquired "considerable property" around the town, something that did not sit well with the majority of his neighbors. In fact, the atmosphere became decidedly unhealthy, so Lobe left Georgia and settled in Kansas City, where he went to work in a meat-packing plant. He purchased an unclaimed parcel of land on the edge of town before sending for his family. They called it "the hole," situated as it was at the bottom of a steep hill.

Lobe's son Edward disliked living in the hole and quit school at fifteen to play professional baseball in the Negro Leagues. He got his start with the Kansas City Giants, then later played for the Monarchs. While on a trip to Sioux City, Iowa, he met one Georgia Baker. The couple conducted a long-distance romance before they finally got married and Georgia moved to Kansas City, where, on 9 September 1933, Edward, Jr., was born.

To survive the Depression, the growing Dwight family planted a large vegetable garden, an act that kept food on the table and created a perpetual love of the land in young Eddie. "I guess I'm a farm boy at heart," he said later.[5]

At twelve, Eddie began to show a fierce independence. Working both a weekly and daily newspaper route, he saved his money and bought a 1929 Model A Ford in good condition. His Kansas driving permit only allowed him to drive during the day, however.

Life in the Midwest had other merits. For example, when Dwight was fourteen, his father "loaned him out" as a farmhand for the summer. It helped bolster Eddie's confidence and further enhanced his love of the land. "They had pigs and horses and chickens," he marveled, and "you ate all that country sausage and those big old eggs! If you grow up in the city, you have no feeling for life. When you're growing up, being molded, I feel there is nothing better for a kid to be exposed to than farm life!"[6]

Dwight attended Our Lady of Perpetual Help grade school and was the first black youth to attend Ward Catholic High School. People said he looked more "like the team mascot at 104 pounds, rather than the school's star halfback." He ran the hundred-yard dash in 9.8 seconds and the two-hundred-yard low hurdles in 23 flat. Later he won the state 118-pound Golden Gloves boxing championship. Dwight also added academic honors to his sports accomplishments by qualifying for membership in the National Honor Society in his junior year.[7]

While he was in high school, Dwight's hormones jumped, causing him to "cast a dark and roving eye at the Sumner High School
majorettes." In particular, shapely fourteen-year-old Sue Lillian James
"caught his fancy." Observers of this romantic interlude were hard
pressed to say just who fell for whom. Sue later said that "it took
about three months for me to say hello to him—he was too persistent!" Dwight, on the other hand, says he showed only "some small
interest in the girl." It was evident to *him* that it was *she* who was
the persistent one.[8]

While in college, Dwight became more serious about flying and went
to a local library to study the subject. As he tells it:

> In 1951, about 33 of us [students] went out to Lowry Air Force
> Base [Colorado] to take the pilot's test. I [was] so possessed with
> this airplane stuff that I'd been doing sample tests for pilot training
> since junior high. . . . [In] the tests that they give you [there were]
> airplanes [turned in] all directions, math tests, physics tests, [and]
> acceleration tests. So I'd been unwittingly preparing. . . . I was
> the only one of [the] 33 who passed! I just zoomed through the
> tests. And it all came out of the books in the library![9]

In August 1953, after graduating from Kansas City Junior College,
Dwight joined the air force, which quickly cycled him through three
of its schools. He took his airman basic and cadet preflight training
at Lackland Air Force Base, Texas, and primary flight training at Malden
Air Base, Missouri.[10]

Although his desire to become a pilot burned as brightly within him
as ever, Dwight's first two rides into the wild, blue yonder were un-
settling. "The first flight I ever had in the air force scared the pants
off me. I had forgotten what the sensation felt like," he recalled, thinking
back to his earlier experience in the Piper Cub in Kansas City.

The next day the instructor let Dwight fly the plane. "It was the difference between night and day!" he later exulted. Fear of flying never
bothered him again, and he finally earned his wings and became an officer in 1955. That same year, Sue Lillian James, the girl he had shown
only "some small interest in" while in high school, became his wife.[11]

Assigned to Williams Air Force Base, Arizona, Dwight became even
more excited about flying when he began jet aircraft training. It was

a "fantastic" experience, driving him to "really take to jets," and become the first pilot in his class to solo in the T-33 jet trainer.[12]

Dwight remained at Williams Air Force Base for two and a half years, performing duty as a jet flying instructor. He also attended night classes at Arizona State University in nearby Tempe, graduating in 1957 "with distinction" and a degree in aeronautical engineering.

After Williams, Dwight was stationed briefly in Japan, where he flew B-57 jet bombers before returning to Travis Air Force Base, California, to become chief of collateral training—the Strategic Air Command's vaunted ground education program. He held that post for three and a half years.

In 1962, news of the accomplishments of American astronauts and Soviet cosmonauts filled front pages and the airwaves as the space race heated up between the two super powers. Dwight, caught up in all the excitement, began dreaming of joining the astronauts' ranks. An air force captain by then, Dwight was also the proud father of daughter Tina Sheree, seven, and five-year-old Edward III. Gazing first at his children, then looking out into space, Edward Joseph Dwight, Jr., silently vowed he would become the world's first black astronaut.[13]

But it was a difficult time to be black in America and aspire to reach the stars. The nation roiled with racial unrest. A little more than six years before, seamstress Rosa Parks had challenged the bus segregation ordinance in Montgomery, Alabama, releasing racial furies. In 1956, 101 Southern congressmen called for and got massive resistance to the Supreme Court's desegregation rulings. National Guardsmen, called out by Arkansas governor Orval Faubus in 1957, barred nine black students from Little Rock's Central High School. Blacks challenged restaurant segregation in Greensboro, North Carolina, with lunch counter sit-ins in 1960. And in July 1962, it took three thousand federal troops to ensure James Meredith's safe admission to the University of Mississippi.

All of this caused a chilling stir deep in the hearts of desegregationists as they responded to the ominous muttering of the phrase, "We don't want no coon on the moon!"[14]

But Edward Joseph Dwight, Jr., ignored the blatant discord and submitted his application for test pilot and astronaut training. While he waited for a response, the moon continued to wax and wane as it had for millions of years.

CAMELOT AND CAPTAIN DWIGHT

The nation deserves an accounting—a full accounting—of what
really happened in Ed Dwight's case. And so does every Negro boy
and girl who ever aspired to the stars.
                                            —Charles L. Sanders
                                            Ebony, *June 1965*

It all began with a telephone call from the White House to the
Department of Defense. There was no arrogance in the caller's voice;
only a simple question was asked:

"Does the Air Force have any Negroes in the new aerospace research
pilots' course being set up at Edwards Air Force Base in California?"

After what was probably an extended pause came the answer: "No,
there aren't any."[15]

It was an ordinary enough question, but the call came from an
extraordinary source. Had it come from an ordinary White House,
the reaction might have been mild, nothing more than grist for a worka-
day tale some government employee could tell at a weekend gathering. But this call came from the *Kennedy* White House, that place
called "Camelot," which had seen the beginning of civil rights "sit-
ins" and had sent troops to get a black man into a university in the
Deep South. It was a White House that had used its influence to gain
Martin Luther King's release from jail. Perhaps the recipient of the
call knew all of this and felt a bit like a person in a closed garage
slowly filling with carbon monoxide. In any event, the reaction was
predictable: something had better be done—and rather quickly. The
innocuous-sounding call thus became something of an edict.

The air force swiftly launched a search for a black pilot with the
right amount of flying time, the "right academic background, and
one who could meet all the other stringent requirements." Fortunately,
air force personnel officers didn't have to look too far, for it was at
about that time that Capt. Ed Dwight's application reached them. It
didn't take the air force long to decide that Dwight, who had logged
more than two thousand hours in the air and held an aeronautical engineering degree from Arizona State University, was the right man for
the job.[16]

The decision was quickly followed by a letter from President Kennedy, according to Dwight, advising him of his selection and intimating, among other things, that the opportunity would give him the chance to "be one of the greatest Negroes who ever lived."

Excited, Dwight approached his air force supervisor. "Do you know what this means?" he exulted. "I'll probably end up on the cover of *Ebony*!"

"What's *Ebony*?" replied the officer, his face blank, proof of his ignorance of the existence of the premier national magazine chronicling the achievements of African Americans.

Dwight saw the handwriting on the wall as official word of his selection was passed down by his air force superiors. "Their attitudes," Dwight remembers, "were not favorable. It had to do with giving up power," a position Dwight later said went back to an inbred reluctance to let "black folks do things."

"You know," his air force bosses warned him, "if you risk it and you lose, you've lost it all!" That was the name of the game. He was in the regular air force. If he left the regular air force to do this "astronaut thing," there would be no coming back. Dwight remembers thinking:

> If I was successful, I would be madly successful. I'd get promoted fast; leave there a brigadier general at least. But if I failed, there was no coming back. I was told that. I ran the risk.[17]

It was worth the risk to Dwight. At that point he probably could not have been more proud to be part of the air force. It was exciting stuff, this chance to go into outer space and perhaps be one of the few people ever to set foot on the moon. Dwight wanted to be an astronaut, to stand tall with the other officers chosen to begin the seven-month course at the Aerospace Research Test Pilots' School at Edwards, commanded by the famous test pilot, Col. Charles "Chuck" Yeager.

In the beginning, Dwight was able to develop a close camaraderie with his fellow students—the kind of camaraderie found on football teams before a big game. They all, as he remembers it, were "going into a pressure pot." And the pressure was the same—no matter who you were, where you came from, or what the color of your skin. The people in charge defined the end results: "Once you go through this pressure pot, we will have molded you into the greatest set of entities that ever existed!" To a man, the new students were "scared to death." Dwight recalled that

> Going in, there's fear of the unknown. You look at each other and you say, 'Man, we're about to go through this grinder, and we're about to be ground up into hamburger!' We didn't know whether they were going to cut our balls off, whether we were going to lose fingers or our heads were going to be shrunk so that we didn't recognize them. [Then] all the [stuff] comes out about all these tests you've got to do, all the things you've got to get into. You didn't know what was going to happen, whether you were going to spin out or whether you were going to get kicked out![18]

The stuff coming at them was formidable and would probably stagger the average person's imagination. The list sounded awesome: Computer theory; orbital and flight mechanics; astronomy; chemical, nuclear, and exotic propulsion; guidance and control; aerothermodynamics; project management. Each candidate would be required to fly a modified F-104 fighter to rarefied heights and practice rocket power and ballistic control operations, reentry corridor simulation, and energy management. There would also be space vehicle simulator training and instruction in bioastronautics designed to familiarize the candidates with the physiological factors of spaceflight.[19]

Through it all, according to Dwight, the initial camaraderie he established with his fellow students continued to exist, despite signs that things might be different where he was concerned.

A sixth sense told Dwight that Yeager and his faculty were privately telling his compatriots "this nigger's going to mess up your stuff!" Still, it was Dwight's feeling that the other students didn't care about that, for they had all started out being "great friends." But once everyone found out that their "heads weren't going to get cut off or our peckers weren't going to be smaller or that we weren't going to be washed out," a subtle attitudinal change became apparent.[20]

It became a game of survival. His fellow students began to realize that everyone had better "look internally [and] look about for our own survival, at who might be standing in the way of [success]." The someone who was obviously in the way, it seemed, was "that Dwight," the

"Kennedy boy," the "guy who doesn't belong here." The guy who was the possible roadblock that might keep one of them from being selected by NASA. Somewhere inside, said Dwight, each candidate believed *he* might be the one who might have made it if not for Dwight. He remembers thinking that it was those who were less secure who must have become convinced "that 'this nigger' [doesn't] belong here, [so] everybody's up for grabs!"

Such feelings were undoubtedly heightened because everyone in the course knew that even if they successfully completed the training, there was no assurance NASA would choose any specific person over another to be one of its future spacemen. Nevertheless, Dwight tried to maintain a positive outlook. He was quoted in a 1963 interview as saying, "But if I get further training after leaving here, my chances of selection are good!"[21]

Furthermore, the school's faculty fostered an intentional fuzziness over each candidate's relative standing within the group. There were no grades, no rankings. It was a kind of "in factor," a Sword of Damocles hanging over everyone's head. It was a way to "keep everybody on their toes, and created monstrous insecurity" in every student. People began turning on each other as they vied for the golden "slot." Dwight became a target, or so he thought, because it appeared to him he was the one student who, because of presidential involvement, was guaranteed selection for astronaut training. To his fellow candidates that meant his presence would lead to some other guy getting kicked out. The rationale thus became, "if Dwight is removed as a factor, then this slot would be opened up. Everybody," according to Dwight, "put themselves in that position."

So Dwight's life became one of misery. His attempts to socialize with other students failed. It was Dwight's sense that people were working to undermine whatever chance of success he might have. "My reception down there was less than amicable," he remembers, "and I caught hell! I couldn't tell anybody about it. It was the same kind of things that [Lt. Gen. Benjamin O.] Davis [, Jr.,] talks about when he went to West Point. Isolation. People not talking to you."[22]

But Dwight was not one to sit idly by and take the changed treatment silently. He complained about it, even traveling to the White House to discuss the treatment he was receiving. Soon after that, investigators from the attorney general's office showed up at Edwards. Dwight had complained about the "things they were throwing at him [that] they weren't throwing at other people," about it being apparent that the word was out and it had been communicated to his "classmates, instructors, and staff" that he was not to succeed.

Yeager and company began to feel the pressure:

> Every week, it seemed, a detachment of civil rights lawyers turned up from Washington. . . . The lawyers squinted in the desert sunlight and asked a great many questions about the program and treatment of Ed Dwight and took notes. Yeager kept saying he couldn't see how he 'could simply jump Dwight over these other men.' The lawyers would come back the next week, squint, and take more notes.[23]

It was about this time that someone at the school told Dwight "they were going to slow-roll him" out of the school. Dwight goes a bit farther, saying Yeager "was told that I was not to graduate, and that he was to use whatever power and resources he had to [ensure] that I would not graduate."[24]

According to NASA official Dr. Curtis M. Graves of Washington, D.C., Dwight said that he had "confronted Yeager on the issue."[25]

Dwight later described the unsavory confrontation in more detail in a fifteen-page report covering his experiences at Edwards. He described Yeager as simply a "high-ranking officer at the school," undoubtedly because, as a serving air force officer, Dwight feared possible retaliation. But it was indeed Yeager "who called Dwight into his office, ordered him to sit down, and," according to reporter Charles L. Sanders, "subjected him to a line of questioning that dripped with racism."

"Who got you into this school?" Yeager supposedly wanted to know. "Was it the NAACP or are you some kind of Black Muslim out here to make trouble? I hear you're a 'Kennedy boy,' so did President Kennedy send the word down that you're supposed to go into space? Why in hell would a colored guy want to go into space anyway? As far as I'm concerned, there'll never be one to do it. And if it was left to me, you guys wouldn't even get a chance to wear an air force uniform!"

Sanders notes that Dwight asked for and got permission to "speak freely to the officer."

"Sir," Dwight coolly replied, "you've done nothing more than make me more determined to prove that a Negro can do anything a white man can."

This reply, according to Sanders, "infuriated Yeager." But whether Yeager was angry or not, shortly after this hassle, Dwight was graduated number eight in his class.[26]

Phase II training now lay before him, the high-powered postgraduate course dealing primarily with aerospace research. Dwight applied for admittance. Apparently not trusting official channels to process and approve his application, he wrote to Kansas senator Frank Carlson, telling of his desire to be selected for advanced aerospace research pilots' training, citing the fact that he was the only black in the program at the time. On 21 March 1962, Senator Carlson wrote the White House on Dwight's behalf, attaching a copy of Dwight's letter and indicating he had followed Dwight's career for a number of years because he was a constituent from Kansas City.

"From a layman's point of view," wrote Carlson, "I think this young man's potential is something that could be considered." It was for that reason, Carlson went on, that he forwarded the matter to the White House rather than directly to the air force. "I will personally appreciate any interest you might be able to give this case," Carlson concluded.[27]

Less than a week later, the White House prodded the air force to act swiftly in Dwight's behalf and draft a reply to Senator Carlson telling him that

As you know, the air force has announced the selection of Captain Dwight as one of the 14 air force officers selected for the next class of the aerospace research pilot course, which begins June 17, 1963.[28]

Shortly after that reply was sent, President Kennedy, as if on cue, delivered a civil rights message to the nation on June 11, 1963:

This is one country. It has become one country because all of us and all the people who came here had equal chance to develop their talents. We cannot say to ten percent of the population that you cannot have that right; that your children can't have the chance to develop whatever talents they have.[29]

Whether or not Colonel Yeager heard Kennedy's message, the chagrin apparently still burned. Yeager still saw Dwight's presence as a simple case of "Kennedy leaning on the Department of Defense; the Department of Defense leaning on the air force, and the air force leaning on him," and continued to take a dim view of the whole "Dwight Affair," as it had become known.

The fires grew hotter.

General Curtis E. LeMay, the air force chief of staff (about whom President Kennedy had a number of reservations[30]), phoned Yeager when word of Dwight's selection reached him.

"Chuck, Bobby Kennedy wants a 'colored' in space. Get one into your course!"

"Well, General, it's gonna be difficult! We have one applicant, a captain named Dwight, who came out number twenty-six. We already published our list with the fifteen who made it, and it's going to be embarrassing to republish the list with Dwight's name on it because now everybody knows who the first fifteen are!"

"Okay, I'll just tell them they're too late for this first class," General LeMay replied. He undoubtedly delivered that message to the Kennedy administration. Then, as Yeager later wrote, "A 150mm shell" came zooming in from the White House. "By God, you *will* have a black pilot in that program—*now!*"

General LeMay was on the telephone again.

"Do what you have to do, Yeager, but *get that colored guy in!*"

"Okay, General," Yeager replied, "But what I think we ought to do is take at least fifteen students in the first class, instead of eleven, and make *him* number fifteen. Give me a little more money and I can handle this man in the school!"

LeMay grunted his approval. Edward Dwight was in.[31]

But the bottom line was that Dwight really was unwanted and unwelcome; "he was being set up for a fall, because the chances of NASA *accepting him as an astronaut appeared remote in any event.*" [Emphasis added.] Furthermore, Dwight's selection for the aerospace school was baffling because race had never been introduced as an issue. To an outside observer, however, it must have been even more baffling to learn that the immediate reaction to Dwight's involvement in the school was that he would fail even before he began.[32]

Two questions ultimately needed to be answered. First, why would

Dwight's chances of acceptance be remote—even before he completed Phase II training—without a chance to prove himself? Second, why was his automatic failure expected? As far as Dwight was concerned, the scenario grew more mysterious and sinister by the day.

The premise on which the program was based was grand: it stipulated that a pilot could either do the job or he couldn't—allegedly there were no other variables. Grand premise or not, review of the initial selection process reveals some interesting factors, especially when one realizes that the screening of applicants who were eventually to form the core of the next NASA group actually began in 1961, *before* the now-famous telephone call from the White House to the Department of Defense. There were the usual thorough screenings since this was to be the first group at the aerospace research pilots' school. The staff culled the applications, pulled the most promising, checked their military records and forwarded the results to the selection committee at the Pentagon. The men's backgrounds were reviewed, personal interviews were conducted, and their evaluations by superiors were considered. Many men were eliminated from further consideration at that point. Dwight was not part of this process.[33]

The final selection committee then met. Colonel Yeager was part of this activity. The actions of the selection committee resulted in the compilation of a list of the *first eleven astronauts*. In his autobiography, Chuck Yeager says of this list:

> Actually, we had *twenty-six* names in order of preference, but we didn't publish our list that way. We just named eleven guys alphabetically as the members of our first class, and listed the first three or four alternates in case any dropped out. [Italics added.]

He goes on to laud the quality of the men on this list, adding that their presence "added tremendously to the prestige" of his school. It was then that the telephone calls from the White House and General LeMay came, asking if there were any black pilots in the published list of eleven potential astronauts. Yeager says he replied that only one black pilot had applied, and he *was number twenty-six on the list*.[34]

According to another source, however, there were actually only *twenty-five* prospective astronauts on the original list, and Dwight was later added to it, bringing the total to twenty-six.[35] Apparently, it was Yeager's solution to what he then regarded as an intolerable situation emanating from that telephone call: "I was informed that the White House wanted a black pilot in the space program!"

Yeager's gushing praise for the men on this list obviously did not include Dwight. He wasted no time getting out the unvarnished word: Dwight was "an average pilot with an average background." His talents were not exceptional. He could certainly fly well enough in a squadron and probably "get by," but it was more than problematical to expect that he could compete in the space course against the "best of the crop of experienced military test pilots."[36]

The situation seemed to border on an obsession with Yeager, to the extent that he began making statements that were insupportable as fact. "In those days," Yeager said, "there were still comparatively few black pilots in the Air Force, but Dwight sure as hell didn't represent the top of the talent pool." Yeager remembered black pilots with whom he had flown (e.g., Emmett Hatch and Eddie LaVelle), but "guys of their quality didn't apply for the course. Dwight did!"[37]

Yet Dwight, selected by the air force because of his record and educational background, must have come very close to the "top of the talent pool." If he didn't, the service's personnel selection process was mysteriously askew. Furthermore, because the search for a black pilot had been triggered by the president himself, the air force's screening was undoubtedly thorough. Finally, there were 1,300 black air force officers on active duty at the time in the continental United States, many of whom were pilots.[38] Others were overseas and within two years would begin flying combat missions against North Vietnam. Although they represented just under 2 percent of all officers in the air force, the numbers were vastly greater than Yeager's off-the-cuff assessment suggests.[39]

In any event, a press release announcing Dwight's selection for the next class at the Aerospace Research Pilots' School (ARPS) was issued by Yeager's command on 30 March 1963. The following day, newspapers were full of the news. The *Washington Post,* under a headline reading "First Negro Designated Space-Flight Candidate," carried the story as its lead:

> The first Negro has been selected for possible participation in future U.S. manned space flights, it was disclosed yesterday. He is Air Force Captain Edward J. Dwight, Jr., of Kansas City, Kansas, who is among 14 new candidates chosen for the Air Force's

aerospace research pilot program at Edwards Air Force Base, California.[40]

Despite his commandant's attitude toward him, Dwight entered ARPS Phase II training in the summer of 1963. He took all the tests and underwent even more in-depth physical examinations.

Pride in Dwight's selection spread quickly around the country, especially in black communities. On 1 April 1963, James H. Browne, president of the Kansas City-based Crusader Life Insurance Company, sent a letter of thanks to the president:

> Truly a greater honor has never come to Kansas City, Kansas, than this gesture on your part. All Kansas City, Kansas, joins me in extending thanks to you and assures you that you will never regret having made this wonderful selection.[41]

Dwight's mother, father, and four sisters out on the Kansas plains shared in that pride. When reporters asked Dwight what they felt, he described them as being "pretty excited."[42] On 4 April 1963, his parents wrote a letter to President Kennedy that expressed their sentiments as follows:

> It is with heartfelt gratitude that we write to thank you for the great honor that has been bestowed on our son, Captain Edward Dwight of the Air Force.
>
> This goal has been in his heart for a long time. As parents, we take a great deal of pleasure in the fact that he has gained his objective. We also share in the honors that are being bestowed upon him. We are an ordinary family, but we have tried to give our children the best education we could afford and we have taught them to live as good Catholics should.
>
> Again, from the bottom of our hearts, we thank you and may God bless you in all your endeavors.[43]

As early as 30 March, Dwight was being hounded by reporters at Edwards Air Force Base.

"Captain Dwight," they chorused, "are you the first Negro to be selected as a trainee for the United States manned space program?"

"Affirmative!" beamed an effusive Dwight.

The Washington, D.C., *Sunday Star* reported in its 31 March 1963 issue that Dwight spoke in a crisp, military way, as his voice "packed both pride and excitement into [the] one word."

"Do you hope to go all the way, Captain Dwight? Be rocketed into space someday?"

"Yesiree, by all means!"[44]

On 12 April, Senator Carlson received confirmation from the White House that Dwight had been selected "as one of the 14 Air Force officers . . . for the next class of the Aerospace Research Pilot Course, [beginning] on June 17, 1963."[45]

Dwight may not have been so cocky and good-spirited had he known what had begun to militate against him, now a kind of Kennedy envoy, a messenger from "Camelot" representing the new president's determination to *force* this black man into the astronaut's sacred arena. "The school looked like the Ed Dwight case with a few classrooms and some military hardware appended."[46]

While Dwight underwent his baptism of fire at Edwards, space exploration picked up speed. On 15-16 May, astronaut L. Gordon Cooper orbited the earth twenty-two times in his *Mercury-Atlas 9* vehicle. On 14 and 16 June, the Russians launched *Vostok 5* and *6*, orbiting the planet eighty-one and forty-eight times, respectively, with cosmonaut Valentina V. Tereshkova, the first woman in space, aboard the latter spacecraft.[47]

Edward Joseph Dwight, Jr., looked to the stars despite the obstacles facing him. Others savored space, could he not expect to fulfill *his* dreams?

A DREAM DEFERRED

Ed Dwight dreamed magnificent dreams. He imagined himself and his fellow astronaut trainees exploring the moon in tracked vehicles or on unicycles, perhaps even riding in pressurized cabins with legs. He envisioned what it would be like to walk in pogo-stick fashion, leapfrogging through air devoid of gravity. He saw himself living in a manned moon base, his survival dependent upon specialized powerplants and hydroponic farms. And there were the rocks to be mined while diamond-shaped space vehicles blasted off from the lunar base, bound for the outer planets.

At home, his small son brought Dwight back to earth.

"How high is the moon, Daddy?" "How soon will you come home from the moon?" "What color is the man in the moon?"

Then came the inevitable question, which seared Dwight's soul: "What color are *we*, Daddy?"

Ed Dwight may or may not have had answers to all of his son's probing questions, but he strove to protect his children with a kind of studied caution in his replies, "using words that had meaning to their young minds." The depth of his son's questions surprised him, while his daughter appeared to be something of a muse about the whole thing.[48]

Besides the miseries Dwight experienced at the hands of Colonel Yeager and company, a lighter side lifted his spirits from time to time—that gaudy round of publicity events NASA encouraged potential and real astronauts to engage in: interviews, speaking engagements, accepting awards and other forms of public recognition.

On 14 July 1963, the Los Angeles Urban League presented Dwight its annual National Preparedness Award, recognizing him as the first African American to enter the preparatory course for possible astronaut training.[49] Attired in air force blues, a splash of ribbons riding his chest, his silver pilot's wings sparkling, Dwight traveled across America speaking to students and community groups. Years later, he recalled, "Prior to Kennedy's death, I was living awfully high on the hog. I had a private secretary. I was sending out 5,000 press photographs a month and I made 176 speeches the first year."[50] Dozens of citations and awards were bestowed on Dwight by organizations across the country.

Dr. Charles Lang of Los Angeles prepared a filmstrip about Dwight's training activities that the NASA Spacemobile Educational Program used widely. According to Roscoe Monroe, who was associated with that program, "I know what I saw in the reaction of black youngsters who looked at Captain Dwight and how they reacted to his message—it did a lot of good. He was the closest person to an astronaut our group could identify with."[51]

Dwight constantly reiterated to adult audiences that he was "one of fifteen men who may be headed to the moon or anywhere else in space. If it's the moon, it's okay. I want to make my contribution. I have no fear of 'out there.' I'd like it. First, I wanted to be a pilot, then a jet pilot. I never dreamed of being an astronaut until it became the latest in flight. I simply applied and made the grade. I am proud I was selected."[52]

He had "hundreds of things to say" to black children. Loath that he could not make them see it all that very minute, Dwight lectured with conviction: "What we face every day is lack of qualifications. Maybe it has been [a] parent's lack of guiding, but when high school graduation comes, it's too late to start thinking about what we're going to do! Preparation should begin in grade school." He also sought to tell kids about the many opportunities he believed awaited them if they would make an effort to find them. Like an old sage eschewing mistakes made decades before, he said, "It's ridiculous we don't get anywhere until we're old. You think I'm young! I'm *old* for my field. I look around me and I see young men in their twenties with degrees—fully qualified!"[53]

Dwight had a message for America. It was a message of pride in the country and its flag, a message bespeaking faith in the official government policy requiring that equality of opportunity be provided to every person in the armed services—a faith abiding in the hearts of all black servicemen and women of the era. He espoused it with smiling fervor in almost every news interview and speech: "There are no racial barriers for anyone who wants to be a man in space. All that counts is whether you can do the job. We guys in this space business are joined together in brotherhood!"[54]

Ed Dwight believed, or tried to believe, that he was a member of a viable team. And why not? His government was spending nearly a quarter of a million dollars on training designed to prepare him for the air force's highly touted Manned Orbiting Laboratory (MOL) project, a mission that called for crews of two or more astronauts to spend extended periods in a thirty-foot-long, canister-shaped vehicle determining how the military might make better use of space. NASA's selection of individuals to serve on that team was imminent; all that was needed was the Defense Department's approval to proceed with hardware acquisition.[55] A big question remained to be answered: Would the "brotherhood" of which Dwight had spoken so glowingly welcome him as a member? When queried on that score, a Defense Department spokesman replied simply that "constructive action is underway in regard to Captain Dwight."[56]

But in the real world in which Dwight lived, the action wasn't so constructive. In NASA, where the *real* astronauts worked, they called speaking tours similar to the ones Dwight participated in a "Week in the Barrel." According to Walter Cunningham, the nickname derived from "the old story about the sourdough," teetering on the edge of drunkenness, who came in from an Alaska mining camp "looking for a woman—any woman." The man's physical need was so overpowering that his compatriots pointed him toward a back room where there was a barrel with a big hole in the side in which he could satisfy himself. The inference, suggests Cunningham, related to astronauts who had yet to fly in space. "A week in the barrel could be embarrassing—a standing ovation from [the] citizenry . . . when all [you had] done was [fly in] from Houston."[57]

In Dwight's case, being in the barrel could be interpreted literally, with the hole in the side intended to accommodate the classmates who accompanied him on those speaking tours. Ovations awaited him along the way, of course, and the shining promise that glimmered in the eyes of black youngsters and adults alike at his accomplishment warmed him and made him proud. But there was also a dark side to the reception he received in his travels across America. Although he tried to ignore it, the fact of it returned like a nightmare:

During that time, I was kind of in a party phase of my life, I suppose. And I hung out at the [officer's] club because when I went down there, I went with blinders on, like I was part of the club. You know, part of the "big club," and I acted that out. [Going to] the officer's club, dancing, and things like that. And I did get orders not to dance with any more white women. Trouble was, it was the white women [who] asked me to dance! [The authorities] "invited me" to Alaska and [to several other undesirable places] if I kept doing it![58]

Despite the glitter and glad-handing he experienced on the lecture trail, Dwight remembers that there was "an incredible amount of social discrimination." When it came to accommodations, he was frequently the only one without a room in which to sleep. "They seemed," Dwight remembered, to operate "in collusion with the people in the restaurants" where they were scheduled to eat, and he often "wouldn't get served." The same treatment was observable in the many country clubs to which they were invited across the country, where the astronaut trainees were in great demand as guest speakers.

Rather than fight it, Dwight persevered. "I just thought that was part of the penalty I had to pay for being there," he said later, acknowledging the treatment he received was not uncommon for African Americans of the period.[59]

Meanwhile, Colonel Yeager's dim view of Dwight's abilities grew. Yeager later maintained that Dwight's abilities were so lacking "we set up a special tutoring program to get him through the academics because, as I recall, he lacked the engineering [background] that all the other students had."[60]

Perhaps Dwight's degree in aeronautical engineering simply didn't count. Or perhaps Yeager could not accept the fact that this "boyish looking" black man had somehow outstripped him and was on the pathway to the stars, a road closed to Yeager himself. Maybe it was simply empathy; Yeager had experienced his own "academic problems" in test pilots' school. The difference between the two, Yeager postulates, is that *he* had a good tutor who could "explain the most complicated problems in understandable language," whereas Dwight's tutors did not.

Yeager further observes that Dwight worked hard, as did his tutors, but adds that "Dwight just couldn't hack it . . . didn't keep up in flying." Yeager claims to have worked with Dwight on his flying, but he noted that "our students were flying at levels really beyond his experience. The only prejudice against Dwight," Yeager recalls, wagging a literary finger, "was the conviction that he was not qualified to be in the school" in the first place.[61]

The almost religious emphasis on Ed Dwight's "academics and qualifications" seems a bit spurious when the academic qualifications of earlier astronauts are examined. Atkinson and Shafritz support Edward R. Murrow's questioning of the validity of the qualifications of the original *Mercury* astronauts. Of the seven, Malcolm Carpenter and John Glenn had no college degree. The remaining five had degrees comparable to Dwight's.[62]

Despite the general attitudes toward Dwight and the mystery surrounding the "qualifications" game, Dwight, thinking he was at least on the right track, applied for astronaut training. He had, after all, completed Phase I of the experimental test pilot program and was one of the fourteen candidates selected for the Phase II course. It was no empty conclusion; it was from this group that the air force recommended pilots to NASA.

Dwight's flying record and classroom ranks placed him mid-range in the standings. Optimism should have abounded. Instead, his status and chance for a shining future swiftly degenerated.

"Any improvement in Dwight?" General LeMay asked Colonel Yeager at a banquet in Washington, D.C.

"No, sir. We're having a lot of trouble just trying to keep him from getting so far behind the others that it will be hopeless. He's just not hacking it!" Yeager answered.

The banquet was half over.

"Chuck," said the general, "if you want to wash out Dwight, I'll back you all the way!"

At that, Yeager wrote later, "I almost fell out of my chair!"

It did not quite come to that, at least not right away. Dwight "hung on," in Yeager's words, and "squeezed through."[63]

Shortly, however, the proverbial hammer fell. Although placed among "the select eight men from his class who were recommended without qualification" to NASA by the astronaut selection board, the board's recommendation apparently did not sufficiently move NASA officials. In the fall of 1963, NASA passed over the young black officer from Kansas City, Kansas, and chose two of his classmates instead: Capt. Theodore C. Freeman of Haverford, Pennsylvania (killed on 31 October in a T-33 jet crash near Ellington Air Force Base, Texas), and Capt. David R. Scott, who went on to walk in space and on the moon.[64]

Stung, Dwight struck back, calling and writing to people in authority with the potential clout to reverse or alter the NASA decision. "All hell broke loose," Yeager recalled. He was hauled on the carpet. Powerful Dwight supporters demanded to know why the black officer was not selected. It was the school and the way it was run, some said. Dwight himself charged racism, as did many of his friends across the country. Congressmen Richard S. Schweiker and Robert N. C. Nix of Pennsylvania announced plans to launch an investigation.

The air force's chief lawyer flew out to Edwards to personally take charge of the case. Pressed for an explanation, Yeager's demeanor became white hot.

"You do have a case of discrimination here," he boomed. "The White House discriminated by forcing us to take an unqualified guy. And we could have discriminated by boosting his grades because he was black!"

After a silence that was probably protracted and palpable, Yeager allowed that "discrimination" was the wrong word. Still, he figured that he had made his point.[65]

Dwight continued to fight back, traveling to Washington to make his case in the Pentagon. His intensity prompted an official to say later:

> There's no question about it. Dwight was going to the moon and he took all possible steps to get there. He didn't back out of it, and didn't flunk out of it. He felt very disconsolate that they could not *prove* to his satisfaction that he wasn't qualified.[66] [Italics added.]

Hobart Taylor, Jr., executive director of the President's Committee on Equal Opportunity, visited Edwards to meet with Dwight and discuss his problems. After their meeting, Taylor said: "Dwight is an intelligent, balanced, decent sort of fellow who believed there were certain people who didn't want him to succeed."

Arranging for Dwight to meet with VIPs on Capitol Hill, Taylor "hope[d] that an expression from the Hill might stop what was going on." It did no good. Nor had Dwight's fifteen-page paper addressed to the Defense Department earlier, in which he'd cataloged the discriminatory deeds done to him—as he perceived them. According to one Washington source, "Dwight's report had gone all the way to the top . . . even Secretary McNamara had a copy of it."[67]

As far as the Pentagon was concerned, it seemed that Dwight had committed a cardinal sin with his stinging complaints. "Let's face it," said the Washington source, "Dwight bucked the 'system' by complaining about discrimination. The military takes a lot of pride in its policy of 'no racial bias in the armed services.' When a guy bucks the system, he's not going to find many people willing to carry the ball for him."[68]

The countenances and backs of Colonel Yeager and his staff stiffened when a group of black civil rights lawyers and congressmen arrived at Edwards. Yeager met with them.

"I am the commandant of this school," he announced, "but the truth is that I lack the college education to qualify as a NASA astronaut. It so happens I could care less. But if I did care a lot, there isn't a damn thing I could do about it, because the *regulations say I must have a college degree.*"[69] [Italics added.]

While the black congressmen and civil rights lawyers pondered what Yeager's tirade had to do with NASA's failure to select Dwight as an astronaut, the colonel pressed on.

"Captain Dwight may care a lot about becoming an astronaut. Well, he gave it his best shot and he just didn't make it. Now, here are his complete school records from day one! Let's review them page by page."

Yeager says that the civil rights lawyers carefully studied Dwight's records and "were satisfied that prejudice was in no way involved in this case. The group had no idea that [Dwight] had received special tutoring and was shocked to see his poor grades."[70]

Given the absolute control teachers or instructors have over student grading, the question arises whether Dwight's grades were accurate as presented. The surprise is, an educator noted, that none of the civil rights lawyers or congressmen present ever asked it. If one of them had, perhaps it would have been moot anyway since Yeager had command authority over the aerospace school. Clearly, Yeager had the men from Washington buffaloed. The record he had presented to them showed unequivocally that Dwight had failed.[71]

Not everyone at Edwards agreed, however. Colonel Thomas U. McElmurray, the deputy commandant of the ARPS during Dwight's tenure, later said that

> Dwight was perfectly capable of being a good astronaut on his own merits. He was perfectly capable of doing it. He would not have been the number one, but if it was important enough to this country at that stage of the game to have a minority early in space then the logical guy was Dwight. But it wasn't important enough to *somebody in this country* at that stage of the game to do it. Dwight was not incompetent. He was graduated number eight in his test pilot class of sixteen. You mustn't say he was mediocre. You didn't graduate unless you were pretty doggoned good. Every man who graduated could have been a test pilot or he would not

have been graduated. We were ethical from that standpoint.[72] [Italics added.]

How, then, did Yeager so blind the men in the Washington delegation that none of them ever questioned his actions? Perhaps the temper tantrum did it. By his own admission, Yeager got mad. So mad, he let it be known, that he "wanted to file charges against Dwight." He wanted to charge Dwight with insubordination, especially after Dwight had brought charges of racism against him and "couldn't make them stick."

But the air force ignored Yeager's request for a court martial. It had already taken enough flak over the "Dwight Affair."

Yeager continued to fume. He knew that in those days and times it had become "fashionable" for government agencies to "advertise themselves as equal opportunity employers." The air force, Yeager said, had been that way with him from the start, and "I would never deny anybody else the chance to prove his worth, no matter who or what he is!" But what Dwight had done struck at the very core of Yeager's being. Dwight had "called into question not only my professional integrity," Yeager later wrote, "but most basic, [my] loyalty to the Air Force!" Yeager says he had experienced prejudice himself because of "his ways and accent." There were, he said, those in the service who had pegged him as "a dumb, down-home squirrel shooter."[73]

SHUT OUT

A man always has two reasons for doing anything—
a good reason and the real reason.
—J. Pierpont Morgan

Although Ed Dwight grew up in a family that stressed excellence and education, his hard work and many accomplishments were not enough to get him to the stars. Although he had survived ten years of stiff competition as an air force officer, logged more than two thousand hours in the air as a jet bomber pilot, and had trained other pilots, he was unable to clear the last hurdle—the dogged racism that continued to hound the armed services and NASA.

There is little doubt that Colonel Yeager was Dwight's personal devil at Edwards. Two observers, Dr. Curtis M. Graves, former deputy director of NASA's academic affairs, and aviation historian Martin Caidin, agree that Yeager stifled Dwight in the ARPS.[74]

But NASA made the actual selections, and it didn't take a rocket scientist to figure out where the agency stood on the issue of race when it announced the latest slate of astronauts in the fall of 1963:

What part, if any, do *genetics* play in astronaut selection? Personnel records indicate that a man with brown hair and blue eyes *may have an advantage* in being selected an astronaut. *There are 19 out of the 30 with brown hair, seven blonds, two redheads, and one each with auburn and black hair. Sixteen of the group have blue eyes; eight brown; three green; and three hazel.*[75] [Italics added.]

One can only wonder what Dwight—who had been notified earlier in the summer that the NASA selection committee did not believe he was "as highly qualified as the candidates selected to participate in the later phases of the program"—would have thought had he read that NASA press release.[76]

A little more than a month before Dwight's class graduated at Edwards, whatever furies existed in America were unleashed. President Kennedy was fatally shot in Dallas on 22 November, and his accused murderer, Lee Harvey Oswald, was killed shortly thereafter by a man named Jack Ruby. Any hope Dwight might have had of assistance from the White House evaporated like steam from a whistling tea kettle, and within days of the assassination he received orders "to get the hell outta there!"[77]

Standing in the ranks with the fifteen other pilots completing ARPS Class IV at Edwards, Dwight listened to Gen. Bernard A. Schriever, commander of the Air Force Systems Command, wax eloquently about their accomplishments and futures. While Dwight could take pride in his work at Edwards, he knew in his heart that he would never, ever fly in space. His dreams had been destroyed—if not by Colonel Yeager and NASA, then by an assassin's bullet. He had been shut out of the astronaut business.

Only two of Dwight's classmates made the NASA astronaut list. Navy and Marine Corps pilots who didn't get selected returned to their respective services for duty. Several of the air force graduates remained at the Flight Test Center at Edwards, and some of them were chosen to serve on the school's staff.[78]

Dwight later observed wryly that he was told he was being assigned to Germany as a liaison officer for that country's then nonexistent space program. Incensed by the perceived slight, he refused to go. Soon after that he was assigned to a bomber test group at Wright-Patterson Air Force Base, Ohio—an assignment his fellow ARPS graduates thought was "the worst possible one a guy can get."[79]

Dwight found life in Ohio both boring and demeaning. When he wasn't flying, he was stuck behind a "small desk in Building 206 of Area C on the huge base" outside of Dayton. That wouldn't have been so bad if Dwight hadn't known that the "C" designation was a hold-over from the days when the air force was segregated and meant the area was for "colored" airmen.

Off base, the situation was even worse. Dwight's efforts to provide his family with a comfortable home were stymied by real estate agents who ignored his "silver captain's bars and air force uniform," and saw only his black skin.

"We're very sorry, but that house was *just* rented," some said.

"There are a lot of repairs that have to be made on *that* house before it can be rented," others laughed.

Finally, a Catholic layman who had seen Dwight's picture on the front of a church publication offered to rent him a home in suburban Huber Heights. Not long after that

the harassment began. [Dwight's] auto took the most punishment: grease was smeared over the spark plugs, air was let out of tires, and at night the vehicle was pelted with rocks. Shouts of "niggers go home!" met the family almost every day. Dwight finally decided to move after a brick was thrown through a window and his daughter, Tina, was showered with broken glass.[80]

The pressure was more than Dwight and his wife, Sue, the girl he had loved since high school, could bear. They decided to get a divorce— a difficult decision because both were Roman Catholics. Dwight, who kept the children, was forced to send them to live in Kansas City with their grandparents because of his duty commitments.

He began to think about resigning his commission. Not only would it free him from the constant reminders of his recent failure, but it would get him away from the snarling, vicious racist acts with which he was constantly confronted. But Dwight couldn't bring himself to submit the paperwork. His dreams of the stars—of going to the moon and beyond—still burned brightly within him. He fought off the temptation to run and hide and resolved to keep fighting for redress.

Meanwhile, as Ed Dwight struggled with his personal demons in Dayton, Ohio, the first rumblings of catastrophe concerning the so-called Dwight Affair were surfacing in the nation's capital.

The previous autumn, while Dwight had been finishing his training at Edwards, a former newspaperman working as an assistant to a long-time Democratic congressman approached a black colleague at one of the many business-mixed-with-pleasure gatherings so common inside the beltway.

"Here's something you might do something with," he whispered, leaning close to his friend's ear.

The black newsman's eyebrows arched and he turned toward his informant, straining to hear over the booze-driven babble. "Yeah? What?"

"Remember the Negro astronaut?"

"Yes," replied the newsman, his interest piqued.

"Well, he's been dropped from the space program! Interested?"

The reporter nodded. The press of people around them, the snippets of errant conversations—it was all too distracting. "Listen," he said, "we can't talk in private about this here. How about lunch in a few days?"

"You've got it," the congressional assistant said, and with that they melted into the crowd.

At lunch, the black newsman was all ears. At first, it seemed as if his informant was from another planet or, at the very least, had received bad information. He called Dwight "Wright," and had him assigned to the wrong state and air force base. But, observed the reporter, Charles L. Sanders, "the essence was there." What he needed was a little research to bring the story into focus. He needed contacts. Could the informant provide Sanders the name of someone in authority willing to talk?

"Let me check my source," said the tipster, "and I'll call you."[81]

*   *   *

Two days later the call came. The tipster said he'd struck a vein of pure gold: He had the name and phone number of a Defense Department official who not only knew the case inside out, but was willing to talk about it. The congressional staffer said the man was nervous because Defense Secretary McNamara had issued strict guidelines about talking to members of the media, but he was willing to speak if he could be assured it would be in absolute confidence. Sanders agreed that the man's comments would be strictly off-the-record.

"I've been warned about talking to reporters," the Defense Department official told Sanders when he called, "but there's smoke here and there may be fire. Let's go with it."

The two men talked late into the night. The official told Sanders about the "Dwight case from the day it began in 1961." He described the White House's involvement and the air force's response. He talked of Dwight's enrollment in Phase I of the test pilot program and his subsequent graduation in 1962. He discussed Dwight's hassles with a "high-ranking officer" at the school, his selection for Phase II training, NASA's rejection of him, his subsequent reassignment to the backwater job at Wright-Patterson, and Dwight's propensity to fight back. The information, while not specific, provided plenty of signposts for Sanders. He began the long process of following up on the many leads the official had provided him.

The air force responded quickly enough with dates, numbers of people enrolled in the aerospace program at Edwards, and other mundane information. Questions bearing on the issue of racial hostility toward Dwight were stonewalled, however. One air force information officer told Sanders, "We have no information concerning any reports of alleged racial antagonism" at Edwards. Sanders's queries about why NASA failed to select Dwight drew a figurative shrug. No information was available, he was told. Furthermore, the air force refused to "acknowledge that Dwight had ever applied for the [astronaut] program."[82]

If anything, NASA's responses were even more vague than the air force's. "It is NASA policy," said a press officer, "to never publicize personnel matters involving individuals whose applications have been turned down."

When Sanders persisted in his efforts to ferret out information, Julian Scheer, head of the agency's office of public affairs and senior aide to then-NASA Administrator James E. Webb, got hot under the collar. Scheer denied that the air force "had ever recommended Dwight for the NASA astronaut program at Houston," and said that, furthermore, "to my knowledge the air force *never* recommended anybody." Scheer then stepped out on a limb and declared, "And one other thing, it was my impression, speaking off the top of my head, that Dwight *never finished his training at Edwards!*"[83] [Italics added.]

The conflicting information Sanders got from the Pentagon and NASA only heightened his interest. He plunged deeper and deeper into the mystery.

SOMETIMES A "HIT DOG" *DON'T* HOLLER!

On 2 July 1964, a little less than a year after Capt. Ed Dwight was bounced from the air force's Aerospace Research Pilots School, President Johnson signed the Civil Rights Act into law. The long-sought legislation forbade racial discrimination in most privately owned places of public accommodation and gave the attorney general the authority to file civil suits on behalf of the victims of discrimination. Voting discrimination was also outlawed, and a commission was created to "investigate alleged racial discrimination by employers and labor unions."[84]

Despite the enactment of that historic legislation, riots erupted in the north that summer. When a fifteen-year-old black youth was killed in New York City, riots broke out in Harlem and Brooklyn, and the violence soon spread to Rochester, Jersey City, and Philadelphia. That same year, the bodies of three young civil rights workers (two whites and a black) were found buried under an earthen dam in Mississippi, where they had been left after being murdered.

In 1965, the civil rights movement changed its tactics and began promoting voter registration. On 1 February, when protesters led by the Rev. Martin Luther King, Jr., attempted to march from Selma to Montgomery, Alabama, they were greeted with tear gas, bullwhips, cattle prods, and clubs. Black men, women, and children were beaten to the ground. Several days later, a sympathetic Unitarian minister from Boston was murdered. The federal government sought an injunction against Alabama to permit the march, and President Johnson told the nation:

I speak tonight for the dignity of man and the dignity of democracy. I urge every member of both parties, Americans of all religions and of all colors, from every section of this country, to join me in that cause. At times, history and fate meet in a single time, in a single place, to shape a turning point in Man's unending search for freedom. So it was at Lexington and Concord. So it was a century ago at Appomattox. So it was last week in Selma, Alabama.[85]

The world paused, looking for long moments at Highway 82 in Alabama as whites and blacks marched and sang together behind a phalanx of federal troops and National Guardsmen.

The summer of 1965 promised to be long and hot. Racial tension mounted and the nation's attention focused on the predominantly black Watts area of Los Angeles, which seemed about to explode. But Charles Sanders's article about the injustices suffered by Ed Dwight exploded in the pages of *Ebony* first.

Newspapers blossomed with the news about Dwight's failure to become an astronaut. The story was a hot one, linked as it was to the racial tension that plagued the country. News of the alleged failure of an African American most people thought had already achieved success held special allure.

On 3 June 1965, the Washington, D.C., *Evening Star* proclaimed that Dwight, the "first and only Negro to get through the Air Force space pilot school, was recommended for astronaut training but was not selected by the civilian space agency for that program." It quoted the Defense Department's succinct statement that Dwight was "accorded the same rights, privileges and treatment as the other students in the Air Force School." NASA's official response, also quoted in the *Evening Star,* was more specific:

A formal objective rating system based on flight experience, academic background and supervisory ratings was developed and used by a preliminary selection committee in rating the candidates to make sure that the best qualified were selected as finalists to be considered for the 14 available astronaut positions. Of the 136 candidates, 102, including Captain Dwight, were eliminated by the primary selection committee, leaving a group of *34 finalists, of whom the 14 best were chosen.* Selection is made on a best-qualified basis, without regard to race, religion or sex. Captain Dwight did possess the basic qualifications; he did not score sufficiently high to be selected under the rating system.[86] [Italics added.]

The *New York Times* and the *Los Angeles Times* also carried the story. *The New York Times* quoted Dwight's denial of the charge that he had been eliminated from the space program because of his race— a statement he made after flying to China Lake Naval Air Station, California. "The charge," he is quoted as saying, "apparently had some information out of context."

Although it was against NASA policy to discuss any individual's qualifications, the agency issued a statement of general principle concerning Dwight: "If he was not selected as an astronaut, it does not mean he was not qualified. It means that someone more qualified was selected ahead of him."

The *Los Angeles Times* article added only that Dwight "does not know why he was turned down as an astronaut."[87]

The next day, the *Bakersfield Californian* reported that Dwight had gotten his back up when the air force claimed that he had been assigned duty as a bomber test pilot because of his "special qualifications." Dwight acidly replied that he "was assigned as a bomber test pilot with no bombing experience!" He also disagreed with the notion that the assignment he currently held was one for which "he is very capable," as claimed by the air force.[88] The same day, the *Washington Post* ran a photograph of Dwight with a cutline noting that he had "apparently been dropped from the program because of a letter he wrote about 'racial pressure' in the aerospace school."[89]

On 6 June, astronauts James A. McDivitt and Edward H. White II pushed Dwight off the nation's front pages with news of their successful *Gemini IV* launch and subsequent space walk. Edward White grabbed the world's attention as he wheeled freely in space, apparently loving every minute of it. White kept up an almost continual banter with McDivitt inside the spacecraft, sharing with his space companion and the world below vivid descriptions of what it was like: "The sun is blinding, but it's quite nice . . . I can sit out here and see the whole California coast."[90]

There was at least one perplexing moment during White's space walk, however. As White was working outside the spacecraft, McDivitt told him to slow down so he could take White's picture. A long pause followed, after which McDivitt exclaimed, "You smeared up my windshield, you dirty dog!"

The world wondered what it was that White had done. It took a call from President Johnson to solve the mystery after the two had splashed down in the Atlantic. After extending an invitation for the pair of astronauts to join him at his Texas ranch, the president drawled, "Major, several million people in this country have been wondering for three days what you were doing to Jim's windshield when he called you a dirty dog."

Without going into the mechanics of how one goes about it in space, White told the president—and the world—that he had voided his bladder. "There wasn't much [else] I could do," he explained sheepishly. "We worked pretty fast—there wasn't much I could do about it."[91]

As usual, none of this was lost on the Russians, who first profusely congratulated the United States on the success of the *Gemini IV* spaceflight, then took the opportunity to criticize America for allowing racial prejudice to "creep into the American space program." The Soviet news agency Tass "revived Dwight's charge against the air force 'that he was rejected for astronaut duty because he is a Negro.'"[92]

In a comprehensive analysis of the relationship between science and the space effort, authors Joseph Atkinson and Jay Shafritz note H. L. Nieburg's comments on the Dwight story, adding that "such regrettable news items reflect other aspects of society and dull even the brightest moments of our national program, and may have more powerfully affected the American image at home and abroad than the *Gemini* flight that occurred the same week."[93]

The Tass observation was, in fact, an expansion of a similar one made several years earlier by Edward R. Murrow while he was head of the USIA. Murrow at the time was worried about further alienating African nations, and had warned the White House that failure to include a black in the space program was the sort of thing that could sour relations between America and predominantly black Third World countries.

News of Dwight's "failure" had a devastating effect on the psyches of American blacks. As early as 11 June, Cheryl Aaron of Chicago wrote to NASA wondering why astronaut Dwight had been kicked out of the space program. NASA responded that Dwight was not "kicked out . . . he was never in the astronaut program in the first place, *but only a candi-*

date." The agency referred Aaron to the air force, which it said ran an astronaut training program "quite separate from NASA's."[94] [Italics added.]

In August, two months after the *Ebony* article appeared, a bumper crop of dissensions sprouted in the magazine's "Letters to the Editor" section. Rage simmered. Anger and disillusion with the country's military services boiled over.

"I spent ten years, nine months and seventeen days in the United States Air Force," wrote Edwin J. Lewis, Jr., of Long Island, New York. "I find that Captain Edward Dwight's experiences were very similar to incidents that are everyday occurrences. The Air Force is saturated with individuals who cannot conceive the idea of integration . . . these people are determined to keep the USAF officer cadre as white as possible."

John Brown, Jr., of Chicago, wrote to say that he had served in the army for ten years, but had to give it up because he never found the promised equal opportunity.

Perhaps one of the most damning letters on the subject came from Larry Wood, of Maywood, Illinois, who wrote:

> The treatment of Mr. Dwight and the mistreatment of so many Negro servicemen serves as a source of discouragement to young Negroes seeking "a career" in the armed forces. . . . As I hear, read and see the plights of Negro servicemen, their treatment by their white "buddies," their treatment by their white commanders, and the general hurt and demoralization of these men, I wonder if the American uniform is worth wearing.

And Randolph Williams of Washington, D.C., wasted few words: "He got what is known in the Air Force as 'the shaft'!"

In those days, according to one observer, there was likely to have been a mighty chorus of black airmen who were ready and willing to supply the proper closing to Williams's statement: "Right up the old gazoo!"

One ray of hope shone in all the letters to the editor, and that came from 1st Lt. Edward Carwine, who, after reading about Dwight and relating Dwight's experiences to his own career, "was not sure of any irregularity" since he personally hadn't "been subjected to racial discrimination." But there Carwine's quite civil and hopeful attitude changed.

His words became those of an avenging angel, and one could almost see the flash and flail of his terrible, swift sword. "But if," he continued, "investigation reveals that Captain Dwight was sidetracked because of his color, those responsible should be severely dealt with! There is no place in the armed forces for racial prejudice, intolerance and discrimination."

Earlier in the year, congressmen Robert Nix and Richard Schweiker kept the air force and NASA hopping. In April, Representative Nix demanded to know why Ed Dwight was not selected for NASA's manned spaceflight training program. Richard L. Callaghan, the NASA assistant administrator for legislative affairs, responded by providing Nix the same numbers the agency later trotted out to mollify the media in the wake of the stir caused by the Sanders article.

Callaghan concluded his letter with what became NASA's stock reply. He wrote that although Dwight possessed "the basic qualifications, he did not score sufficiently high to be selected under the established rating system"—a system built around high qualifications and objective evaluation procedures "as rigid as we can make them."[95]

Hobart Taylor, Jr., a member of the White House staff, also wrote to NASA headquarters in April requesting details as to why Dwight was not selected for astronaut training. The letter was passed on to the Manned Space Center (MSC) in Houston for a reply that incorporated most of the same policy statements, but provided additional detail.

Robert R. Gilruth, the MSC director, defended NASA's selection procedures by making it clear that the agency's initial selection criteria involved the careful review of "forms of relevant experience, flight experience record, application for federal employment (SF 57), a supervisor's rating of the candidate, and the transcripts from respective universities" in order to ensure all candidates were highly qualified. In Dwight's case, wrote Gilruth:

The assessment of the applicant's qualifications, as pertaining to flight crew requirements, indicated that Captain Dwight was inconsistent in the manner in which he performed his test missions. The overall evaluation of the supervisor listed Captain Dwight as an "average" candidate, which is the fourth level of five choices.

Further, a review of his ranking in the test pilot school, which he had attended earlier, indicated that he had graduated in the *lower third of his class, lower than any other Air Force nominee.* [Italics added.]

The last sentence quoted above conflicts with the earlier mentioned recollection of Col. Thomas U. McElmurray, the school's deputy commandant, who said Dwight graduated eighth in a class of sixteen. The NASA response goes on to note that Dwight's

college transcripts showed that he was awarded a Bachelor of Science degree from Arizona State College ["with distinction," was included in the original draft here, but was deleted in the final version]. Although his grade point average was acceptable, his course work was largely at the sophomore level and below, and there were no upper-level scientific or engineering courses of any significance.

Of course, one question immediately arises: How does one get a bachelor of science degree, with distinction, completing course work "largely at the sophomore level and below," and with *no* "upper-level scientific or engineering courses of any significance" from a school with a reputation like that of Arizona State University?

NASA's bottom line was that Captain Dwight's "experience, recommendations, and educational background were substantially below those of the other candidates submitted by the Air Force. He was, therefore, eliminated from the selection, at a time when 102 out of a total of 136 active candidates were eliminated, including 14 out of 26 Air Force candidates."[96]

A couple of months later, shortly after Sanders's story about Dwight was published, Representative Schweiker, a member of the House Armed Services Committee, told the *New York Times* that he had independently confirmed information regarding the allegations made in *Ebony* and had cited his findings in a letter to President Johnson requesting an investigation as early as February of 1965. The president's response, said Schweiker, was "very perfunctory," and he promised to send another letter to the president seeking an immediate investigation of the "serious charges" made by Dwight. Furthermore, Schweiker added, he "believed the charges of discrimination were true."[97]

Bitter and buffeted by the racism he had encountered around Wright-Patterson Air Force Base in Ohio, Dwight was not through lashing out. Although by his own admission he "didn't have time to read *Ebony* and *Jet*—there were too many other important things to do"—he did keep track of events in the majority media.

On 24 September 1965, astronauts L. Gordon Cooper, Jr., and Charles Conrad were featured in a *Baltimore Sun* article that left Dwight fuming. The two were ostensibly on a goodwill tour, flying from Nairobi to visit Jomo Kenyatta at Kenya's Keekerok Game Lodge.

"This is the first thing I've flown since *Gemini V!*" exclaimed Cooper giddily as he stepped down from the Aztec aircraft and shook hands with Kenyatta. He and Conrad were twenty minutes late, having gotten lost while buzzing over buffalo in the desert scrub.

Kenyatta and the astronauts exchanged gifts—including a twelve-foot-long Masai spear, a symbol, said Kenyatta, of their victory.

Cooper beamed and joked that, "at last we've [got] something to stick into our director of operations. We've been wanting to do this for a long time!"

After they finished exchanging pleasantries, the astronauts toured the game preserve with Kenyatta, who showed them lions lolling in the bush and wildebeest and zebra grazing. Then they returned to the airstrip where Cooper and Conrad boarded their Aztec and flew on to Nairobi and then Lagos, Nigeria, the next day.[98]

In Nigeria, Cooper incurred the wrath of Ed Dwight, who read about the *Gemini V* astronauts' press conference there while seated at his little desk in Building 206C at Wright-Patterson Air Force Base.

When asked about the possibility of black participation in the U.S. space program, Cooper replied in part: "When we find [a woman or] Negro with the right qualifications, they'll be selected—presently no Negroes [or women] have been found to be anywhere near qualified."[99]

When Dwight read those words, he exploded. After having gone through all that he had—and to a certain extent was still going through—Dwight was in no mood to countenance such a callous remark from the likes of L. Gordon Cooper or anybody else! On 30 September 1965, he sent a letter to President Johnson. The typewriter keys probably smoked as he churned out two and a half pages of single-spaced text.

Dwight wasted little time on pleasantries, but instead got right to the heart of the matter:

if it is true that Colonel Cooper did, in fact, make these statements, he did so as a representative of the United States government. I feel as a Negro American that this rationale is untenable
and totally unacceptable. These statements are a direct affront
to the American Negro citizen, and indirectly can have only harmful
effects to our policy of good international race relations with the
African countries.

Dwight's logic was cogent, reflecting the same concerns expressed
earlier by Murrow. Dwight added that he took

strong issue to Colonel Cooper's implication that the American
Negro is so backward and unqualified that he is incapable of
performing space functions. . . . I am fully qualified in all respects
to perform space flight. . . . It is not my intention to question
government policy, but in light of the intense social upheaval in
progress in this country, Colonel Cooper's statement is a blight
on Negro progress. He has demonstrated a lack of insight into
the real Negro problem here and abroad. A man of his stature
does not smack the Negro in the face with such a discouraging
attitude, and then expect the Negro to have faith in the American way, and to exercise the drive and determination to excel.
He could at least have exhibited a positive attitude. We, as a nation,
can ill afford to alienate these black nations.[100]

On 4 October, the White House referred Dwight's letter to the NASA
administrator for a "direct reply." The referral form attached to the
letter, signed by presidential assistant Paul M. Popple, indicated that
Dwight's letter "reveals intention to leave active military service because he feels the Negro is being discriminated against in the space
program."[101]

NASA's Julian Scheer received Dwight's letter on 15 October, with
instructions to respond only to those portions regarding "the Cooper
comment" and Dwight's nonselection for NASA astronaut training.
The air force was ordered to deal with the other charges made by Dwight.[102]

NASA's response to Dwight took the palliative approach, noting
that the White House had asked it to respond to that part of the letter
"in which you discuss remarks made by Colonel Cooper in Nigeria."

The NASA official who drafted the reply continued:

> Since I was with Colonel Cooper, I feel qualified to respond. I
> know, because I responded to another part of the same question
> in . . . [a] conference, that there was absolutely no intent on
> [Cooper's] part to reflect on your qualifications or those of any
> American.

The remainder of the response to Dwight simply regurgitated official rationales already given concerning Dwight's nonselection as an astronaut.[103]

Robert F. Freitag, NASA's director of field center development, forwarded copies of the correspondence to Donald K. "Deke" Slayton, the astronaut-turned-administrator, for proper filing and safeguarding. In his cover letter, Freitag noted the material's "sensitive nature," and explained that the reply contained "our comment on Gordon Cooper's *alleged* remarks made while in Lagos, Nigeria."[104] [Italics added.]

Thus were the fires Dwight had tried so hard to ignite so deftly extinguished.

There is an old saying in African-American folklore, usually delivered tongue-in-cheek by elders to persons involved in questionable, sometimes shady behavior who, for all intents and purposes have been found out, but continue to loudly proclaim their innocence.

"Hit dog always hollers!" they announce, their countenances reproving, their voices tinged with disgust.

But such proverbs are sometimes found wanting. This time, the "hit dogs" didn't holler at all. Instead, they deftly dodged Ed Dwight's volley of verbal and written "rocks"—an expression of the outrage he felt over the racism he had both perceived and experienced.

There may have been a "yelp," but there was plainly no hollering as they quietly closed the book on the Dwight Affair.

PARADOX

As far as Ed Dwight was concerned, the real reason he was not selected to become an astronaut was, pure and simple, racism. He viewed Colonel Yeager, commandant of the ARPS, as his chief antagonist, and saw the staff and faculty and his classmates as collaborators. They became the devils on whom Dwight could focus his frustration. There are, however, other factors that contributed to Dwight's nonselection.

A strange admixture of human frailties and the attitudes prevalent in American society and its politics of the time combined to thwart Dwight. Some observers contend that racism, although certainly a factor affecting the decision not to select Dwight for astronaut training, was only a minor consideration. Dwight, they argue, was caught on the horns of multiple dilemmas.

Of foremost importance was the relative inexperience of the new president, John F. Kennedy, and his brother, Robert, the attorney general, as they dealt with the racial problems sweeping the country.[105] Although well intentioned, both Kennedys were forced to deal with issues that, until then, were only peripheral to them. Faced with a full-blown civil rights revolution, they sought a number of quick fixes—not least among which was getting a black American into the space program—intended to mollify the greatest possible portion of the black electorate.

Such quick fixes might have worked had President Kennedy lived. It was he, after all, who issued the directive that led to Dwight's selection for the air force's astronaut training program. The attorney general, on the other hand, provided the clout. In fact, the fine hand of their administration was evident right up to the time the list of names of ARPS students recommended for selection as astronauts was provided to NASA. Despite this, resistance to their not-so-subtle pressure permeated the program.

Colonel McElmurray, Yeager's deputy at the ARPS, said that there was nothing about Dwight himself that could have accounted for the atmosphere he ran into when he arrived at the school. Nevertheless, McElmurray admits that Dwight was justified in feeling the way he did about his reception, although he says Dwight's treatment stemmed from the fact that he had been sent to the school because of political connection, and was regarded as "that Kennedy guy." Such resistance was not without precedent. According to McElmurray:

You have to understand the test pilot school to understand that real well. For example, [there was] the Korean ace [who] didn't have an engineering degree. That was an absolute, hard requirement, [but]

he got there by connections. He didn't even get a diploma signifying completion of the school. He was resented by the people in
the school. Of all the air force schools, that one was probably the
most nearly even-steven [and] objective. . . . There was not any "fix-
ing" of anything much there. . . . You earned what you got![106]

As for Dwight, McElmurray recalled that "Ed was a very capable
fellow! He was a smart guy [and] a pretty good flier. He was not number
one in his class, but he was as good as the middle of the run that we
brought through the course."

Nevertheless, Yeager had called Dwight incompetent. He'd emphatically
proclaimed that Dwight couldn't cut it academically. More than that,
he'd pooh-poohed Dwight's flying ability. If Dwight was so competent and smart, why would Yeager say such things about him? After
pondering the question, McElmurray replied:

Well, I certainly wouldn't propose to speak for Yeager, but Yeager,
like so many exceptional guys who have been at the top for a
long time, tend to judge [others] from the level of the top of the
heap. . . . Again, I don't speak for him, but when evaluating graduates
who came out of there, he [was probably] looking at the first and
second guy in a class [and] saying, "Okay, those are the quality
guys! The rest of them—let them go do some job somewhere [else]."
He [was] inclined that way because he was a top-of-the-heaper
himself. [So what if] Dwight did not perform in the top 25 percent of his class? . . . But judging, say, the [top] 75 percent of
the class, Dwight did well. He was not [incompetent, a failure
academically, or a poor pilot.][107]

Still, Dwight viewed Yeager as a racist and a bigot. McElmurray,
when told of Dwight's interview with the "high-ranking officer" at
Edwards mentioned in Dwight's fifteen-page report on his school
experience, launched into further defense of his former boss.

"In all fairness," he said, "I think that if a regular Caucasian had
[used] political influence to get into the class, Yeager would have made
exactly the same comments that he did." McElmurray added that the
use of the terms "black" and "white" was simply an enabling factor

for the purpose of quick "identity," and was not the basis for resentment of Dwight. Rather, resentment toward Dwight was born of the fact that many believed he had sought political influence to get into the class. Yet, said McElmurray, "it's my understanding that [Dwight] didn't ask [anybody] to be sent out there."

In that, McElmurray was correct. Dwight had simply applied for astronaut training. The political decision to actively seek a qualified African-American astronaut candidate was made independently by the White House. Unfortunately, according to McElmurray, Yeager and his staff weren't aware of that. For all intents and purposes, Dwight was seen as a "shoo-in," and that was that as far as they were concerned. This fact, more than any other, McElmurray believes, hurt Dwight. He explained that competition for the slim number of NASA astronaut training slots was extremely keen, and said there was "strong resentment" at the thought of someone obtaining one by any means other than the "objective evaluation of all the candidates" in the program. In short, even had Dwight's visage been as white as snow, his academic and flying performance, which ranked him in the middle of the pack, were not good enough for NASA or the air force, which nominated "only about the top three or four" graduates from a class.[108]

Even so, the fine hand of the Kennedy administration remained apparent. "I remember when we were doing all of this," continued McElmurray, "we were told: 'You *will* go down the list until you include Dwight!"[109]

McElmurray's account rings true. At the time the *Ebony* story broke, the official air force and NASA responses almost never failed to note the number of other candidates who, in addition to Dwight, were not selected. They were undoubtedly the difference between the "top three or four" in Dwight's class and his ultimate ranking of eighth in a class of sixteen.

This is the exercise that probably moved McElmurray to say in an earlier interview, "we were ethical from that standpoint."[110] To be ethical, the ARPS staff felt that they simply could not discriminate by selecting the third or fourth top student, pass over those in between and submit Dwight's name. They decided it would only be fair to include *all* the students within the specified range in order to reach Dwight.

Thus did Capt. Ed Dwight, ostensibly by the slenderest of margins, miss his chance to become an astronaut. The odds are great that, had President Kennedy lived, NASA would have been directed to select Dwight.

"The greatest thing that could have happened," McElmurray suggested, was for Dwight to "have come in Number One" in his class.[111]

When he did not, Dwight began fighting back. Charge and countercharge. Bitterness and acrimony. Accusations of racism and bigotry. Bringing down the establishment on the heads of Yeager and the ARPS staff by citing the untoward treatment Dwight perceived he was the victim of—treatment in which racism undoubtedly played a part, because Dwight was, in his own words, "the nigger who's messing up their stuff."[112]

But Dwight was also a political pawn; a "shoo-in," an opportunist by fiat whom Yeager and company were loath to accept. Racism, the color of Dwight's skin, his alleged poor performance, and so-called objectivity became weapons used to deny him his goal. Once the fulcrum in the person of President Kennedy was removed, Dwight's dreams of catapulting into space were dashed.

In the final analysis, he may have shot himself in the foot with his racial caterwauling, for even though Yeager, McElmurray, and the school staff still thought him a "pretty good guy," the problem, as they saw it, was that he was "diminishing himself." They felt no real resentment at his harangues. They believed that Dwight had been dumped on by the system. In their view, when the Kennedy administration told Dwight: "We want you to go do this and we're going to assure you that you get through this," it set the stage for his ultimate disappointment and embarrassment.[113]

The late John "Mr. Death" Whitehead, a member of the now-famous band of African Americans nobody thought could fly during World War II—the Tuskegee Airmen—and a graduate of the experimental test pilots' school at Edwards long before Dwight ever showed up, suggests that part of Dwight's problem may well have been "his attitude." Whitehead said Dwight went about it the wrong way, that he beat himself. "Hell," Whitehead recalled, "Dwight wasn't the first black man to attend the flight test center schools at Edwards! But we all got through without a problem." In fact, added Whitehead, L. Gordon Cooper suggested that Whitehead himself consider becoming an astronaut. Whitehead said he turned it down because "if there was a severe racial problem in those days, it was with NASA. I told Cooper I was tired of dealing with it."[114]

Perhaps the saddest commentary on the Dwight Affair may be that Dwight could have been the top man in his class with perhaps a little more effort on his part. The evidence suggests Dwight was certainly capable of it. But perhaps the knowledge that he was the "Kennedy boy [who] was going to make it, no matter what" held him back.

For all his bombast, Dwight is a very precise person, a perfectionist *and* an idealist. He was prone to being deceived and bamboozled by others. That appears to be precisely what happened when he reported to the ARPS. By his own admission:

> It [was] like being out on the ocean going into a storm without knowing it's coming. I walk in there like I'm bad, and they turn me around. I was so naive. I said, "Well, this is what is hard about the air force." I didn't know they were raking me over the coals.[115]

There was a difference in the way Dwight appeared to others in the school and the way he saw himself—"I walked in there like I was bad!"—which left Yeager with the firm conviction that Dwight was clearly the wrong candidate.[116]

His life in a shambles, his first wife long gone, Dwight secured custody of his children and married again, only to see that marriage dissolve in thirty days. He was, he later remarked, "about to go crazy," when he met his third wife, Barbara, with whom he had grown up in Kansas City. She helped bring him to ground. Still, all that he had been through gnawed at him.

Perhaps he thought that his letter to President Johnson complaining about L. Gordon Cooper's indiscretion in Nigeria, in which Dwight reminded the chief executive of his qualifications, might still save the day. After all, he recalled, "They promised me a flight if I wouldn't talk to the press."[117] That was probably a pipe dream, for the president was angered by the articles featuring Dwight's pot shots at the air force alleging racial discrimination.[118] President Johnson was the wrong man to approach with mewling protestation, breast-beating, and foot-stomping. With LBJ, loyalty was everything. To attack the agency that fed one, in this instance, the air force, was a serious breach of loyalty in Johnson's book.[119]

So it was that Captain Dwight and his career went right down the tube. President Johnson was already casting about for his *own* black astronaut. Dwight was perceived as damaged goods; he had become too closely associated with JFK in the public's mind.

Furthermore, as far as the air force was concerned, Dwight was in a worse situation than Deke Slayton, who had been sidelined by a heart murmur. When advised of Slayton's problem, General LeMay, then air force chief of staff, reasoned, "If he can't fly for NASA, how can he fly for the air force?"[120]

Dwight knew it was over. Even though he had made it to the major's promotion list, he knew he

> couldn't stay. I mean, there was no military career. [My pass-over by NASA] destroyed it. It was over. You don't stay in the military after making a clown out of yourself, after [that] kind of exposure. What would they do with me? How could I accept a regular air force job, work with regular people, or do regular things? I mean, I [was] constantly going to be on somebody's list. . . . There was nothing to do but resign.[121]

He was probably correct, for the air force, although realizing that its efforts to eliminate racism within its ranks weren't perfect, had been the first military branch to fully integrate after President Truman issued his 1948 executive order to end segregation in the armed forces. Naysayers or not, the service was proud of its record as far as discrimination was concerned. Dwight had sullied the air force uniform. Black officers like Col. Daniel "Chappie" James, Jr., who later became America's first black four-star general, were touting the air force and the progress it had made, insisting that *excellence of performance* was the ultimate guarantor of success in the military.[122]

In 1966, Ed Dwight resigned his air force commission.

To his credit, Dwight did not allow his life to go flat. He opened a chain of restaurants in Denver, but soon found them unprofitable. He next tried working as an aviation consultant, then joined a group that established a jet training school for pilots certified in propeller-driven aircraft. At that point his dream exploded in his face. His six instructors, departing on a flight without him one day while he was closing a real estate deal, crashed fifteen minutes after takeoff, killing all aboard. "It scared me," Dwight said later. "I haven't flown since." He then dabbled in real estate for an extended period and was quite successful, building condominiums and other properties in Denver's more exclusive neighborhoods. He once declared himself "the only black in Denver who could get a $100,000 loan on my signature." But he lost it all during the recession of the 1970s by staying in the market too long after his partners effectively bailed out.[123]

Fate brought Dwight full circle, back to his favorite childhood pastime— sculpture. After earning a MFA degree at the University of Denver, he taught there for a period. Lucrative commissions soon followed. He made renderings of Hank Aaron and Dr. Martin Luther King; of Herb Alpert and Jackie Robinson. As the guest of honor at the Denver Marriott Hotel in 1984, kicking off the Republican National Committee fund drive, his art spearheaded an auction of bronze eagles. A lone eagle, "Visions," sold for $19,000; smaller eagles for $1,000 each. Edwin Meese III was there. So was Miss America of 1958. The childhood "pastime" parlayed itself into a craft worth some $1.2 million to Dwight, along with the status that came with being a respected sculptor.[124]

Programs for Dwight's unveilings unfailingly refer to him as "America's First Black Astronaut Trainee." Conversations buzz. He is often regarded with awe. People wonder, wide-eyed, how his life might have been different had President Kennedy not been killed. Dwight unabashedly accepts the accolades and tells all who will listen that the reason he never went into space was "100 percent the death of Kennedy." His "aviation career" had been a nightmare. "I thought I was a white boy. If I could have found myself before, I would not have walked in [the Air Force] expecting something from them."[125]

Dwight refuses to believe the McElmurrays and Yeagers, or the media, which reported that he failed to become an astronaut because his class rank was simply too low. As far as he is concerned, it was racism and JFK's untimely assassination.

To this day, the Dwight Affair is a chapter in American history the federal government and almost everyone connected with it would prefer to forget.[126] Official histories of the Air Force Flight Test Center mention Dwight, confirming that he graduated from both Phase I and Phase II of the ARPS, but fail to address his ultimate assignment, as they do the subsequent assignments of his classmates. As for Dwight's fifteen-page report, if it still exists, it probably lies moldering in some far-flung archive, "perhaps part of [a collection of] papers the government isn't ready to release at this time."[127]

Looking back, it seems as though America ultimately sought to exorcise the memory of Ed Dwight's travails. But less than a decade after the Dwight Affair became history, one observer noted:

> While little can be done about NASA's past policies, that agency has plenty of time to work out a program of recruiting nonwhite astronauts. . . . Everyone helps foot the bill for the space program [and] NASA has an obligation to include all segments of society. . . . [When that obligation is fulfilled,] then the thwarted efforts of Edward Dwight would be redeemed.

Although those sentiments were too late for Dwight, he has few regrets:

> My involvement was fun. I enjoyed it. I wouldn't change anything. I'm glad it turned out the way it [did] . . . because I wouldn't be [an artist] today. I'd still be living in that shit . . . caught up in the aftermath and the afterglow, trying to live it like the rest of those guys.[128]

CHAPTER 2

THE FIRST AFRICAN-AMERICAN ASTRONAUT-DESIGNEE

Maj. Robert H. Lawrence, Jr.

It is with great pleasure that I congratulate you on selection . . .
to the Manned Orbiting Laboratory [program]. . . . [It] marks you
[as] an outstanding officer . . . a member of an elite group.
—*Gen. J. P. McConnell, air force chief of staff,*
to Capt. Robert H. Lawrence, Jr.
20 June 1967

The F-104D *Starfighter* crouched silently on the Edwards Air Force Base ramp. A proud century series fighter aircraft, its lines evoked images of speed, even though it sat stock-still, casting angled shadows across the tarmac in the desert sun. It was a bullet with wings. Jazzy. Fighter pilots loved the *Starfighter*. This one bore the number 57-1357 on its tail and belonged to the ARPS.[1]

It was the afternoon of 8 December 1967. Air force majors Harvey J. Royer and Robert H. Lawrence, Jr., walked toward the waiting jet. Major Royer, the ARPS's chief of operations, was scheduled for a proficiency mission as part of his Phase II curriculum orientation.

Major Lawrence, already designated as the air force's first African-American astronaut, was going along as copilot in order to maintain the high degree of flying proficiency he had already demonstrated. When they reached the plane, Royer climbed into the front seat, followed by Lawrence, who settled into the rear of the cockpit. After a normal preflight check, the whine of the jet's powerful General Electric J79 engine pierced the arid air. You could feel the power at the other end of the runway. It shivered your timbers; caused your innards to undulate.[2]

The *Starfighter* was fun to taxi. When you jiggled the throttle out of idle and pulled it back, that juiced-up, crazy engine would go *woooooh*—like the Super Chief riding a straightaway. Some pilots liked to shock people around the flightline that way. They would sneak up on them at idle, then goose the throttle and make the engine roar—just to see them jump![3]

Lawrence and Royer probably played this game as they taxied their needle-nosed, stubby-winged interceptor toward the runway. When they reached the far end of Runway 04, the tower cleared them for takeoff. They locked down and throttled up, then began their power roll. It was 1458 hours, Pacific Standard Time. Once airborne, they climbed like a rocket until, within a matter of seconds, they were twenty-five thousand feet above the Edwards runway centerline on a heading of 130 degrees.

What they were about to practice had been used as a training tool in the ARPS program since 1961. At that time, planners had sought a way to simulate the in-flight mechanics of space and reentry vehicles. The skills and experience required to master those mechanics were considered necessary for test pilots and astronaut trainees. Early on, while training pilots to fly the X-15, instructors noted that the F-104 *Starfighter* in "dirty" configuration (i.e., with landing gear extended, speed brakes down, and drag chute out to increase aerodynamic drag) closely approximated the X-15 in unpowered flight.[4]

But the F-104, with its long, needle-nosed fuselage, and hypersensitive avionics, was a totally unforgiving rascal under certain conditions. Even one of the school's former commandants, nationally acclaimed test pilot Col. Charles "Chuck" Yeager, augured one in. He lost control, they said.[5]

Jack Broughton best described the problem:

The F-104 boundary layer control system gave some people a lot of trouble. The wing was so small [that] you had to blow engine bypass air over it at low speeds to make the wing think it was going fast enough to support you. . . . If you got too low and had to add power, the boundary layer air came on [and] the wing gave too much lift and forced you almost straight up. When you cut power, you lost all the boundary air and the wing let you down like a high-speed elevator.

Repeating the process several times could result in "approaching the runway in square-cornered oscillations and you never caught up." The only real solution was to make a perfect approach—or go around and try again. But operationally, Broughton concluded, "it doesn't always work out so that you have those choices." It was for these and other reasons that production of the F-104 was discontinued in 1959.[6]

Royer and Lawrence were on a standard ARPS lift/drag mission. The plan called for them to make two simulated X-15 approaches until fuel depleted to 3,500 pounds or less, two "clean" (i.e., wheels up) lift/drag approaches until fuel burned to 2,500 pounds or less, and two dirty lift/drag approaches. It was a sanctioned training routine designed to evaluate student performance under exacting conditions—essential practice that satisfied the goal of providing pilots trained to perform under demanding circumstances.

As they went through the drill that afternoon, things went horribly wrong for Lawrence and Royer. An approach that was probably too low. That sudden, gut-wrenching lift pilots feared. Maybe they had boundary air problems—or experienced the oscillation Broughton described. No one will ever know for sure why, but the F-104 smacked into the runway left of the centerline, twenty-two hundred feet from the approach end, its underbelly blossoming fire. Both main landing gear collapsed on first contact. The canopy shattered. The F-104's fuselage dragged along the runway for over two hundred feet, then took to the air again, sailing madly down the runway for another eighteen hundred feet. Royer ejected. Then Lawrence punched out. At the four-thousand-foot runway marker, the ship veered left and, 235 onerous feet later, the twisted wreckage left the runway and skidded to a stop in the sand. Royer was seriously hurt. Lawrence's shattered body landed seventy-five yards from the wreck. He was still strapped in his ejection seat. His chest was crushed; his heart lacerated.[7]

The first African-American astronaut-designee died instantly, less than six months after being congratulated by the air force chief of staff upon his selection. In a letter to Lawrence, Gen. J. P. McConnell wrote:

Ahead of you lies adventure, challenge and an opportunity to serve the Air Force and the nation such as few men have had. Your tasks and responsibilities will be extraordinarily demanding. I am certain you will measure up to them.[8]

Robert Henry Lawrence, Jr., gave full measure; he was the ninth U.S. astronaut to die.

In the Edwards Air Force Base officers' housing area, Barbara Lawrence puttered about the house, looking forward to a friend's promotion party the couple were to attend that evening. Their eight-year-old son, Tracey, was playing with neighborhood friends several houses away. As usual, it was serene out on Community Road, where the Lawrences lived. The faraway sound of growling jet engines complemented the usual routines. Barbara listened absentmindedly to music on the local radio station as she went about her work.[9]

Suddenly, the idyllic setting cracked like shattering glass. A news bulletin blared. There had been an aircraft accident. Crewmen were forced to bail out.

Oh, Barbara thought, I'll have to ask Bob who it was when he comes home! She had long before accepted the dangers inherent in her husband's profession. She was never afraid. After all, she said later, "it was what he wanted to do—and if I was not willing to deal with that, I would not have been there in the first place." She knew that Bob Lawrence would not have been happy doing anything else. And, too, she knew that he was a capable man who was content with himself.

In spite of that, her breath caught and her pulse quickened when she glanced out the front window and saw a familiar Volkswagen pull up. Things seemed to move in slow motion as she watched Col. Eugene P. Deatrick, Jr., the ARPS commandant, and Lt. Col. Robert T. Herres, a member of her husband's class, get out and walk slowly toward the house. Her heart pounded when she saw the tears staining Herres's cheeks.

Barbara opened the front door. For a moment, silence reigned as their eyes met. Deatrick's face was etched with solemnity; Herres's glistened with tears. She knew then that her husband had been involved in the accident she'd heard about just moments before. Still, she refused even to think of the possibility that he was dead.

"Is he badly injured?" she asked.

Deatrick and Herres simply stared. One of them may have muttered, "We're sorry, Mrs. Lawrence," but she couldn't remember for sure what was said. She only remembered that at that moment she knew her Bob was dead and the reality of it struck like a sudden hail storm, taking her breath away.

"Where's Tracey?" one of the officers asked, noting that her young son was absent.

"H-He's over at a friend's house—playing," she stammered. "He's supposed to be home by four o'clock." That hour was rapidly approaching. The accident occurred at 3:22 P.M. "Let's just let him stay there."

"No," she recalled hearing one of the officers say, "the news is all over the base and somebody might tell him. We'll go get him. We're so terribly sorry, Barbara."

The air force is a closely knit society, and the death of anyone in the service, especially in the line of duty, is deeply felt. That fact alone made Tracey's retrieval easy. The father of the boy Tracey was visiting had gone home from his job on the flightline. He had heard about the accident, knew that Major Lawrence was dead.

Before he could finish telling his wife about the crash, she interrupted him and said Tracey was outside playing with their son. He squeezed her hand and rushed out, then gently ushered the boys into the house. Deatrick and Herres arrived a few minutes later and took Tracey home.

After they left, Barbara patiently explained to her eight-year-old that his father was dead. She watched his eyes fill with tears as he struggled to comprehend the shocking news. She tried to comfort him. She hugged him tightly and told him that although his daddy wouldn't be coming home again, she would always be there—to protect and love him. They sat together on the edge of Tracey's bed. Suddenly, his eyes lit up and his small face contorted with an anger she had never seen before.

"Why did you have to tell me?" he cried.

A sinking feeling overwhelmed her. She felt like the messenger who was killed for bringing bad news.

Later, Barbara said she discovered a spirituality in her son she was not aware he possessed. He told her of how he had known that morning that something unusual was going to happen that day. He told her of how he was usually asleep in bed when his father left early for work, but how, on that morning, he'd been up and awake and had seen his father just before he left the house. He told her of how their eyes had met for a long moment and then his father, a wan smile on his lips, had said simply, "Good-bye, Trace!"

Years later, Tracey Lawrence recalled the moment and remembered how unusual it had seemed. There was something spiritual about it, something prophetic. It was as though they had both known Robert would not be coming back. Ever.

After telling Tracey about his father's death, Barbara thought of her husband's mother and sister. They had every right to know what had happened. Picking up the receiver, she dialed the numbers in tandem. "I don't think," she later recalled, "there was anything in my life that was harder to do than that."

It was Friday. Barbara and Tracey boarded an airliner and flew to Chicago on Sunday, escorting Robert's body home for the funeral. On the way, with the plane's droning engines as a backdrop, Barbara recalled how it had all begun. She thought of how they'd met in 1952: he a sixteen-year-old graduate of Chicago's Englewood High School, and she a fourteen-year-old grammar school graduate. Of how they'd met at a party given by a girl's club at Saint Edmond's Episcopal Church. Of how, when it was over, she'd dutifully waited for her parents to pick her up. When they were late, Bob had felt moved to wait with her in the February cold. They stood there together for forty-five shivering minutes. Finally, fearing he'd miss the late connection with his trolley, he reluctantly caught the last bus.

Barbara's eyes misted as she recalled how, when her parents finally arrived, she'd insisted they follow Bob's bus and give him a ride home when he got off to transfer to the crosstown trolley.

For all of that, it had not been love at first sight. Long months later, however, Barbara experienced a great awakening when she found herself at his school, Bradley University in Peoria, Illinois, and saw Bob practicing the 440 and 880 on the track. She admired his style and grace—and the fact that he was very popular, with loads of people around him. They exchanged letters after that and soon began to see each other regularly. Not long after, she knew *he* was the one.

After completing his bachelor's degree in chemistry at Bradley and distinguishing himself as cadet commander of the Bradley ROTC, Bob had gone away, with a commission in the air force reserve, to become an instructor pilot in Germany, where he taught German pilots to fly.

The steady drone of the airliner strengthened her resolve. Tracey sat comfortably next to her, strangely introspective for an eight-year-old. She looked at her son and remembered how she had accepted her father's college graduation gift—a trip to Germany to marry Robert—and thought of how she had made his life hers:

> I was the only one of my three sisters who was not totally career-oriented. My attitude, when I got married, was that what Bob wanted to do, that's what we did. [It] was his life and we were support players to that. . . . You made that decision when you got married.

After Lawrence transferred to the regular air force and made a career commitment, the service sent him to graduate school at Ohio State University, where he earned his doctorate and wrote a dissertation about the reaction of tritium rays to methane gas.

Compared to the open-endedness of time, theirs had been a relatively short trip together. It had been structured but challenging. It was the way Barbara's husband had been. Balanced, always planning for the future. He was an individual whose mind was never at rest. He was always seeking change in a very structured way so that he would never, if he could help it, be caught off guard. In eleven years he had become a major and a senior pilot, logged over twenty-five hundred flying hours (more than two thousand of them in jet aircraft), taught others to fly, and had served as a research scientist in the air force weapons laboratory at Kirtland Air Force Base, New Mexico.

Barbara then recalled Bob's discovery of the astronaut program, and of how he longed to be involved. He had queried the air force and NASA, then submitted applications to both. The air force was interested, but he was repeatedly rejected by NASA, the first time in early 1961.

At long last, Lawrence received an official letter telling him he'd been selected for the air force's astronaut program, along with Maj. James A. Abrahamson (who later became a lieutenant general and NASA associate administrator for spaceflight), Lt. Col. Robert T. Herres (who went on to become a four-star general and commander of the air force's Space Command), and Maj. Donald H. Peterson. They were to be part of the air force's MOL program, which called for two men to ride a *Gemini B* capsule into space atop a *Titan IIIC* rocket, make contact with an orbiting laboratory, and spend a month or so in the satellite conducting various experiments before returning to earth in the *Gemini* capsule.

Barbara remembered her husband's modesty when news reporters asked how he, a Negro, felt about being selected for the prestigious space-pilot training program. "Race was incidental," he had replied, the choice "probably a culmination of the great deal of training and help a lot of people put in to prepare me." He gave the credit to others, declaring, "It's an expression of success that they should enjoy instead of me. Perhaps I have been more fortunate than others in the opportunities that have come my way."[10]

The announcement of Lawrence's selection apparently displeased some Americans. Letters began to pour in. Some threatened his life. These, he turned over to the air force's intelligence branch. On the heels of this came NASA's final rejection letter, signed by the venerable Deke Slayton.

Undaunted, the Lawrences had gone to Edwards Air Force Base. No one brought up the subject of Ed Dwight. Most of the people associated with him had gone. Colonel Yeager had been reassigned in 1966 to command a combat wing in the Far East. They were treated very well at Edwards, Barbara recalled. For a few magic months, it was Bob Lawrence's time in the sun—and the family thrived on it. Perhaps that is why, when the plane carrying Lawrence's body home landed in Chicago, his wife was able to speak words that stirred the hearts of those who heard or later read them:

Bob's death is quite a personal loss to Tracey and myself. He gave us a love and security that will be a tremendous void in the days and years ahead. However, he gave his life doing the thing that he wanted most—preparing to be an astronaut. Every day of his life has been given toward that goal. I am most proud of him, as an air force officer and as an American. I hope all of [you] share this pride with me. Thank you for the courtesy you've shown all of us.[11]

An air force spokesman then stepped to the podium and advised the media that memorial services would be held at a Chicago funeral home on 12 December, followed by similar services on Tuesday at the First Unitarian Church on the University of Chicago campus and at the Edwards Air Force Base chapel.

Not all Americans were courteous, though. Nor did they grieve.

On 11 December, a disgruntled San Franciscan clipped a news article about Lawrence's death from a local paper, inserted it in an envelope, then scrawled a note to Mrs. Lawrence. Signing it "An Anonymous American," the miscreant wrote, "Good riddance to that nigger. He was just a Johnson flunky. White Power!"

Another anonymous writer announced, "I'm glad he's dead. We don't want no coons on the moon!"[12]

Condolences from President Lyndon Johnson and the announcement by Talman W. VanArsdale, Jr., president of Bradley University, her husband's alma mater, of the establishment of a scholarship fund in Bob's name served as a counterbalance to the racist writers' biting remarks. It was only fitting that the scholarship fund would recognize outstanding black students who wanted to study chemistry—Lawrence's major field.[13]

Born 2 October 1935 in Chicago, Robert Lawrence was the son of Gwendolyn and Robert Lawrence, Sr., a disabled veteran. His parents were divorced when he and his sister, Barbara, were very young. Their mother later remarried, bringing Charles Duncan into their lives as stepfather.

They were poor, but it was not the grinding poverty associated with life in today's ghettoes. Charles Duncan worked as an underwriter for the Veterans Administration and later in the circulation departments of various periodicals, and Bob's mother worked as a civil servant for more than twenty years.

There were few frills, however. Like many young blacks of that era, Bob Lawrence improvised and made his own wooden scooters, with which he burned up the Chicago sidewalks. Born into a different kind of black culture, he was surrounded by people who believed in striving, in making something of themselves despite the racism that existed in the country. Black parents sought to impress upon young minds the importance of religion and of the need to learn and become somebody. Lawrence's family chose to follow the teachings of the Christian Scientists. This, according to Bob's mother, was perhaps most responsible in shaping her children's characters. "This may sound unbelievable," she recalled, "but I don't know of any occasions when I had to discipline my children; they had a discipline that must have come from within."[14]

And Bob Lawrence had discipline—plenty of it! When his mother bought a piano that included a plan for reduced-rate lessons, she counseled him on "the importance of making all his lessons." Later, after being hit by a truck on the way to his piano teacher's, Bob got up, dusted himself off, and refused to allow the pleading truck driver to take him to the hospital. He told the stunned driver that he didn't dare to miss his lesson! It was discipline that allowed Bob to master the difficult Rachmaninoff piano compositions and thrill the occupants of the Good Neighbor Apartments on the corner of Twenty-Third and South State streets with his renditions of them.

Lawrence's elementary school friends called him "BobJunior"—the words run together without pause—and watched, fascinated, as he built and flew model airplanes and ardently played chess. They rejoiced with him as together they snatched chunks of ice from the back of an old man's delivery truck, not realizing, perhaps, that he intentionally left the chunks of ice there just so they could get them.

Despite exuberant outbursts, Bob Lawrence possessed a dedicated, serious, scholarly mien. Every Christmas, his mother recalled, he wanted "a bigger and better chemistry set." He was enrolled in Englewood High School by age twelve. Biology fascinated him, chemistry beckoned, and hamsters became his roommates of choice at home. Once, he interceded for his animal friends when a hamster bit someone at school. The police came and removed all the rodents, turning them over to local health authorities. Later that evening, Bob showed up at the station pleading for the animals' release. The record shows that he got them back.

After graduating from high school in the top 10 percent of his class, Lawrence entered Bradley University, where hard work and his dedication to discipline earned him the rank of cadet lieutenant colonel in the campus air force Reserve Officer Training Corps program. A classmate remembered Lawrence as being "brilliant, very conscientious . . . always military-minded and very, very strict." Never too proud to do what he had to in order to be successful, Lawrence worked as a waiter in the campus cafeteria to help finance his studies.[15]

It was at that point that Lawrence's future wife, Barbara, the daughter of Dr. and Mrs. Henry Cress of Chicago, entered his life. They began dating, and in March 1956, he was commissioned a second lieutenant in the air force reserve after being awarded a bachelor's degree in chemistry.

A new Bob Lawrence emerged. Flying became his passion. As a grown man, he could still be mischievous at times. His natural father, Robert Sr., recalled Bob's penchant for speed, how he drove his Porsche like the wind. Once, while they were driving down the expressway, the elder Lawrence was moved to counsel his son, "Man, you're flying too low!" But Bob only laughed. It was fun. There was a natural chemistry between the two. "I didn't see him that often," said Robert Sr., "but when we were together, we always had a ball!"[16]

After marrying Barbara and completing his tour in Germany, Lawrence entered Ohio State through the Air Force Institute of Technology as a doctoral candidate. His grade-point average soared above 3.5 even though his course load included such challenging subjects as nuclear chemistry, photochemistry, chemical kinetics, and advanced inorganic and thermonuclear chemistry. "He was," a friend said later, "so heavy!"— the black way of saying Lawrence was very intelligent. "He wasn't satisfied to simply make it on his own natural ability. He was confident he could achieve something if he worked hard. He wasn't pushy. He didn't talk about himself much. But Bob knew that if he did something well, it would not go unrecognized."[17]

For all of his seriousness, Bob Lawrence could laugh. He thought it was a hoot when H. Rap Brown, upon discovering that America wanted to send up a black astronaut, quipped that the country wanted to do it "just so's they can lose that nigger out in space!"[18]

Lawrence's own evaluation of what he was about is contained on the dedication page of his doctoral dissertation, which he completed in 1965:

This work is dedicated to those American Negroes who have spent their lives in the performance of menial tasks struggling to overcome both natural and man-made problems of survival. To such men and women, scientific investigation would seem a grand abstraction. However, it has been their endeavors which have supplied both the wherewithal and motivation that initiated and helped sustain this work.[19]

Some observers worried that Major Lawrence's death was no accident. The fact that rescue people on the scene had cut his body from the ejection seat before the cause of the crash could be determined caused some people to speculate that he had been assassinated. Such feelings are not unusual, given the anger stirred up by the Dwight Affair and the charges of racism that were still rampant at the time.

John Whitehead, himself a graduate of the Edwards test pilot school, remained unconvinced. "Perhaps there were racists around, but I can't imagine anybody doing anything [like] *that*."[20]

On 12 December 1967, the Rev. Ben Richardson, delivering the eulogy in Chicago at Major Lawrence's funeral service, put a life ended too soon into perspective:

He lived out his days inextricably bound . . . in the company of the several races and creeds of men—lived as if he believed that the ultimate reach of man's social existence is to be found in a milieu harboring a grand existence of respected differences and the thoughtful resolution of human problems. His life proved that living such a relationship with his fellow man, hastened his own self-realization. The world gives the assurance that without this mode of dwelling, there may be no future for anyone. The monument he leaves, then, because it suggests a means whereby man can inhabit earth joyously, engenders hope and a cause for optimism.[21]

Donald Peterson, who later flew on NASA space shuttle mission STS-6, confirmed that description of Lawrence: "He was the kind of person you thought an officer should be; greatly admired; easy to be around." Lieutenant General James A. Abrahamson concurred, adding that Lawrence was "very impressive."[22]

Pressed by the media, Gwendolyn Duncan offered a final accolade for her son. "I have been proud of my son ever since he was born and proud of everything he has done," she told reporters. At the time Lawrence was selected to serve as an air force astronaut, she considered the ultimate goals of spaceflight worth the risk. "After all," she observed, "if it weren't for Columbus, there wouldn't be an America!"[23]

Ebony staff writer David Flores saw Lawrence as a hero in the true American tradition who,

> In so doing proved, finally, what black people in this country have long known—*that excellence has no color.* For young black boys . . . should they seek to be heroes in the traditional manner or of another kind, it is the legacy one courageous black man left them.[24]

Robert Lawrence's death marked the end of minority participation in the astronaut program for a lengthy period. More than a decade would pass before NASA again seriously considered minority males and women for employment as astronauts and offered them a chance to make the cherished leap into space.

TURNABOUT

One is reminded of Alice's distraught question in Wonderland:
"Would you tell me, please, which way I ought to go from here?"
"That depends a good deal," replied the Cat
with irrefutable logic, "on where you want to get to."
—Milton M. Gordon in
Assimilation in America: Theory and Reality

Ed Dwight and Robert Lawrence were both looked upon as participants in the air force Manned Orbiting Laboratory program, which was discontinued in 1969, when funding was withdrawn. Of the two men, NASA probably would have more readily accepted Lawrence. After all the bad press generated by the Dwight Affair it could not have afforded to do otherwise.

With President Lyndon B. Johnson's affirmative action executive order following hard on the heels of the 1964 Civil Rights Act, and the subsequent passage of the Equal Employment Act of 1972, NASA was forced to give serious consideration to minority hiring.

On 12 September 1973, the NASA Manned Spaceflight Management Council met in Washington, D.C. Dr. Dudley G. G. McConnel, the assistant administrator for equal opportunity programs, outlined the chief objectives: Discrimination within NASA *must* be removed in both fact and appearance. The new policy targeted all programs and functions. Managers were instructed to support the planning, implementation, control, and evaluation of the equal opportunity program at every level in the agency, and to verify that established goals were met.

An Equal Opportunity Action Plan was unveiled. The plan listed the key elements for Equal Employment Opportunity (EEO) staffing and training. It also provided detailed goals, time tables, and methods for measuring performance against the plan. The plan further projected end-of-year numerical goals and wage categories for minority hiring through calendar 1977.[25]

Establishment of an equal opportunity program advisory board was also directed. Its goals: helping NASA assess the programs and methods used to attract top minority and female applicants. The board was also tasked to look at "allocating the adverse impact" of certain existing Civil Service regulations.

Finally, a complete review of functions and planned memberships in a NASA-wide equal opportunity council was planned. Affirmative action goals for the Kennedy Space Center (KSC) space-shuttle launch and landing facilities construction work force were being coordinated to ensure that minority workers available in the KSC area were being used.[26]

With those actions, NASA began an astounding turnabout in its treatment of women and minorities—its start fueled by the scrawl of the president's pen. In 1963, the Soviets launched the first woman cosmonaut. Although it had no women astronauts, the United States had, in 1961, appointed internationally recognized pilot Jerri Cobb as a consultant to the NASA administrator. She was followed by Jacqueline Cochran. Both women advised the agency on how best to develop qualification guidelines and programs for women astronauts.[27]

*   *   *

By February 1974, equal opportunity program meetings at NASA were lively affairs, with open and candid discussions among participants. Equality of involvement was called for in discussions about the recruitment of women and minorities. Greater involvement of middle managers and supervisors in the affirmative action mix was also encouraged.

What were the obstacles that seemingly hindered recruitment of minorities and women? The small number of candidates and lack of middle manager and supervisor involvement leapt to the head of the list. Even where these managers and supervisors *were* involved, someone noted, none had the authority to make on-the-spot commitments. More important, there were "few minorities within reach of the Civil Service Register," a problem undoubtedly carrying over from previous NASA practices. Federal salaries for mathematicians, administrators, and scientists were not competitive with those in private industry. Furthermore, promotion was slow in NASA. The agency writhed under the glaring spotlights affirmative action and equal opportunity programs focused on it. Some staff members thought there were other things wrong with the agency's image. For instance, applicants weren't being matched with the right people within the space centers, which, from an outsider's perspective, made for an image that was "decidedly poor."[28]

The agency resolved to overcome these problems. A recruitment program was ordered, not only for entry-level positions, but for higher-level posts as well. Even more important, NASA's brass got into the act. "It is imperative," wrote Dale D. Myers, a NASA administrator, "that we establish optimistic goals that can be obtained by concentrated effort and the personal attention of each center director."[29]

As defined in 1974, the effort would not only be evident in flight activities, but throughout the NASA work force. Supervisory staff members were directed to attend the space centers' human rights seminars, conducted by the Equal Opportunity Office. Each directorate was ordered to develop an affirmative action plan and select a responsible individual authorized to speak on behalf of his organization in "developing and implementing [these] plans." At the Goddard Spaceflight Center, meetings were opened by stressing that "the key word is equality—equality because it is right!"[30]

During the second quarter of 1976, agency officials determined that most equal opportunity/affirmative action program/entry-level profes-

sional hiring goals could be met by minorities and females graduat-
ing from the "co-ops" (recruitment "feeder" programs in colleges and
universities). Efforts were made at Howard University, the Massachusetts
Institute of Technology, and Houston-Tillotson College to recruit blacks.
Hispanics and native Americans were actively recruited at New Mexico
State University, the University of Texas at El Paso, and Texas A&I
University. One oriental male was being considered for employment
in the third quarter of fiscal year 1976.[31]

Word soon began to spread that NASA was changing its style.

Enter Nichelle Nichols, the black star who played Lieutenant Uhuru
on the hit television series *Star Trek*. She was upset because she sensed
her role was being cut as the weeks passed. She chafed at the perceived slight and "wanted to quit." Although she had been excited about
the show in its first year, the erosion of her part caused her to seek
out the show's creator, Gene Roddenberry, and tell him about her plan
to leave.[32]

"Don't do it," Roddenberry counseled.

Providentially, Nichelle soon met Dr. Martin Luther King during
his travels around the country. She told him how she felt about her
diminishing role and that she wanted to ditch the show and "get on
with my career." She still remembers Dr. King's response. He looked
at her in that special way people living at the time recall so well. Incisive.
Fearless. Determined. Nichelle thought he would take her side—console her and commiserate with her. She thought he would say something like, "No, don't take that. Go on with your career!" Instead, he
looked at her in a completely different way, the timbre of his voice
weighty, as though he were delivering a Sunday sermon.

"You *must* stay," King told her. "You don't understand the effect
you are having! Not only on young women, but everybody's mind and
attitude is changed immeasurably because *you* are there!"

So she had stayed.

In 1977, NASA called her in as a consultant. For almost a year,
the agency had actively sought women and minority applicants for
astronaut training. They had expected a deluge of applications, but had
received only a trickle.

"Why," NASA officials asked Nichols, "are women not responding? Why are minority people not responding? Why are we having
all these problems?"

Strolling across the Houston Space Center grounds with astronaut Alan Bean, Nichols asked the major a question. "I'm talking now," she began, "about including women and minorities in the astronaut corps, because, after six [rounds of] selections, it's still an all-white, male astronaut corps. Well, [NASA's] credibility is [about] zero with minorities and women! What about integration of the corps?"

Bean's response was partly incredulous, partly apologetic, but Nichols detected a ray of hope.

"First of all," Bean said, "I'm kind of surprised that we've got a credibility gap. We tried to do what we [promised]. Previously, you know, we had to have so much training—you had to have engineering [and] flight training. . . . We're looking very much forward to having an integrated [astronaut] corps and I just hope that we get a big response. I think we've got something like sixteen hundred applications now, of which two hundred are from women, and we certainly need more than that—certainly more [from] minorities."

But it was more than just numbers to Nichols. She really wanted to see both men and women in the space shuttle. She had a vested interest, she thought, "because I wanted to see that our *Star Trek* universe lived—men and women of all colors [in space.]"

NASA found no fault with that. But how to get more people to apply?

"I think you need to get someone with credibility," Nichols replied. "Someone with high visibility; [someone people] see on television and in newspapers." She advised NASA to launch a "media blitz" employing well-known people the public would believe.

Like who?

"Like Bill Cosby or Coretta Scott King," said Nichols.

NASA's response was tongue-in-cheek: "How about Lieutenant Uhuru?"

That is how it came to pass that Nichelle Nichols—sitting in front of a battery of communications monitors in much the same fashion as she did on *Star Trek,* but dressed in the blue coveralls of an astronaut—found herself delivering a NASA recruiting pitch on national television:

Oh, Hi! I'm Nichelle Nichols. It kind of looks like when I was Lieutenant Uhuru on the starship *Enterprise,* doesn't it? Well, now there's a twentieth century *Enterprise,* an actual space vehicle built by NASA and designed to put us in the business of space—not merely space exploration. NASA's *Enterprise* is a space shuttlecraft, built to make regularly scheduled runs into space and back. Now, the shuttle will be taking scientists and engineers, men and women of all races, into space—just like the astronaut crew on the starship *Enterprise.* That is why I'm speaking to the whole family of humankind—minorities and women included. If you qualify and would like to be an astronaut, *now* is the time! This is *your* NASA!

Applications poured in. Suddenly there were more than a thousand from both women and men!

The spacecraft Nichols described was the new space shuttle system, a reusable space vehicle that had been on the drawing boards for more than a decade. It was the answer to the tremendous waste of expensive space hardware required in the *Mercury, Gemini,* and *Apollo* programs. It is a system that carries everything required to do its work in space, without jettisoning anything from the primary ship, then reenters the earth's atmosphere and lands safely. As Nichols pointed out, the first operational shuttle was called the *Enterprise.* It was the grandson of the old air force *Dynasoar,* which never flew, and a distant cousin of the X-1—which shot Chuck Yeager through the sound barrier in 1947—and the X-15, the first "winged vehicle to penetrate the fringes of space itself." The Space Transportation System (STS) as it was formally known, cost more than ten billion dollars to develop. The manned orbiter vehicle was boosted into space atop a giant, external tank that supplied liquid hydrogen and liquid oxygen fuel to the shuttle's three main engines. Two mammoth solid-fuel rocket boosters helped kick the whole thing off the launch pad and through the dense lower levels of the atmosphere.

The *Enterprise* was a final NASA test bed. It first flew atop a specially equipped Boeing 747, gathering data about its glide performance. On later test missions it detached from the 747 and performed a critical series of approach and landing tests. After the successes NASA experienced with *Enterprise,* the program got a green light and three more orbiters were built.[33]

*   *   *

Because a president's pen scratched a signature on an executive order and people listened to a television actress's impassioned pleas, men and women from "the whole family of humankind" would represent America in space far sooner than anyone thought.

Thanks to a NASA recruiting effort begun in 1976, the agency's minority hiring program was a far cry from what it had been. It was a stellar turnabout, leading to a new reality and providing *all* Americans an opportunity to reach the stars.

INTO THE CIRCLE

America's space effort burgeoned during the decade following Robert Lawrence's death and NASA's decision to recruit women and minorities. Astronauts who orbited the moon in December 1968 sent back televised views of the barren surface. Between July 1969 and December 1972, American astronauts made six lunar landings, brought home a total of 845.2 pounds of soil and lunar samples, and spent 299 hours, 58 minutes, 2 seconds on the moon's surface. Three *Skylab* missions were flown and deep space walks were made in 1971 and 1973.[34]

Fascinated by this panoply of achievements in space, minorities and women could only watch and thrill. Although affirmative action programs were in place in NASA, astronaut positions continued to be dominated by white males. Following the "media blitz" inspired by Nichelle Nichols, aspiring minority astronaut prospects across the country completed and submitted applications. In mid-December 1977, a list containing the names of forty new space shuttle astronauts reached NASA administrator Dr. Robert A. Frosch.

According to the *Washington Post,* Frosch was unhappy with the selections. The Johnson Space Center staff held its collective breath. Worried about the military look NASA was assuming, Frosch questioned the fact that thirty of the selectees were from the armed forces. Since this list was also to include minorities and women, he was distressed to see that it included only two black pilots and three women scientists. Frosch wanted to be "darned sure there aren't more qualified blacks and women who could be added," and called for another look at the list of candidates.

That relook was providential. Within weeks, a new list was announced.

It contained the names of thirty-five prospective astronauts, including six women, three black males, and one oriental male. The lucky thirty-five came from an applicant pool of more than eight thousand, over fifteen hundred of which were women.[35]

Christopher Columbus Kraft, then director of the Johnson Space Center, pointed out that in 1967, the last time NASA had selected applicants for astronaut training, few qualified blacks and women were chosen. "The rewarding thing," Kraft said, "is that there were large numbers of qualified minorities and women this time around. We had no problem finding women and minorities who were qualified and highly motivated as to what they wanted to do."[36]

The real difference, though, was that in 1967 NASA apparently was not really looking for women and minorities. Furthermore, the odds are that a number of qualified women and minorities could have been found that year if only NASA had made the effort. Even when pushed to consider the option, the answers supplied almost always produced a slanted playing field, placing a career as an astronaut just beyond reach of the average black academic.

James A. Michener, in his fact-based novel *Space,* describes how a black high school principal argued with a newly-elected senator over the absence of blacks in the space program. Beginning by displaying NASA-provided photographs of the thirty-six astronauts chosen up to that time, the principal pointed out that the cost to train them was at least three million dollars each and that blacks helped foot that bill with their taxes. What was more, one of them was from the senator's hometown![37]

"Not one black face among them!" snapped the high school principal. And this, when "we blacks compose about twelve percent of the national population. There ought to be about four of our young men in these photographs!"

He then produced photographs of NASA's Mission Control staff. The faces were all white. "By proportion, Senator, we should have twelve or thirteen black faces in *that* fine snapshot. We have none!" His voice tinged with disgust, the principal ended his peroration by asking: "Why do you always cut us off from the best parts of national life?"

The senator then verbally pilloried his staff, ending with, "How do you account for this?"

"The problem never came up," replied a staffer.

"And *that's* the problem!" roared the high school principal. "Nobody ever noticed that one of our nation's greatest enterprises was lily-white! Nobody gave a damn!"

Michener's fictional senator called an urgent Monday morning meeting. All would be present, including a high-level NASA official. At that meeting, the NASA official admitted that he'd served on three selection committees. They'd tried hard to find qualified Catholics, Jews, women and "especially black pilots," he said. It was a matter of "good will. We were not bound by religion, sex or color." It was the qualifications, or lack thereof, that eliminated these people, the official asserted, handing out mimeographed sheets listing NASA's alleged criteria:

- B.S. degree in science or engineering.
- M.S. degree in science or engineering (advised).
- Military flight training.
- Test pilot school graduate.
- Graduate university training.
- Solid mastery of mathematics, physics, combustion engines, calculus.
- Service with a flight squadron.
- Test pilot experience in at least two dozen types of aircraft.

"It's very simple, gentlemen," the NASA official told the committee members, "you find me young black men who have subjected themselves to training as rigorous as this and I'll lead the battle for their selection!"

Clearly, this was the biggest snow job since the great blizzard of 1888, in which four hundred people lost their lives! Review of the selection requirements published in any of the NASA astronaut job announcements will verify that.

After touring several universities, including three with engineering schools and two without, members of Michener's fictional senate committee concluded that they could not find *a single black man* pursuing the hard, scientific training needed to qualify him for astronaut selection.

This, too, was probably a smoke screen, for if the search had been conducted at predominantly white schools, the results would not have surprised anyone. It is a fact that many blacks applied to and were rejected by schools that were all lily-white.

Michener's fictional senator was infuriated. "Goddamnit, I want a black astronaut," he snapped, even if the standards had to be lowered "to the third grade level. . . . And don't tell me that it can't be done!"

Such an act would be inane, suggested the NASA official. The whole program would be endangered. "The entire program will be shot to hell right here in Congress if you don't find us a black astronaut," Michener's senator angrily riposted. "When the next photograph is taken of Mission Control, I want to see at least four black faces in there!" If the senator couldn't have his astronaut, well then, he'd settle for minority representation in Mission Control.

That idea seemed mindboggling to the NASA official. "Doing what?" he asked, his voice containing an air of impudent stubbornness.

"I don't give a goddamn what they're doing!" shouted the senator. "They can be knitting for all I care, but I want them in there!"

Later in the year, writes Michener, "They found an exceptionally well-trained young man who was 'gifted in meeting people.' Lacking 'calculus and flying experience,' he was given the job of liaison with the press, in which he performed superbly!" Later, a black from Alabama, another from California, and a third from Massachusetts were found with qualifying scientific backgrounds. According to Michener, "That sea of radiant white faces was speckled more realistically."

It was an entirely new ball game. NASA had come a long way. Of its twenty-two thousand employees, more than 7 percent were black. At the Johnson Space Center, 6.4 percent of the thirty-three hundred were black.[38]

On 31 January 1978, Johnson Space Center director Christopher Kraft introduced the thirty-five new astronauts to the world. A diverse group, considering the requirements for the job of astronaut, they were immediately subjected to a hectic round of press interviews and photograph sessions. The six women were: Anna Fisher of Rancho Palos Verdes, California; Dr. Shannon W. Lucid of Oklahoma City; Dr. Judith A. Resnik of Redondo Beach, California; Sally K. Ride of Stanford, California, a research physics assistant; Dr. Margaret R. Seddon, resident surgeon at City of Memphis Hospital in Memphis, Tennessee; and Kathryn D. Sullivan of Cupertino, California. The entire group would serve on space shuttle crews as mission specialists, a combination of flight engineer and scientist.

"I don't feel like I'm a pioneer," said Resnik, responding to a question posed to all six women. "I feel like I'm one of those persons selected to be an astronaut and it's a coincidence that I'm a woman!"

Reporters' pens and pencils scrawled; minicassette tape recorders were pushed closer.

"I think," she went on, "the six of us have always gone after the things we wanted; most of them are, to a certain extent, unusual. Some of us had more obstacles than others, but we have overcome whatever was in our way and this is another step in the pursuit of a continuing career."

At the center of this media session were the three black astronaut candidates who stood posing for the cameras, their hands touching a model of the new space shuttle. Guion S. Bluford, Jr., occupied the foreground. Slender. Dark. Spare. Distinguished. He wore a modest "natural" hairstyle. Frederick D. Gregory was in the center. Handsome. Curly haired. Pleasant. Then there was Dr. Ronald E. McNair, distinguished from the two military men by his ever-present sunglasses, white-lapeled jacket, high-rise shirt collar, larger, sideburned "natural," and flamboyant tie with a fat windsor knot.

Thirty-seven-year-old Fred Gregory, an air force major and the first prospective black shuttle pilot selected by NASA, handled the media attention with quiet aplomb.

"How do you regard your selection as a shuttle pilot?" a reporter asked him.

"I look at it as being a very well-qualified person to perform a function for the United States." He had flown helicopters. Performed as a test pilot. "Driving on a highway was more dangerous than flying," he said. And what was more, he'd flown aircraft larger than the shuttle. Like the Boeing 747. "Aircraft without engines, too," he added.[39]

Air force major Guy Bluford, thirty-five, came from an assignment at Wright-Patterson Air Force Base, Ohio, where he was chief of the Aerodynamics and Airframe Branch. When asked if he thought the money allocated to train him for the nation's space program would be well spent, Bluford replied that it would give him a chance to use his skills as a pilot and engineer.

McNair, the youngest of the trio, at twenty-seven, spoke bluntly at times. "I think the very people who don't think the government is justified in spending the money on the space program help justify the

existence of NASA," he said. "If people want to continue to have more
and better color television sets, they're going to have to spend money
on science.[40]

Air force captain Ellison S. Onizuka was the last of the minority
selectees. The thirty-one-year-old from Kealakekua, Hawaii, was assigned to Edwards Air Force Base as chief of engineering support at
the test pilot school. Onizuka, a third-generation Japanese-American,
had wanted to be an astronaut since he was seven years old and first
watched *Sputnik* fly overhead, he told reporters. Gregory said he shared
that dream. His selection also fulfilled a childhood desire to fly in space.
Onizuka and McNair, thinking about minority group members who would
follow, said they hoped to serve as role models. What they were about
to do was awesome. McNair summed up all their feelings: "Becoming an astronaut is a far-fetched dream—out of this world!"[41]

They were given until 1 July to get their personal affairs in order.
At that time they would report back to Houston to begin two years of
rigorous training designed to prepare them to fly or serve as crew members
aboard space shuttles in the 1980s and possibly into the 1990s.

The spacecraft in which they were to fly was, in itself, an out-of-
this-world, far-fetched dream. Its central entity, the orbiter, was, without
doubt, one of the most complicated spaceflight systems ever devised.
It was a booster at launch, a spacecraft while in orbit, and an aircraft
during reentry and landing.

NASA designers teamed with experts from Rockwell International,
the prime civilian contractor, in countless technical staff and planning
meetings and exchanged thousands of communications as the project
moved forward. They worked closely together to develop a specialized avionics package and a thermal protection system designed to keep
the orbiter's aluminum skin from overheating during reentry, when
hellish temperatures well above steel's melting point threatened to destroy
the orbiter.

Special carbon tiles were created to counter the hellfire. Reusable
black tiles partially covered the vertical stabilizer and areas around
the windows of the cockpit. White tiles made by a different process
were used to insulate the fuselage sides, most of the vertical stabilizer, the upper wing surfaces, and the Orbital Maneuvering System.
A miraculous manufacturing process was employed in both instances,

beginning with common sand refined into fibers of pure white silica and ultimately mixed with deionized water and other chemicals molded in plastic. Excess liquid was squeezed away, to be fired in a microwave oven and made cohesive through heat and pressure in yet another oven, through a process called sintering, at over 2000° F.

Under no circumstances could the orbiter weigh more than 155,000 to 160,000 pounds in its infancy, because of budgetary limits. A main propulsion system had to be devised. A cooling system. A hydraulic system. A mechanical system that included all the payload bay doors and associated mechanisms. An adequate communications system, auxiliary power units, and fuel cells also had to be incorporated. All these systems had to work flawlessly and be developed within tightly prescribed budgetary guidelines.

The shuttle astronauts would fly in a spacecraft whose controls were unlike anything ever seen before. The system was linked to four high-speed digital computers, arranged in backup settings, with a fifth computer independent of the other four. More than that, the four computers and their backup would talk to each other about 440 times per second—processing incoming data, comparing data, sending out information. Together, they contained the most sophisticated software programs ever developed for spaceflight.[42]

It was to be a system that was partially reusable, retaining the ability to deploy satellites and sustain its crews while in orbit. It would be a space station of sorts, in which research could be carried out until a larger, permanent space station was developed and orbited.

As miraculous as the space shuttle these astronauts would fly was, it was a few steps removed from the vehicle originally planned because of budget restrictions. Now, only three main engines would lift it from earth. Fuel and oxidizers from a mammoth external tank (ET) provided their lifeblood. After burnout, the solid-rocket boosters would separate, be recovered from the ocean, and refurbished. The ET was expendable, destroying itself upon contact with the earth's atmosphere after separation from the orbiter. When the mission was complete, the crew would bring the orbiter back to earth for a runway landing and refurbishing for another mission.

The orbiter itself, looking a bit like a conventional aircraft, weighs one hundred fifty thousand pounds empty. It is 122 feet long; 56 feet, 7 inches high (with landing gear lowered); and has a wing span of 78 feet. The crew compartments are located on two levels in the forward section. The upper deck closely resembles the cockpit of a modern jetliner, with two flight positions up front—the mission commander on the left, the pilot on the right. Between the two sit the flight computer and navigational aids console. Flight control instruments, including some fourteen hundred switches, surround the two stations. Three cathode ray tubes (CRTs) stare "like eyes focused on a technological world bursting with facts and figures and data." Identical sets of controls face both pilots, providing real-time displays of important data.

Behind the pilots are positions for two mission specialists on the flight deck, one of whom acts as flight engineer during launch and recovery, assisting with reading checklists and helping monitor flight instrumentation on even more control boards. From their vantage point, the payload bay can be seen through windows providing a long view, facing the rear. Two overhead windows allow visual observation.

Accessible by ladder is the middeck, home of additional mission and payload specialists. Up to seven (and sometimes eight) people can fly aboard the shuttle. Here also are facilities for sleeping, meal preparation, and personal hygiene. Below the middeck are the avionics bays, storage, environmental controls, and related systems. Behind the crew compartment lies the payload bay, the primary area containing mission cargo.

The new star voyagers faced weeks and months of study, training, travel, and orientation. Of unraveling the secrets of this conglomeration of man's engineering and design prowess. Of "trying out NASA, while NASA tried them out."[43] Beyond that lay the most fantastic ride any human being born in the twentieth century could take: to be blasted from Mother Earth, through the density of her atmosphere, into quiet, awesome space, hundreds of miles into what the earthbound call "the sky"; privileged to see us and our works as we can never see ourselves.

Questions proliferated. Bluford, Gregory, and McNair responded, wondering again about their immediate futures. Despite the stark brilliance that went into development of the Shuttle Transportation System (STS) and the engineering skills evidenced in the concept, the three of them, along with their comrades, were only on the cutting edge of America's space age. They were part of a giant leap past the very expensive *Apollo-Saturn* system and a new day. The orbiter not only represented the latest specialized technology, it also required special people.

That they were African American signified only snippets of the reasons they had been chosen out of thousands to participate in the space shuttle program. It had to do with each of them, what they had become as men and as Americans. But because they were seen as America's first three "official" black astronauts, it was difficult at first to get their fellow countrymen to understand that. In a telephone interview, Fred Gregory said, "I would hate to think that I was chosen—or any of the women or minorities were chosen—because of tokenism. I think my qualifications were adequate—super—to be chosen."[44]

Later, in 1981, Ronald McNair observed:

People with self-doubt, people who are afflicted with this business of believing that something is bigger than you are, should know that it's not true. Everything is big when you are on the outside looking in and don't know what's going on. Everything is complicated, but once you're thoroughly prepared, you're prepared like everybody else and you can conquer the obstacles like everybody else. So identify [your] goals and go for them. Don't let anyone or anything cause you to deviate from your objectives.[45]

Guy Bluford insisted in his quiet, unassuming way that his road to NASA was based upon a "lifetime passion for aeronautics" and that he "never encountered obstacles to his development because of racial barriers."[46]

Inspired by the trio's accomplishments, another black man sought to make the grade despite initial doubts. He was marine, a 1968 graduate of the U.S. Naval Academy. A naval aviator with over a hundred missions into North and South Vietnam, Laos, and Cambodia. He was a man who knew firsthand what the *Flight of the Intruder,* the novel about the A-6 fighter, was all about. A near-graduate of the U.S. Naval Test Pilot School at Patuxent River, Maryland, Charles F. Bolden, Jr., had already overcome a boatload of obstacles in his life. Still, he doubted his chances for a career as an astronaut. Until then. According to Bolden:

I never had an interest, never had a legitimate interest in being an astronaut as a kid. I just figured that was impossible, so I didn't even think about it. After a tour in Thailand and coming back to California, NASA advertised they were going to select a group of people to be space shuttle astronauts. They said all you have to do is apply. I said, "I'll try it," and then I changed my mind.[47]

It was indeed possible, however. Guy Bluford, Ron McNair, and Fred Gregory had already joined the hallowed ranks of U.S. astronauts. In a relatively short time, so would Charles Bolden.

In July, the new astronauts returned to Houston to begin their training. The odyssey of America's bronze star voyagers began in earnest. They toured all the NASA installations within the first few weeks—the Johnson Space Center, the Dryden Test Center, Ames, Langley, and the Cape— to observe what went on in NASA and learn the specialties of each of its components.

They were trained in all the basic skills required to do the astronaut's job. Emergency escape procedures. Parachuting over land and into water. Survival. Tests. Centrifuge. The chair, where they intentionally try to make you sick, then train you how *not* to be sick in space. On space- flight and astrophysics. Becoming "experts" in the ramifications of missions they would be expected to fly.[48] Study and more study, within a structured program of classes. Guy Bluford recalled that:

It was exciting. We spent a lot of time in classrooms [and went on] a lot of field trips. You came in every morning with books. Three or four hours of class. They had science classes. They had to equalize the plan because people had various backgrounds. So they [gave] us science courses, space shuttle courses, [courses on] how the management worked—the paperwork [and] how you got things done.[49]

After being checked out in the T-38 jet trainer, they went to Rockwell International's west coast facility to see the shuttle, which was still being built.

The classroom skull work lasted six to nine months. The schedule called for two years of candidacy before becoming a full-fledged as- tronaut. But NASA's management changed its mind after the new candidates began working on various projects in support of the first shuttle mission, STS-1. Guy Bluford became a mission specialist af- ter just one year. They were deep into it. Into development of the system of the Remote Manipulator System (RMS)—the robot arm—working with the Canadian designers and engineers. Into SAIL, the Shuttle Avionics Integration Laboratory, and FSL, the Flight Systems Laboratory—mockup shuttle cockpits in which Bluford flew simulated "ascents and entries and in orbit," checking out the shuttle software.

Camaraderie between the three black astronauts grew, as did their respect for what each had already accomplished. Gregory and Bluford, the "military types," the "city slickers." Ron McNair, a kind of "alter ego" with a "country" personality. A civilian. Regardless of their varied backgrounds, they were comfortable with each other when it came to the business at hand. They could run together in that scenario. Gregory, an Air Force Academy graduate. Bluford and McNair, both Ph.Ds. McNair's from the Massachusetts Institute of Technology, Bluford's from the Air Force Institute of Technology.

Piloting and flying were new skills to McNair, but he was always up for it, seeking the needed backseat time—that precious four hours a month.

"Hey, Guy!" It would be McNair, that infectious smile glittering.

"Yeah?"

"I see you've got an airplane! Can I fly with you?"

"Sure!"

Bluford recalled that "we'd go up together and fly around the country. It was a very enjoyable experience.[50]

A fleet of five orbiters was planned for shuttle operations. *Enterprise,* the first, was used strictly as an atmospheric test vehicle. *Columbia,* which made the first successful launch, was joined by *Challenger* at the Kennedy Space Center in 1982. *Discovery* was finished in October 1983, and *Atlantis* arrived in 1984. Slight modifications were made in each succeeding orbiter, based upon flight experience. By the time the new astronauts completed their training, a remanufactured *Challenger* would be ready to go operational.

The first shuttle missions were two-man shakedowns. John W. Young and Robert L. Crippen took *Columbia* into orbit on 12 April 1981, circling the earth for two days, six hours, twenty minutes, and fifty-three seconds. They landed at Edwards Air Force Base after making thirty-six orbits and logging over a million miles in space.

Joseph H. Engle and Richard H. Truly did it again in November, carrying the first cargo aloft: radar that produced images of the earth's surface that looked like photographs, and sensors capable of distinguishing clouds, land, and oceans by measuring the amount of carbon dioxide in the center of the troposphere. They also tested the fifty-foot-long, Canadian-built robot arm to see if it moved as advertised.

In March 1982, Gordon Fullerton and Jack Lousma took *Columbia* up again, this time for a full week, holding the orbiter in various constant attitudes to test its reactions to continued harsh sunlight and darkness, further testing the robot arm, and performing other experiments while circling the earth 130 times.

Mission STS-4 was launched on 27 June 1982. Astronauts Ken Mattingly and Henry W. Harsfield, Jr., stayed up for seven days, 112 orbits, and 3.3 million miles. Mission STS-5 employed a four-man crew aboard *Columbia*—Vance D. Brand, Robert Overmyer, Joseph P. Allen, and William B. Lenoir. They went up on 11 November 1982, and theirs was the first truly operational shuttle flight. Calling themselves the "Ace Moving Company," they deployed a pair of two-thousand-pound communications satellites during extravehicular activity (EVA). While he was out there, Lenoir tested tools to be used in the future to repair the nonfunctioning *Solar Max* satellite.[51]

On 4 April 1983, Paul J. Weitz, Karol J. Bobko, Donald H. Peterson, and F. Story Musgrave took *Challenger* into space. Old for this kind of business—their average age was 48 years, 3 months—they were known as the "Geritol Gang." They hauled aloft the biggest communications satellite in the world, the Tracking and Data Relay Satellite (TDRS) that relayed voice and data to the ground for future shuttle missions, making manned ground stations obsolete and increasing the data-handling rate.

Then came STS-7 and *Challenger,* a mission full of firsts, on 18 June 1983. Bob Crippen became the first astronaut to fly the shuttle twice. Sally Ride became the first American woman to fly in space. They were joined on the first of five-person crews by Frederick Hauck, John Fabian, and Norman Thagard, the first of the "Class of 1978" astronauts to fly.[52]

The African-American astronauts were all smiles. One word described the electricity in the air: Launch! Guy Bluford was going to fly on *Challenger* with the STS-8 crew.

CHAPTER 3

THE FIRST AFRICAN AMERICAN IN SPACE

Col. Guion S. Bluford, Jr.

Stories about the coming flight titillated listeners. STS-8 was to be the first "night flight" launch. The landing was also to be accomplished at night. Part of the original mission involving the second huge Tracking and Data Relay Satellite was canceled because of a component failure in the first TDRS. The crew was in deep training and planning, commanded by the navy's Capt. Richard H. Truly, seasoned veteran of the second shuttle flight. Excited rookies Daniel C. Brandenstein, Dale Gardner, and Dr. William Thornton were champing at the bit.[1] Perhaps the biggest story of all, however, was the inclusion of the name Guion S. Bluford, Jr., on the crew manifest.

Bluford's home was usually a very quiet place. It was no different now. One son was away at Texas A&M University; the other was attending high school. Linda and the boys usually took for granted what Guy did for a living. "They're not into the aviation [and] space side. They don't get all enthusiastic as I do," Bluford would say. But the media's trumpeting got the better of them. Because of "the articles in the newspapers and the attention the media gave" to his impending launch, "they got excited because they saw the excitement surrounding my getting ready to fly." Not one to "take his work home with him," he felt and saw that *this* time they "were interested. I know they were excited!" he said.[2]

But the name of the game for Bluford and the crew to which he was assigned was deep training for the coming flight. They nestled in the simulators, experiencing a simulated countup and the motion associated with actually flying the shuttle during ascent, orbit, and reentry. They familiarized themselves with upcoming mission objectives. They learned about the 260,000 commemorative envelopes

to be placed on sale by the Postal Service for $15.35 each, the proceeds to be split with NASA. About the eight other "Getaway Special" canisters aboard, and the 8,500-pound "dumbbell," fifteen feet long and thirteen feet high, called the Payload Deployment and Retrieval System (PDRS), to be used to demonstrate the ability of the robot arm to handle heavy objects, simulating movement of even larger items on future flights. They planned for the orbiting of the commercial Indian National Satellite, INSAT-1B and setting up for the Continuous Flow Electrophoresis System's fourth flight on the middeck, processing living cells for the first time. They spent long segments of time training in the engineering simulators, becoming expert on the software. They learned to relate what was happening on the screen to the actual programming.

Bluford went through fifteen months of it. Overlearning to the point where what he had to do on orbit was second nature. He worked hard to "put his best foot forward [to] . . . do the best job" he could. That attitude was probably the reason he was chosen to serve as flight engineer for the mission.

But that, an observer noted, was vintage Guy Bluford. He needed to be needed. He unflinchingly faced challenges. He had a sharp, analytical mind, a propensity for conducting exceptionally good research, and possessed an enormous amount of "stick-to-itiveness." He was a quiet, unassuming guy "who could live on bread and water if he had to."[3]

Although Bluford is reluctant to assume the title of "historical role model," people who know him gushingly affirm his fitness. According to Dr. Curtis M. Graves, former NASA deputy director for academic affairs:

If I had to invent someone to be the first in space, he's the one! The reason is that no matter what happens in life, Guy will always be there. You can always count on Guy never to get caught in the wrong place at the wrong time. He doesn't drink; he doesn't smoke; he doesn't chase. He doesn't do any of those things. He is probably the [best] role model that you could've come up with—with one exception: he doesn't [understand] the excitement other people [feel about] what he has done.[4]

Guy Bluford was born 22 November 1942 in Philadelphia, the first son of Guion S. Bluford, Sr., an inventor and mechanical engineer, and Lolita Harriet Bluford, a teacher in the public schools. Growing up with his younger brothers, Eugene and Kenneth, he lived in a racially mixed neighborhood on a middle class street that sprouted the classic row houses of "West Philadelphia." The city became known for its embodiment of the Quaker belief in equality for all men—both before and after the Civil War. Many Negroes flocked there over the years.

The Bluford family was suffused with middle-class values. Guy's parents instructed him and his brothers to work hard and strive for excellence in their personal pursuits. It was not a simple suggestion, but a "hallmark on both sides of the family." Their achievements proved it.

On Guy's mother's side were already-successful educators and musicians: Carol Brice, the contralto; Jonathan Brice, the pianist; and Charlotte Hawkins Brown, founder of the North Carolina black prep school—Palmer Memorial Institute. His father's side of the family included Lucille Bluford, editor of the *Kansas City* (Missouri) *Call,* and one F. D. Bluford, one-time president of A&T State University in Greensboro, North Carolina.[5]

Philadelphia's role in the nation's early development, as well as its reputation for being a haven for the religious and racially oppressed, had a certain appeal to the Bluford family. That aura was catching.

Personal drive, goal fulfillment, and a strong work ethic fueled the Bluford household. Race was never seen as an obstacle. Guy's parents believed that black children *could* develop their talents and "had a moral obligation to do so." Oddly, the "civil rights movements of the late 1950s and early 1960s were not considered worthy of family discussion."

Guy's family nickname was "Bunny." Something of a loner, he kept to himself, savoring crossword puzzles and games that called for mental prowess, such as chess. He had a paper route and achieved the rank of Eagle Scout. Model airplane construction probably fueled his early fascination with aviation. Determined to grasp the dynamics of flight, he studied science and mathematics in junior high school and by high school had decided to become an aerospace engineer. The military also fascinated him. Television shows like *West Point Story* and *Navy Log* were among his favorite entertainment fare. Frederick Hofkin, Guy's high school physics teacher remembered, "He would sit very quietly until I began asking really hard and challenging questions. Then he would come alive!"

For all his probing intellect it wasn't easy for Guy in school. He had to work harder than his brothers. At one time, his mother thought him the "least likely to succeed." His brother, Kenneth, remembered that Guy had to put in long hours and was always a little behind, trying to catch up. A high school guidance counselor regarded him with a jaundiced eye, once advising his parents that "Guy was not really college material and might be better off as a carpenter or mechanic."

The counselor obviously didn't understand the Bluford clan. College was a must for *everybody*. Nor did he understand Guy, who sometimes tends to withdraw within himself, yet is a bright man with very strong determination.

Professorial doubt followed Guy into college, where he enrolled in the aerospace engineering program at Pennsylvania State University. He was the only black student in the engineering school. A professor there remembered that Guy was "not the sort you would expect to be interviewed about twenty years later." But Bluford was diligent, intense, and serious. He enrolled in the air force ROTC program and ended up winning the 1962 Phi Delta Kappa leadership award. After writing a senior thesis, in which he investigated the flight of the boomerang, Bluford obtained his B.S. degree in aerospace engineering in 1964. After graduation, the air force sent him to Williams Air Force Base, Arizona, for pilot training. He was awarded his wings in January 1965 and, after training in the F-4C *Phantom*, ordered to combat duty in Vietnam in 1967.[6]

Bluford thought he was headed to Udon, Thailand, to fly and fight with the likes of one of the few black full colonels he'd ever met while in flying training—Daniel "Chappie" James, Jr.,—and the legendary

Robin Olds, commander of the 8th Tactical Fighter Wing. But his assignment was changed when he stopped off for jungle warfare training in the Philippines: Cam Ranh Bay, Republic of Vietnam.[7]

Cam Ranh Bay. Located some two hundred miles or so northeast of Saigon, it was the home of the 12th Tactical Fighter Wing. Its fighter squadrons had nicknames like *Hammer* (the 558th) and *Billygoats* (the 559th). Bluford's new squadron, the 557th, was proudly known as the *Sharkbaits*.[8]

By the time Bluford arrived in October 1966, almost the entire wing was returning home, having been injected into the Vietnam War all of a piece. There were no beautiful, permanent living quarters like there were stateside. It was tent city for the ordinary airmen, Quonset huts for the pilots, and trailers for the higher-ranking brass. Vietnam was everything it had been rumored to be: temperatures generating discomfiture, humidity at levels not to be believed. It was a chancy world, too. A world of high G-forces and serious air combat. Of fear, elation, and ultimate pride in being the one who helped save a ground-pounder's ass or a forward air controller's life or the rumps of the entire crew of an AC-130 *Spectre* gunship. These things bespoke elan, derringdo, bravery, and experience that would come later. For the time being, however, with the old squadron heads coming home, there was nothing much for Bluford and the other replacement pilots to do. It was boring and primitive. They needed jeeps to negotiate the unpaved roads. There was a makeshift officers' club over in the dining hall where everybody congregated, but that soon became boring and tedious.

To make life tolerable, Bluford and his fellow pilots engaged in secretive talks with wheeler-dealer supply sergeants and a little "midnight requisitioning."[9]

"What ya got?"
"What d'y'need?"
"This is what I can get ya."
"Yeah?"
"Yeah."
"How ya gonna get it here?"
"Why, old man, we'll just *fly* in it to ya!"
"Deal!"
"Wait!"
"What?"

"Ya gotta get us some tools and some lumber."

"Tools? Lumber?"

"Yep."

"Leeme work on it."

That was how the 557th Fighter Squadron's "party hootch" evolved. Each of the squadrons built their own party hootch: a little-bitty bar where the pilots could go and drink.

"Ours was near our Quonset hut," recalled Bluford. "We had a bunch of guys who were good with hammer and nails."

The lolling around soon came to a screeching halt, however. On a morning stroll down to operations, Bluford saw his name on a mission roster. It was time to suit up with all the prescribed equipment. Bluford recalled that the .38-caliber pistol pilots carried was "just enough to get you killed. If you got shot down and you pulled out your .38 and tried to shoot it out, you were dead meat!" Time for briefing. Time to fly that brand new *Phantom* F-4C with those two great big old engines that could generate thirty-five thousand pounds of thrust in afterburner. It was a marvelous machine with a built-in redundance that could bring you home with one engine shot up. Time for a new guy-in-back (GIB). Time to be cautious. Nervous time. He was about to go into combat. Killer-diller time. The real stuff. This wasn't pussy-footing around at MacDill Air Force Base, Florida, dropping dummy bombs. It wasn't flying sorties with empty ammunition trays. There were new rules to learn. Keep it above 5,000 feet, or some slap-happy farmer might blow you out of the sky with an old blunderbuss. Real folks were shooting real ordnance. It brought up the ultimate question: Wonder if I can get outta here without getting killed?

After that first mission, life became a blur for Bluford:

"They need you and your airplane today. Four of you! Fly down to such and such coordinates. . . ." We'd get in touch with the FAC [Forward Air Controller]—who was flying a Cessna 01 or 02 —and he'd say, "Hey, we need to have you drop your bombs over here because the army troops are coming in." So we'd set up a pattern [and] fly around in a circle and one guy would pull in and drop his bombs. We'd make multiple passes at targets marked by the FAC. Then you reformed and [headed] home.

Every two or three weeks there was duty on the Alert Pad. This meant living in the trailer hard by the end of the runway for twenty-four hours. Bluford's and two other crews waiting. The F-4Cs sat majestically by the alert shack ready to dance and boogie with the Vietnamese. One *Phantom* was all decked out with "nape" (napalm) and another looked like a pregnant cow, with bulbous five-hundred-pound bombs and nape. The third looked the same, its bombs seemingly straining to be free. The klaxon sounded. The crews jumped and ran like hell, racing for those cockpits. Somebody out there was in trouble. They needed those bombs and that nape somewhere. The horn was still blowing as they roared down the runway. Once they were airborne, the controller called out the vectors. Then Bluford and company would go out, blow the bastards up, and come home.

Home meant the party hootch—where there was laughter and good spirits and real vitality—nothing like the "O-Club" with its sometimes starchy correctness. The party hootch, where *real* fighter pilots congregated and talked in wild and raucous ways about the stuff they'd done that day. The hootch sure beat hell out of the O-Club when it came to getting to know that "whole bunch of medics and nurses and Red Cross [volunteers] at the nearby army hospital." At least it did until the second black full colonel in Bluford's experience hove into view. He was a quiet man, Bluford recalled, who "handled the administrative side of the wing. Lucius Theus [who retired a major general] jumped up and down and killed off the party hootches." It seemed to have had something to do with hurting the O-Club's revenue, what with all those fighter pilots spending their money carousing in those "itty-bitty party hootches." Colonel Theus was within his rights, but he was no fighter pilot; nor was he a part of that group. He simply didn't understand the pilot's need to have an outlet other than the O-Club. "You either flew or you sat around, read, played tennis, made tapes, or went to the O-Club," said Bluford. The party hootch was much more constructive. But Theus never really understood.

Bluford flew 144 combat missions against targets in South Vietnam and just over the DMZ. Of the latter, some sixty-odd were into the dreaded Route Package VI, the heavily defended Hanoi area. After a while, he said, he actually got used to the war. Missions were routine stuff—until the last one, activated off the Alert Pad. "They vectored us into North Vietnam to drop bombs on an active AAA [antiaircraft artillery] site. Saw more AAA than I *ever* wanted to see!"

It was his last flight. He was almost ready to leave the combat zone, to go home. Bluford suddenly felt nervous again and began flying very carefully. He watched his back at all times, "because you can see the light at the end of the tunnel! And those guys at the AAA site were shooting at us as actively as we were trying to drop bombs on them. We got back all right, but if we could save somebody's rump, the trouble was worth it! I found missions of this type most gratifying."

Putting an African American into space for the first time was a happening worthy of note, thought Dr. Curtis M. Graves, NASA's deputy director for academic affairs. What he was about to do in relation to the coming *Challenger* flight with Guy Bluford aboard was nothing new for him. He'd done it before, inviting famous and interesting Americans down to the Cape to witness a shuttle launch. Graves called them "educational conferences." Fifty educators from around the country had come for the first shuttle launch. Four hundred were on hand for Sally Ride's historical foray into space. Now, he intended to invite two hundred or more black Americans to witness Bluford's historical launch.

Graves's motive, however, involved much more than Bluford's flight. He envisioned a real conferencing of education and enlightenment. He would invite the cream of America's black educators and professionals. The superstars of science and the arts. The unsung NASA employees whose names nobody knew, but who, through daily, skilled contributions, helped support the entire space program. People who had been "doing this stuff for years."

At least two months before the launch, Graves and his staff combed and culled appropriate directories and lists. They made myriad telephone calls: to the presidents of all the black colleges and universities, to the presidents of all the black fraternities and sororities, to famous performers in the arts and sciences.

They invited NASA's "hidden" treasures, civilians who worked in support of all the astronauts: Dr. Julian Earles, of the Lewis Research Center; Dr. Christine Dorten, of the Langley Center; Dr. Patricia Corwing, a psychologist at the Ames Research Center; Dr. Robert Shurney, a contributor to studies in weightlessness and design criteria for moon vehicles.

They also invited such African-American notables as John Jacob, president of the National Urban League; Dr. Dorothy Height, president of the National Council of Negro Women; Dr. William (Bill) Cosby, of television fame; Hortense Canady, national president of the Delta Sigma Theta sorority; Nichelle Nichols of *Star Trek* fame; C. Alfred Anderson, "the father of black aviation," the man primarily responsible for training many of the now-famous Tuskegee Airmen. Presidents of black colleges and universities, members of school boards across the country, and members of the Congressional Black Caucus from the nation's capital.

More than 250 talented black Americans would be present for the launch. Two jetliners were contracted to fly them and many others down from Washington, D.C. In all, Graves said, "there would be about a million people, including three or four thousand certified media" observers watching the beginning of Guy Bluford's journey into space.[10]

While Dr. Graves prepared his invitation list, arranged for transportation to get guests there, and organized a special prelaunch banquet and briefing, NASA readied *Challenger* for its historic flight.

In May 1983, the Indian INSAT-1B communications satellite to be orbited arrived at Cape Canaveral Air Force Station and was placed in its payload assist module. In June, NASA began a three-shift schedule in the Orbiter Processing Facility, allowing for overtime and a nonstandard work week.

On 3 June the twin solid-rocket boosters were stacked on the Mobile Launch Platform. The huge external tank was mated to them by the twentieth. Looking, to the layman's eye, like "a big steel tube rounded off at both ends," it is a marvel of engineering. Sturdy, it is able to absorb propellant pressures from within and absorb external thrust loads at launch of over six million pounds from the two SRBs and the orbiter's three main engines. Actually two tanks in one, a single tank holds 141,000 gallons of liquid oxygen and the other, 385,000 gallons of liquid hydrogen. Together, these power the shuttle's three main engines during ascent. Between the two propellant tanks is an intertank, containing instrumentation, processing equipment, and structures accommodating its attachment to the forward ends of the rocket boosters. Sprayed with an insulating foam, the external tank loomed light brown, almost yellow, in the light.

Payloads for the flight began arriving at the Kennedy Space Center for installation in *Challenger*. On 29 June, *Challenger* itself arrived, flown in from California atop NASA's specially constructed Boeing 747SCA aircraft. After being lifted off, *Challenger* was towed into the Orbiter Processing Facility. Wheeled majestically between the high bays, it rode silently along a predrawn yellow line, its tall tailfin easing through a vertical slot above the building's main doors. Maintenance platforms were moved into position. An army of technicians swarmed over the orbiter, examining the spacecraft for any faults that hadn't been detected before. They tested all systems and loaded payloads into the orbiter's cargo bay. For twenty-six days, the technicians fussed and caressed *Challenger*. The Getaway Specials arrived, were carefully checked, and all twelve were mounted. On the nineteenth, the Indian INSAT-1B satellite was moved to the Vertical Processing Facility to be checked out, verifying orbiter-to-payload interfaces. On the twenty-first, the Payload Flight Test Article and Development Flight Instrumentation were installed.

By the twenty-sixth, the shuttle's turnaround was completed. It was loudly hailed as the fastest to date. On that date, *Challenger* was moved to the Vehicle Assembly Building (VAB) for mating to the external fuel tank and two solid-rocket boosters sitting on the Mobile Launch Platform. One of the world's largest buildings, the VAB soars 525 feet into the air, covers eight acres, and has a volume of 129,420,000 cubic feet—all of it resting on more than forty-two hundred steel pilings driven into bedrock to ensure stability in even the most violent windstorm. Inside, two of four bays are used to join the shuttle's parts before launch.

The solid-rocket boosters are deceiving. They look like slender, metal pencils. Measuring 149 feet in length, together they weigh 2.6 million pounds. At launch, they generate 5.3 million pounds of thrust and leave a trail of smoke and fire across the sky.

Technicians installed parachutes into nose segments, along with the ordnance necessary to deploy them. Then they attached the solid-rocket boosters.

Like the final movement of a great concerto, *Challenger* was lifted up for alignment with the gargantuan external tank, an operation that is, according to Nigel MacKnight, "a sight to make your hair stand on end." Towed along that yellow line, to be sure of precise alignment with a sling lowered from the VAB ceiling, the spacecraft is tethered, then lifted up and up and up as the undercarriage is retracted, rotated "into a vertical position and hoisted slowly right up to the roof of the building then across into one of the high bays" in the structure of the ceiling. The fit is tight. Clearance is measured in inches. The mating is done.

On 2 August the assembled *Challenger* sat resolutely on its huge Mobile Launch Platform as the monstrous Crawler-Transporter, the "Mighty Tortoise," groaned into the VAB to pick up the orbiter for the trip to the launch pad. Powered by two 2,750-horsepower diesel engines driving four one-thousand-kilowatt generators for its traction motors, the Tortoise is as wide as a twelve-lane superhighway. Consuming fuel at the alarming rate of one gallon every twenty feet, it has special systems aboard that ensure the Mobile Launch Platform and shuttle are maintained in an absolutely level configuration. It plods. It grunts and growls, carrying the eleven million pounds of the launch platform and space shuttle 3.5 miles to the launchpad, grinding along at a speed of one mile per hour over a specially built roadway as wide as an eight-lane freeway, its 450 tons of tracks crunching layered river gravel in forty-foot-wide lanes separated by a middle strip. Engineers walked stolidly alongside during the long ride, looking for cracks or potential failure of a vital part, which could signal catastrophe should the shuttle suddenly begin to topple.

At the launchpad, the Tortoise whined, growled, and delicately picked up the Mobile Launch Platform, set down on large, twenty-two-foot-high pedestals, maneuvering within two inches of the platform support points. Its operators changed cabs (one exists on either end) and took their behemoth back to its berth.

Activity picked up in the Launch Control Center east of the VAB. The "firing rooms" are located here. One, dedicated to this flight, had been busy since *Challenger* arrived in the Orbiter Processing Facility. Checkout. Status reports on work being performed. Schedules. Work control. Launch control. Operators seated at consoles and keyboards in semicircled clusters of six. Testing. Monitoring. Ultimately loading the hypergolic fuel automatically. Liquid oxygen tank sequencing. Transporting one hundred forty thousand gallons of supercold liquid one-third of a mile from the oxygen tank to the orbiter's external tank after proper chill down. Technicians pressurized the orbital maneuvering system, the reaction control system, and the helium tanks. After a planned hold for contingency work, pad activities were cleared by 24 August.[11]

Countdown for the third *Challenger* mission began on 27 August 1983. The stream of invited guests and media people prepared to converge on the Kennedy Space Center to witness the historic liftoff. Preparation for the special banquet, briefings, and speeches moved apace.[12]

Sally Ride talked to Guy Bluford about some of the challenges she had encountered as a celebrity. "We talked about the mechanics of scheduling, speaking engagements, and other public appearances," she told reporters. "I'm not sure our experiences are going to be the same." Actually, Guy was glad Sally Ride had gone into space before him. It suited him just fine.

"Let her carry the spear and get the attention," he remarked. "That relieves me. I'm very excited about flying the shuttle," he said at a Johnson Space Center press conference. "I'm not as hyped up about being the first black."[13]

BY THE ROCKETS' RED GLARE

*As I looked, behold, a stormy wind came out of the
north, and a great cloud with brightness round about
it, and a fire flashing forth continually, and in the
midst of the fire, as it were gleaming bronze.*
—*Ezekiel 1:4*, The Holy Bible,
Revised Standard Version

Countdown to launch continued. At T-minus-two days and counting, planes, buses, and automobiles began disgorging invited guests. Dr. Graves's public relations show was on target. An all-day briefing by the NASA "superstars" nobody had heard about before consumed their first day. That evening, the astronauts themselves conducted mission-specific briefings, describing some of the things they would be doing on this mission. The next day, guests toured the space center, then attended a NASA-sponsored banquet featuring budding astronaut Fred Gregory as guest speaker.[14]

The rains came, beating and swirling about the orbiter on the launch pad as it pointed majestically toward the sky. For eighteen hours the rain slashed and sluiced in the wind. Thunder rumbled grotesquely. Lightning crackled and scorched. Prevailing winds swept clouds into the Atlantic, leaving the air damp and hot. A few miles away, luminous alligator eyes searched the liquid turf for unwary prey down on the Banana River.

The inexorable countdown continued. According to David Shayler, it was "one of the smoothest countdowns in the program to date."[15] At T-minus-two hours and counting, *Challenger* sat resolutely on Launchpad 39-A, a glowing tribute to American technology and engineering skill. The 150,000-pound orbiter carried a 65,000-pound payload in its 60-foot cargo bay. Bathed in artificial light, it looked fat, attached as it was to the huge ET and solid-rocket boosters perched over the blast pit.[16]

Graves's invited guests arrived aboard four buses and filed into the bleachers from which they would view the launch. Rain pelted; umbrellas glistened under the floodlights. Plastic coverings, raincoats, and newspapers protected coiffed hair. Shoulders bowed against the wind-driven dampness as would-be onlookers wondered if this launch would be scrubbed. Some thought of leaving. It was a chance they couldn't take. There *could* be a miracle and they'd miss the show! The wives of all the astronauts were taken to the top of the tall VAB, "out of the way of the press, in case something happened."[17] Bluford's wife and two sons looked out toward Launchpad 39-A, their hearts fluttering a bit.

After a 10:00 P.M. breakfast, the astronauts were driven to the launchpad around midnight, took the elevator to the white room, and entered the shuttle. After completing the equipment checks, they prepared for blastoff. Strapped into their contoured seats, the crew powered up the auxiliary units. Captain Truly and Commander Brandenstein busied themselves on the flight deck. Mission specialists Gardner, Thornton, and Bluford waited as box-like "filling stations" pumped liquid oxygen and hydrogen into the belly of the mammoth external tank. Scheduled liftoff time, 2:15 A.M. EDT on 30 August approached. A hold was ordered. Weather parameters across the board were "No Go!"[18] The crowd in the bleachers and members of the assembled media held their breaths.

*   *   *

Guy Bluford had been "as happy as a clam" back in 1977. As chief of the Air Dynamics and Airframe Branch in the air force's Flight Dynamics Laboratory at Wright-Patterson Air Force Base, Ohio, he had been supervising more than forty engineers and was the proud overseer of two wind tunnels.

But the military is never static. Vacancies occur and are filled. Military tradition held that staying on station in one location too long was taboo. An air force pilot, Bluford knew he could not continue to neglect his flying proficiency. Since the job he held was nonflying, reassignment beckoned. People in the know intimated that he would be going back to Training Command. That wasn't what Guy wanted. It wasn't a step up the ladder, but a kind of stagnation; like running in place on a closed track. That ultimate challenge he'd always sought seemed about to elude him.

Bluford had *been* an instructor pilot in Training Command after Vietnam, then worked especially hard entering the graduate program at the Air Force Institute of Technology at Wright-Patterson in August 1972. In 1974, he was awarded his M.S. degree in aerospace engineering with distinction, and in 1977, was nearing completion of a doctorate in aerospace engineering with a minor in laser physics. Successful defense of his dissertation, "A Numerical Solution of Supersonic and Hypersonic Viscous Flow Fields Around Thin Planar Delta Wings," was the final hurdle. Serving as an instructor pilot in Training Command with a doctorate in aerospace engineering hardly seemed the way to fly, he thought.

"So I started looking for a job," Bluford recalled—just as NASA began looking for astronauts for the space shuttle. The field was suddenly opened up to include people who had credentials other than "test pilot." *Pilot astronauts* and *mission-specialist astronauts*. It wasn't the easiest of decisions. He almost mulled it over in his mind too long. At the last moment Guy said he decided to put in an application "to get into the program." The air force selected him as a mission-specialist astronaut, despite extensive flight time and experience; the NASA selection board had concurred.

Guy said he was surprised to learn he'd been one of the thirty-five selected from among the more than ten thousand considered. What he found most exciting was the way he, McNair, and Gregory were greeted by NASA when they showed up. "NASA really rolled out the red carpet for us," he recalled in a 1991 interview, a satisfied smile on his face. It had not always been that way, however.

Guy was not unmindful of how the national scene had changed since the civil rights revolution. There had been Lawrence in 1967, and Dwight before that. For whatever reasons, African Americans somehow missed catching the brass ring in the world of astronauts. The stories about their experiences were memories by the time Bluford was selected.[19] But he had his own scars from the civil rights wars. The denial, for example, of housing for his family when he was a second lieutenant as he prepared to go fight for America in Vietnam.

Seventeen minutes after scheduled liftoff, the rain stopped and the wind died. It seemed almost miraculous. Visibility was tolerable. Countdown resumed. T-minus-ten minutes and counting. Invited guests and members of the media peered from under dripping umbrellas and sodden, makeshift coverings, their hair matted.[20]

Bluford was honored to be the first black American chosen to venture into space, but that fact was not uppermost in his mind. Instead, he thought of the enormity of leaving planet Earth. Of flying higher into the firmament than most men had ever been. Fear was not an issue; there was no time for that. "It was," Bluford recalled, "like preparing for an exam. You study as much as you can, the better prepared you are, the less frightened you are about taking the exam."[21]

The exam grew closer as the countdown dwindled to T-minus-thirty seconds. Second hands swept across watch dials; digital prompts pulsated on the faces of electronic clocks. Launchpad 39-A glistened under powerful searchlights. The 154-foot-high external tank seemed somehow larger, its 28.6-foot diameter fatter. The two 150-foot solid-rocket boosters flanking the ET seemed to glow, providing their assent to the coming test. The orbiter, its nose pointed toward the heavens, shone with an unearthly whiteness.

Computers had taken over the countdown. The propellant tank vents were long closed. Couch-bound, Truly and Brandenstein stared fixedly at the instrument panels. Bluford and the other mission specialists lay cinched into their seats. Every indicator was green as the countdown moved to T-minus-fifteen seconds. Out in the darkness, cameras set to record the launch began their maniacal, electronic song.

"Liftoff!"

The roar shook houses miles away. Flames flashed and blazed into huge, wedge-shaped deflectors, sending searing exhaust from the solid-rocket boosters into a forty-two-foot trench underneath the launchpad, roaring out the sides, white smoke and brilliant orange flames billowing into the air. The temperature around the launchpad soared to 6,000°F, as the "rain birds" strategically placed around it disgorged three hundred thousand gallons of water onto the pad in thirty seconds, cushioning the shuttle from acoustic energy damage generated by the powerful boosters. Night turned into momentary day as someone observed that, even though it was 2:32 A.M., they could read their newspapers in the monumental glow. Birds, thinking themselves ensconced for the night, took momentary flight, silhouetted against the bright fire. Some died, killed by the sheer level of noise.[22]

"Ooohs" and "aaaaahs" soughed through the crowds on the ground. Some wept. Others cheered as the orbiter leapt into space, grudgingly at first, then headed out over the Atlantic, a fitting denouement to a brilliant spectacle.[23]

"This has to be one of the most spectacular things I've ever seen!" exulted John Jacob, president of the National Urban League.

Former pro-basketball star Wilt Chamberlain said, "I think it was fantastic. Awesome is the word!"

Barbara Lawrence, wife of astronaut-designee Robert Lawrence, killed in the 1967 aircrash, reminisced: "I would have hoped that had Bob lived, this would have happened a long time ago!"[24]

They call it "rocket dawn" when the space shuttle takes to the air in the middle of the night. People from as far away as North Carolina saw it light their skies.

Inside *Challenger,* Guy Bluford and the crew thought it was like being in the middle of a great bonfire, riding in some strange elevator through roaring flames. It was a major surprise. They'd purposely turned down the cockpit lights so they could look out the window— just in case they had to land. But it was a night launch, and when they lit the rocket boosters, they "lit up the cockpit so much that whatever night vision we were trying to maintain was lost," Bluford said later.[25] Mission commander Dick Truly also recalled the shock:

When the main engine started, I could see the reflections from the exhaust all over the tower and then it became much brighter when the solids lit. And as soon as we were away from the tower and began to rise, it looked like you were driving through a fog bank except that there was an internal orange light within the fog.

It got brighter and brighter and continued all the way through the solid-rocket booster burn. When tank separation occurred, it seemed like we were surrounded by flame.

"The SRB separation was like being in the middle of a bonfire!" added another crew member, his voice filled with awe.[26]

Oddly, there weren't many other surprises. "What amazed me," Bluford recalled, "was that the shuttle flew just like the simulator said it was going to fly. The only differences were the motion, the vibration, and the noise. You don't get those in the simulator. When I felt the movement and heard the noise, I thought, Hey, this thing really does take off and roar!"[27]

It was an understatement, for the solid-fuel rockets exerted 5.3 million pounds of thrust in four-hundredths of a second, lighting the entire circle of the sky. "Rocket dawn" dappled the clouds orange, as the orbiter zoomed through and the color suffused. Within two minutes of liftoff, the shuttle was twenty-seven miles above the earth, where the two booster rockets fell away, tiny explosive devices separating them from the great fuel tank. Parachutes soon deployed and the boosters fell into the sea where recovery ships would bring them back. For the next six minutes, the main engines burned, hurling *Challenger* to the very edge of space. As the main engines shut down, the huge external tank jettisoned, tumbling along a ten-thousand-mile arc into the sea. One hundred eighty miles above the earth, *Challenger* slipped into orbit.[28]

About an hour into the flight, Guy Bluford unstrapped from his seat and, although having been trained for the weightless state aboard an aircraft test bed, he had only experienced it at one degree of gravity. It hadn't really dawned on him that, 180 miles into space, he would be dealing with a zero-gravity state. "The next thing I knew," he recalled, "I was floating off the top of the cockpit!" It wasn't panic that took over, but the searching for a viable answer to the simple question: How do I get down from here? He began wiggling around for a while, trying to figure out how to move about the cabin. It was a new experience, and he quickly found that the rules were somehow different in a weightless state. You learn to push off walls and ceilings because you realize you can't walk around like you used to. It was like floating around in water, but without any water. The bulky space suit and helmet made him feel clumsy as he made unintentional mistakes as he went about flipping switches. But, after two hours, he began to get the hang of it. To his surprise, it was loads of fun:

> You figure out what you can do at zero-G and it's fascinating. I mean, it doesn't take much to get things floating across the room. . . . I like to walk on walls and ceilings and all that sort of stuff! Zero-G is nifty! It's like [you're] a kid who's just picked up a new toy! [You're] fascinated with this new toy! And you play with it for a while. Zero-G is the same way. . . . It's really great![29]

Bluford speaks in a kind of "gee whiz" tone, his voice a well-modulated sing-song, not unlike the way a youngster sounds who's learning to speak while discovering the world and all that is in it. The difference is you know you're talking with a mature, well-educated gentleman, who's perfectly aware that beyond the initial "fun" of existing in a weightless state at zero-G, certain physiological effects are taking place, not all of which are yet understood. Minerals can leach from the bones, reducing the rate of bone formation. Muscles can atrophy when not properly exercised. Blood collects in the head and chest. The face becomes puffy, the nose stuffy. Headaches are frequent. The legs get skinny. And so, Bluford, along with the other crew members, began daily exercises in space while NASA's experts on the ground worked intensely to find the answers as space missions became longer and longer. Happily, it all reverses itself upon return to normal gravity.[30]

By then it was time to go to work and carry out the assignments given STS-8. Before the first orbit had been completed, *Challenger* effected communications through the new TDRS, "sending back the clearest TV pictures ever transmitted through the relay."

The launch had been timed to coordinate with one of the mission's prime objectives—launch of the $45-million Indian national satellite, designed to provide communications and weather information to that country. Twenty-five hours and sixteen minutes into the flight on mission day two, Bluford and Garner popped the INSAT-1B from the payload bay during sunset over the Pacific.

"Roger, Houston, we're happy to let you know that INSAT was deployed on time with no anomalies and the satellite looked good!" Bluford reported to Mission Control.

"You guys have maintained the shuttle's perfect record!" the ground controllers responded.[31]

They knew President Reagan would probably call, so the communications link was established and, also on their second day in orbit, the presidential call came through.

"Guy," said the president, "you are paving the way for many others and making it plain that we are in an era of brotherhood here in our land. You will serve as a role model for so many others and be so inspirational."[32]

Bluford thanked the president. His response was low key because he is a low-key kind of person. Later, he remembered telling the president simply "that I was part of a team. We were doing a great job, and I was pleased to be there. [And] I *was* pleased."[33]

The remainder of the second and third days included runs of the continuous flow electrophoresis system experiments—the electrical separation of biological fluids in space; putting living cells from pancreas, kidneys, and pituitary glands through an electrical field to separate hormone-producing cells from the others. It could be done on earth, but it was faster in space because of the absence of gravity. Bluford ran six samples—two each of pituitary, kidney, and pancreas cells. "We found that we could make an awful lot of product [and were] very efficient making these things on orbit."[34]

Mission days three and four saw Bluford and Gardner working with the fifty-foot mechanical arm while Truly and Brandenstein maneuvered the orbiter. The two mission specialists grasped the 8,500 pounds of steel, aluminum, and lead in the cargo bay effortlessly, picking it up, moving it out into space and back again. It was a test in preparation for a scheduled try at retrieving a wayward, malfunctioning satellite. They called it "pumping iron," holding the huge mass at "varying angles and balance points" to see how the mechanical arm operated.

Bluford and Gardner were also responsible for feeding the six rats on board. They gave them nutrients and raw potatoes "to test their ability to survive in their own life-support module." Dr. William Thornton, at fifty-four, the oldest human ever to fly in space, studied the phenomenon of motion sickness, conducting brain-wave monitoring and eye-movement tests and observing how fluids shifted within the body and how the eyes and nervous system reacted to flashing light and clicking sounds.[35]

On the sixth day, the crew concentrated on cabin stowage preparing for reentry and landing. As engineer, Bluford helped Truly and Brandenstein initiate the 160-second deorbit burn early on the morning of 5 September—at the end of their ninety-seventh orbit and after covering 2.22 million miles in space. Truly flew *Challenger* through the prescribed flight profiles and the blast furnace of the earth's heavy atmosphere, taking manual control below Mach 1. Landing at night, they were guided in by twin, powerful light beacons—one white, the other red—punching up from the vast emptiness of the Mojave Desert. Positioning *Challenger* between the two beams, Truly held the orbiter steady on a steep, nineteen-degree angle of approach to the landing site—carved from the desert darkness by six Xenon arc lamps shining with the power of 4.8 billion candles.[36]

A large, enthusiastic crowd greeted Bluford and the STS-8 crew after landing. Among them were large contingents from the Urban League and the NAACP. Their standing ovation said it all—as if the crew were members of some celestial symphony at the end of the debut performance of a difficult and monumental work of epic proportion. His family in tow, Bluford smiled the slow smile for which he is now famous and said, "I'm really humbled tonight to see so many people out here to welcome us back! I feel very proud to be a member of this team, and I think we have a tremendous future with the space shuttle—I mean *all* of us!"[37]

His Aunt Lucille hugged him and presented him with a proclamation making 30 August 1983 "Guion Bluford Day" in Kansas City.

Later, in the light of day, amid echoes trailing a band that had been playing martial music before an even larger crowd, Guy again had a turn to speak. As he approached the microphone, he noticed that his wife, Linda, hung back a bit. He paused, smiled, and waited. She joined him at the microphone. He said

> I think we NASA people can be proud of the space shuttle because I think it's a very dynamic, capable vehicle that will be doing lots of good work for the next ten or fifteen years. I feel very honored to have flown on STS-8 and to have helped do some of that good work and [I hope] to continue doing some of that good work.[38]

Requests for public appearances poured in from across the country. His was a message of confidence, pride, and dedication that people wanted and needed to hear. Mayor Marion Barry of Washington, D.C., gave Bluford the key to the city. The Congressional Black Caucus feted him with a capitol reception.

Although proud of both the role he has played and of his accomplishments, Bluford is not one to thrive on the hoopla. Nor is he one to put on airs when it comes to dressing up, unless it's absolutely necessary. When Bluford was invited to the Black Caucus reception, Dr. Graves remembered Guy saying he had never worn a tuxedo before.[39] Amazed, Graves, based on his own experiences, remembered that, "Black folks always dress up to do things! But Guy had never done that. He called me to ask, 'How does the tie go on?'" Chuckling, Graves later remarked, "But *that's* Guy! He's different!"

For all of that, and even though Bluford is not remembered as an "electrifying speaker," he still enjoys the opportunity to speak to audiences of black youngsters, to share with them the values his parents taught him. He told a crowd of six hundred at a school in Harlem:

What I want to pass on to you is that it's very important to set high goals for yourself and realize that if you work hard, you will get them. I want you to be the future astronauts in space with me!

And—

If you want to succeed, prepare yourself as best you can for whatever career you have chosen to pursue. Work hard, dedicate yourselves and make the necessary sacrifices. Above all, be diligent and persistent. A lot of times, people give up when they taste a little bit of defeat, but it's important that you set goals for yourself. You should doggedly pursue them until you achieve them![40]

Nobody alive was more qualified to say such things than Guy Bluford. From his early school years through college, and then service in Vietnam, diligence and "being good" earned him a M.S. degree with distinction in aerospace engineering in 1974, and a doctorate, with a minor in laser physics. After Vietnam, he wore the Vietnam Campaign Medal, the Vietnam Cross of Gallantry with Palm, and ten air force Air Medals. In 1983, that same diligence had taken him to the edge of space and back, even though, at times, it disturbed him that probably for the rest of his life, someone would walk up, nudge him in the ribs, and congratulate him on being the "first African American into space."

In Bluford's more lucid moments, perhaps he, like Nichelle Nichols, may be prone to give some of the credit not only to his parents and the milieu into which he grew, but to the Rev. Dr. Martin Luther King, Jr., whose effect on society moved an aged, black Atlantan named Virge Packer, driving his old silver Buick past King's grave the day before Guy's launch, to say:

> When I was young, the Ku Klux Klan hung a boy 'cause a white girl say he looked at her. Driving down to Florida one time, a man refused to sell me gas, just 'cause I was black. But Dr. King, he changed a lot of things. He said there'll come a time when white chillun and black chillun will play together. That happened. I'm sure glad I lived long enough to see things turn out the way they did. All those bad old days, they gone with the wind.[41]

Guion Stewart Bluford, Jr., did Martin Luther King, Jr., one better. People of varying ethnic origins were flying into space; out toward the stars and into the sanctity of a place that perhaps, an observer notes, bespeaks the presence of God, Himself.

And still, the low key Bluford persona impresses:

> I look at my life and I'm amazed that I have had the opportunities to do the things I've done. From a black perspective, my flight on the shuttle was important because it represented another step forward. Opportunities do exist for black youngsters if they work hard and strive to take advantage of those opportunities.[42]

As far as the world knew, mission STS-8 was a huge success. Only later was it discovered that the crew had been inordinately lucky: they had been only seconds away from disaster during the launch. Examination of the recovered solid-rocket boosters showed that one of the carbon-phenolic resin liners (designed to burn down to one and one-half inches as protection from the extreme heat of exhaust gases) had burned down to a mere two-tenths of an inch. Some say that just fourteen seconds' more exposure would have caused an explosion.[43] The possibility of such a tragedy is terrifying. Yet, it was, as they say in the space business, "an anomaly." Something just as chancy could happen on any expressway in America. Nevertheless, NASA delayed its Shuttle 9 launch and conducted a thorough investigation.

Lady Luck had ridden with the STS-8 crew. The so-called color line had been broken in space. In less than five months, another African American would venture into the heavens.

CHAPTER 4

Ronald E. McNair, Ph.D.

THE SECOND AFRICAN-AMERICAN ASTRONAUT IN SPACE

Whoever owned those sprawling cotton and tobacco fields about a half-mile outside the town of Lake City, South Carolina, would probably have doubled over in hilarious laughter upon hearing that one of those little McNair boys would one day be an astronaut. Lake City was Ku Klux Klan country. "Black aspirations" were horselaughs to many majority folks. They'd demonstrated their point of view before, firing shots into Walter Scott's house because "he was out front in the little Voter's League" Lake City blacks were trying to create in those days.

The McNair family was poor. A little over a decade after his birth on 21 October 1950, at harvest time Ronald McNair and his two brothers found themselves in those cotton fields. The work was rough, tough, and brutal. The boys would awaken when the sun first peeked over the horizon to chase away the early morning dew. Shuffling along with other men and women down long rows of cotton. Bending, plucking; always moving forward, dragging long sacks behind. Interminably stooping; reaching. As the sun reached its zenith, the earth glimmered in the heat. Slowly, the welcome shadows grew longer as the day inched by. Their backbones felt "like two razor blades meeting." They wanted to quit. Instead, they called up even more endurance, more strength, for that wage of four dollars a day was a means to an end.

The struggle in those long rows of cotton helped shape Ronald E. McNair. Long years later, he was to remember in an interview: "I gained qualities in that cotton field. I got tough. I learned to endure. I refused to quit!"[1]

As a youngster, he showed that he was special. Although she couldn't write, Ron's great-grandmother learned to read and, while caring for the boys before they were old enough to go to school, taught them to read. They could play for a while, but then "it was time to get out the books," his grandmother recalled. He was reading words by age three. By age four, "he was too smart to stay home, but they couldn't take him in the city school," said Irene Jones, a friend of the family, teacher, and graduate of a black college. They took Ron to Idell Singletary, principal of Camerontown Elementary School, where blacks who lived outside Lake City sent their children. She let Ron in and, when he turned five, transferred him to the black elementary school in the town.

Ron caused something of a stir at once, being the only child who walked around "with his pencil behind his ear always, carrying his notebook in the same position at his side." As he was promoted from grade to grade, the impression of studiousness hung on. Had the term been in vogue, they would have called him "gifted," because he was. Ron soon caught up with his brother Carl, and the two became inseparable. The family bought a set of the *World Book Encyclopedia* and, on Saturday mornings, the brothers (including Eric, the oldest) would spend hours reading through it.

Home was Ron's grandfather's weather-beaten, unpainted house. It leaked in winter—once so bad the ceiling caved in. Ron wanted to stay home and clean up the place.

"No, son," his mother said, "we're going to school. We'll worry about that when we get back."

Pearl, his mother, was dedicated to family, church, and education, and taught in the black schools. His father, Carl, was an automobile mechanic who never finished high school. Nevertheless, he pushed his sons and the boys he coached in baseball to stay in school, study, and be successful.

It was a time when African-American educators and parents knew they were black and had to be better than good in order to measure up. The teachers in the black schools were tough; parents didn't allow their children to go to school unprepared.

Ron McNair caught the drift. In his junior year in high school, his chemistry instructor asked the class to write a paper on what they'd like to be doing in ten years. Ron sat down and counted up the years. He considered all kinds of directions in which he could have gone: music, medicine, chemistry, physics, history—but, in the final analysis, he chose physics because it brought mathematics and science together in a way that was most appealing to him. He envisioned four years of undergraduate study, two years of work, then four more years for graduate study, and he was going to work like crazy to realize those goals!

Valedictorian of his high school class, a star in baseball, basketball, and football, Ron also exhibited great talent as a saxophonist. His strongest interests were music and science.[2] Ron became fascinated with outer space when he was a very small boy. His father recalled that:

Ronald was always the curious type. Back when the Russians launched that spaceship—I think it was *Sputnik*—he would go outside and look up at the sky. He couldn't understand how something that size could stay up there! But the main reason he continued to look up at the sky was he thought maybe something might go wrong and that thing might fall. He wanted to be sure he could see it coming down so it wouldn't fall on him! He became real interested in space then. He must have known somewhere in the back of his mind that he could play a part in the space program.[3]

Ron's aunt, Lela M. Austin, was also a teacher. She had been instrumental in getting his friends Joe Wilson and Toney Graham into colleges and assisting them with scholarship applications. Lela helped Ron get a scholarship to North Carolina A&T, the "agricultural and mechanical college for the colored race."

Tom Sandin, professor of physics and Ron McNair's faculty adviser at North Carolina A&T, remembers the roundabout way scholarships for his second, third, and fourth years of college were obtained. "You had to apply to the state of South Carolina. It was the state's way of keeping blacks out of white schools and their view of 'equality.' Scholarships were given to any black student who would go out of state. With the integration of the schools, the practice stopped."[4]

Caught between a love of music and science, Ron McNair took a battery of aptitude tests to redetermine his real direction.

"You have what it takes for engineering school," his college counselor advised.

So, science it was. Ron earned pocket money playing the saxophone in a rhythm and blues band at campus clubs and high school dances. He also began studying karate. Keenan Sarratt, a roommate, said that "Ron loved the competition, the grace of it."[5] Suddenly, there were a few concerns about Ron's academic progress. According to Tom Sandin, "those concerns were not unfounded," what with all the "outside interests," like being the karate champion, a member of Omega Psi Phi fraternity, playing his saxophone in night clubs—surrounded by a glorious fan club of eager young ladies. And, too, there were rumors of a possible Atlantic Records contract, which could have meant big bucks had the rumor become real. "Ron," sighed Professor Sandin, "was a well-rounded individual!"[6]

It was a kind of upper division replay of the peer pressure that had threatened to steer Ron toward trouble while he was going to the all-black Carver High School in Lake City. Dedicated teachers saved him. Later, he doffed his hat to them: "There were several teachers who recognized that I was going astray. And these were teachers who were capable of conveying knowledge as well as molding character."[7]

Professors Donald Edwards, chairman of the A&T physics department, and Tom Sandin offered Ron a challenge in 1969. Under the auspices of a Massachusetts Institute of Technology exchange program, it was possible for McNair to take his junior year in physics at MIT. They wanted him to do it, for he showed great promise. But at first, Ron didn't want to go. Why leave a comfortable environment in Greensboro to go to a school like MIT, where the pressures would undoubtedly be greater? he thought.[8] Then he thought of how he'd hesitated once before, when offered a football scholarship to Howard University in Washington, D.C., a school many called "the Harvard of black schools." He'd "chickened out," opting instead for A&T because his brother was going to school there and because "they had physics." As it worked out, Ron's studies there provided a reasonable background from which he would attain greater heights.[9] As McNair later observed, he decided to plumb the mysteries of the unknown because he wanted to be a winner and "you can only be a winner if you are willing to walk over to the edge and just dangle it just a little bit!"[10]

The exposure to "renowned scientists at MIT" opened new vistas to Ron, affording him a different view of the field. Returning to North Carolina A&T, Ron graduated magna cum laude in 1971. His brother, Carl, graduated the same year. The entire McNair family breathed rarefied air that June. In addition to the graduation of the two brothers, Eric and "Mrs. Austin's daughter and their grandmother, Mrs. Montgomery, all graduated from high school in Lake City in the same month." Mrs. Montgomery was sixty-five.

After winning a Ford Foundation fellowship, Ron McNair returned to MIT for graduate studies, a glowing recommendation from A&T's Tom Sandin in his pocket. Sandin did not offer his recommendation lightly. He saw a student's ability to be successful and assimilate as being the key. "The change," Sandin said later, "from the essentially all-black atmosphere at A&T to the essentially all-white atmosphere at MIT, plus the added pressures, were not something we wanted to just throw our students into." It was not an empty concern. Michael S. Feld, an MIT professor of physics, noted that after McNair's arrival "it was clear that his background was quite deficient." But McNair "dangled it over the edge," and, as Professor Feld later observed, "he did quite well—he worked very, very hard, and he made up the deficiency."[11]

McNair rented an apartment on Columbus Avenue in Roxbury, Massachusetts. Once he was settled there, MIT and its environs soon became familiar territory. He went to church Sundays, joining the St. Paul's African Methodist Episcopal Church. Later, he founded a karate school for church youngsters. On occasion, Ron traveled to Hartford, Connecticut, where he patronized his uncle Jerry Mack's bar and restaurant. Sometimes Ron would help out in the cavernous bar, playing jazz and blues tunes on his saxophone. Jerry Mack himself would often join in, twirling and plucking his string bass. Jerry Mack's was a place where friends gathered, a popular watering hole. It was a place where you could feel comfortable while sipping sloe gin. You didn't have to talk to anybody. You could just sit there and look. When the conversations took off out of control like an old T-Model Ford and the debate grew raucous, the bar's regulars, people like Elihu Lumpkin, the construction worker, and John Thompson, the bricklayer, would stop in midsentence and look to Ron McNair, the learned man, to act as judge.

"Ron," they'd say, "who's right?"

They knew he knew. He was bright and educated. But Ron didn't want any part of it. "He'd just smile at us—like, 'figure it out for yourselves!'" Then they'd smile to themselves, tightening callused, worn, and gnarled fingers around their little glasses of sloe gin, allowing as how they'd put Ron on some kind of pedestal.

"He didn't want to be there, but we knew better," Lumpkin said.

One day, Thompson was carrying on, wondering aloud why there weren't more blacks in the space shuttle program and saying what a shame *that* was. Ron McNair just let him spew it all out, listening as politely as you please. Finally, Ron smiled and quietly said: "Well, *I'm* in it."

Then he'd gone on being himself, Ron, Jerry Mack's nephew. Serving drinks. Waiting on tables. Joking with the customers. Riffing on the saxophone from time to time. Then the weekend would be over and he'd be gone; back to MIT, the doctoral program, laser technology and physics—until the next visit.[12]

For all of the homespun philosophies there for the taking, it wasn't the ambiance of Jerry Mack's bar and restaurant that radically changed Ron McNair's life. That happened at the Rev. Dr. LeRoy Attle's AME church in Cambridge one Sunday when Ron looked across the congregation and saw beautiful and gifted Cheryl Moore of Jamaica, New York, a public school teacher. Light-complected, sharp-featured, and stylish to a fault, she left his heart in a shambles at the flick of an eyelash. Attractive and unassuming, she matched his quiet inner strength. He, the karate instructor, calmly smashing bricks and breaking boards, showing the youngsters how. She, the Bible school teacher. Both holding forth at the usual weekly church dinner.

Romance came slowly and took even longer to really develop. They'd "find themselves at events" together. It was after such an "event" that sparks first leapt the space between them as he walked her to her car. She suddenly missed him at her side. Curious, she turned and saw him there on the walkway, holding and petting a stray kitten he'd found.

She smiled, a bit amused at the contradictions she found so interesting in this man who broke bricks and concrete with his hands, but who "had enough sensitivity to pick up a cat and pet it."

Time telescoped. They began to go out regularly. Love overtook them. A year and a half later, Ron asked her to marry him. It was a medium-sized wedding held in the church where they had met. "People who knew people" set them up with honeymoon reservations in Bermuda.[13]

McNair's sojourn as a graduate student at MIT was no cakewalk. It was tough. But Ron made up for whatever deficiencies he may have had with intense determination and hard work, a Ford Foundation Grant carrying him through his years of graduate study. In 1975, he received a "traveling fellowship" from the North American Treaty Organization, which allowed him to spend several months studying laser physics in France at the Institute for Theoretical Physics at Les Houches.

Professor Feld stuck with him, supervising, collaborating, and watching. Over the years, Ron performed some of the earliest work in the development of hydrogen-fluoride, deuterium-fluoride, and high-pressure carbon-monoxide lasers.[14] It was like, Ron recalled later, "a five-round prize fight." He'd entered MIT "armed with the gloves of eagerness; cheered on by the great crowd of hope." And, by the fifth round, "that great giant of technology lay stretched out on the canvas!"[15]

But a nightmare occurred during McNair's last year at MIT. The research papers he'd compiled so carefully for his graduate thesis were stolen from the bag containing his notebooks. Normally, it would take at least a year to recreate the research notes, but Ron buckled down and, after many long hours and much "intense work in the laboratory," regenerated the lost data. After months of writing, his thesis, "Energy Storage and Collisional Transfer in Polyatomic Molecules," was accepted by the MIT staff in 1977, and he was awarded a doctorate in physics.[16]

Tired of the Massachusetts cold and snow, Ron and Cheryl looked toward California as an alternative place to live. They moved to Los Angeles, where Ron accepted a position as staff physicist with the Hughes Research Laboratories in nearby Malibu. It was there that NASA's media blitz caught his eye. Ron was particularly interested in the fact that shuttle mission specialists didn't necessarily need a military background. He sent for the brochures and written qualifications, and he was elated to find that he apparently met all the requirements.

"This is what I want to do," he remarked, as he filled out the "stacks and stacks of forms and applications." Security investigators spread out across the United States to check his background. About a year later, Ron was invited to Houston for testing and interviews.

"I knew," he said later, that "they were inviting finalists for personal interviews and physical examinations because I kept close tabs on what was happening by any means possible." He really felt it was something he could do. No stone was left unturned. So confident was he, that "my wife and I started making plans to go to Houston."[17]

At about this same time he called his brother, Carl, by then a data-processing consultant in Atlanta, to announce that he was going to be an astronaut.

"Oh, yeah?" his brother retorted. "And I'm going to be the Pope!"

"I am!" came the insistent reply.

"What makes you think you're going to be an astronaut?"

"Because I applied for it."

"How many other people applied for it?"

"Eight thousand."

"*Eight thousand?* Man, what makes you think you're going to be an astronaut?"

"Because I applied for it, I told ya!"

Carl let the matter rest until, weeks later, tuning in to Walter Cronkite and the evening news, he heard his brother's name announced as one of the thirty-five shuttle astronauts selected by NASA. He called Ron. The news was cause for congratulations. It was, in fact, the way Ron found out he'd been chosen. And when members of the media began calling for interviews, it really began to sink into Carl's consciousness that it was no pipe dream. It was real. His brother was going to be an astronaut!

That Carl was at first skeptical about Ron's being an astronaut was not unusual. He didn't doubt his brother's scientific acumen. It was where they'd come from. "A town of 10,000 to 12,000 people, where the biggest headline in the paper was about Farmer John's mule being hit or something." It was that background and who they were in American society. "We always had," Carl told journalist Bernadette Hearne, "a preconceived notion of what an astronaut was and what kind of a family they came from, and it certainly wasn't ours!" Astronauts came from politically active families, Carl thought, families that had ties to important people in government. They were fighter pilots—which Ron wasn't, or "heroes with five Purple Hearts or something!"[18]

Ron McNair wasn't intimidated by the imposing, twelve-person selection board in Houston. In fact, he rather enjoyed it. He figured they already knew everything about him and just wanted to hear how he'd tell it. There was no point in being intimidated because, as he later told an interviewer, the "examinations left no parts unviolated—physically or psychologically!"

Two months passed before the final selections were announced and he returned to Houston to begin training. He thought the instruction in Houston was one of the more fantastic parts of the overall training program. Courses in astronomy and oceanography were taught. Meteorology and astrophysics. Geology, medicine, "every other scientific discipline you can imagine." The details of spaceflight and the space vehicle. Orbital mechanics. The physiology of spaceflight. Spacecraft maneuver. Ron learned to fly in the T-38 and rode with Guy Bluford and others in low-gravity flights. SCUBA training for underwater familiarization in the Water Immersion Facility, simulating zero-gravity conditions. Caucusing with engineers and space contractors to gain an overview of the interplay of all the orbiter's systems. Traveling around the nation, concentrating on his specific area of responsibility for coming spaceflights. Meetings. Discussions. Fifteen hours a month in the high-performance T-38 jet trainer, studying cross-country navigation and star identification. Doing acrobatics out over the Gulf of Mexico, acclimating himself to flight stress. Practice in formation flying. Spending huge amounts of time in the simulators. Learning procedures and identifying the purposes of a plethora of switches. Talking with the software. Playing with the flight controls, hydraulic systems, and electrical systems. Practicing for payload handling in the Remote Manipulator System.[19]

Public appearances, talking to young people across the land about what the business of astronauting meant to him. Dressed in the astronaut's blue flight suit, the American flag emblazoned on his left shoulder, he told students at Dudley High School in Greensboro, North Carolina, that the shuttle "is going to make available some of the means of life in the future. In solar energy, in satellite communications. It's going to change our whole way of looking at the universe."

And he remembered his amazement and his fellow students' awe before the television at North Carolina A&T State University as they watched Neil Armstrong make his historic moon walk. He shared with them his wonder at the sophisticated technology that made it possible to accomplish such a feat, and described the special significance the event had for him. It was then, he told the students, that "he began to envision himself in a similar role as a space pioneer." The lunar expedition "revealed to him a universe that was his to explore."[20]

The weeks and months sped by as Ron McNair's foray into space drew closer.

While Ron McNair and the next *Challenger* crew prepared for their upcoming flight, the era of space science came of age with the launching of *Columbia* with the European-built *Spacelab I* on 28 November 1983. The six-man crew on mission STS-9 was the largest ever, with John W. Young serving as commander, Brewster H. Shaw as pilot, Robert Parker and Owen Garriott as mission specialists, and going along as payload specialists, Byron K. Lichtenberg and Ulf Merbold (the first non-American to fly in an American spacecraft). They conducted scientific laboratory experiments in the cylindrical spacelab situated inside the payload bay, covering areas of astronomy and solar physics, space plasma physics, atmospheric physics, as well as earth observations, life sciences, and materials sciences on a 24-hour basis, split into two operating shifts. Although relatively successful, the mission was plagued by mechanical problems, glitches in the materials-processing furnaces, and the metric camera for earth photography. The crew exhibited resourcefulness in making repairs, allowing for continuation of scheduled experiments during the first half of the mission. Things went better on the second half of the flight and the mission was extended one day. However, on landing day, *Columbia* lost a computer during the retro burn and within minutes, a second failed. NASA delayed the landing so experts could analyze the problem. After seven hours, *Columbia* finally landed. During the approach, a fire broke out at the root of the shuttle's tail section and *Columbia* was taken off line for what was to be two years of extensive modification and modernization.[21]

*   *   *

When 1984 arrived, McNair was tapped to be the second African American to participate in a space mission.

Not long before the announcement was made, Mae C. Jemison, M.D., an aspiring black astronaut mission specialist, stopped by the Houston Space Center and talked with McNair about the space program prior to submitting her application to NASA. Dr. Jemison said that during the hour they spent talking,

> I was extremely impressed with Ron. I was very much looking forward, if I was accepted into the program, to working with him because he had a lot of strength and character, and lots of different skills, from everything I could gather. He was extremely confident.[22]

Scheduled as the first all-military mission by NASA, mission STS-10 had been canceled because of problems with the upper stages of the military satellite that was to be launched. After being canceled a second time, it was rescheduled and called STS-11 or Mission 41B. The latter designation reflected a new numbering system signifying the fiscal year and the launch center.

Vance D. Brand would be mission commander and Robert L. Gibson was scheduled as pilot. Ron McNair, Bruce McCandless II, and Robert L. Stewart were the assigned mission specialists for the flight.

They would launch two communications satellites and practice for an upcoming attempt at capturing and repairing the *Solar Max* satellite, which had been in orbit since 1980. They would test rendezvous procedures, using a balloon launched from the cargo bay as their target. Two of the astronauts on board would attempt the first free flights by man in space, becoming human satellites as they tested procedures for capturing the *Solar Max*. They would be propelled by jet-powered backpacks called Manned Maneuvering Units (MMU), that had twenty-four jets fueled by cold gas. Bruce McCandless would go first, perhaps as far as three football fields away. Robert Stewart would go next, testing the Remote Manipulator System designed to hold an astronaut stable in space while he worked on orbiting hardware. Finally, they would again try to land the orbiter at the Kennedy Space Center, the mission's point of origin.[23]

Down in Lake City, South Carolina, Ron McNair's mother, grandmother, and other relatives were excited, but not afraid for him. "I'm not worried about my son's safety," his mother said, "because it's been done successfully so many times before." Ron wouldn't be overwhelmed by the experience, she added, observing that, "Nothing's a big deal to him."

In Atlanta, brother Carl said he thought Ron was like a kind of Johnny-come-lately Mr. Spock, the *Star Trek* officer with the pointy ears. According to Carl:

> Ron often feels more than he shows. Like Spock, he'll be going along and there's no emotion, except once in awhile he'll show a hint of it on his face, and then it's gone. When I ask him if he's excited, he'll sit there very quietly for a while, and then he always says the same thing: "This is very serious work! I can't afford to get excited."[24]

But despite his calm exterior, Ron's pulse was racing. He sought out the astronauts who'd been on the *Spacelab* mission for a record eighty-four days.

"What did you do all those days up there for a pastime?" he asked.

"Look out the window," they replied, "just look out the window!"

"Okay!" Ron rejoiced, "I can dig that!"[25]

Ron McNair was going to do more, though. He'd already decided to take along his beloved saxophone and play it as he circled the earth.

At 2:00 A.M. on 1 February 1984, the countdown for the fourth *Challenger* mission began. It would continue for forty-three hours.

RON McNAIR AND THE HUMAN SATELLITES

Truly there is no more beautiful sight than to see the earth from
space beyond. This planet is an exquisite oasis. Warmth
emanates from the earth when you look at her from space. . . .
My wish is that we would allow this planet to be the beautiful
oasis that she is, and allow ourselves to live more in the peace
that she generates.
—Ronald E. McNair, after his first spaceflight

Flying in the swift, sleek, Northrup T-38 jet trainers had been fun for Ron McNair. He loved tunneling through the air at Mach 1.3 or faster; being able to leave the Kennedy Space Center in the afternoon and put his feet under the table in Houston in time for dinner; roving the skies above the United States to attend flight tests of new space equipment or to sit through a contractor's meeting someplace he'd never visited before. But this was different. He was about to go out into the heavens, to orbit the blue and green, cloud-speckled earth every ninety minutes.

On this mission, McNair would be responsible for some seventeen experiments, including operation of a unique Arriflex motion picture camera with a special lens that could encompass half the globe, producing an image that could be projected on planetarium domes.[26] He had come prepared for the role, with a movie director's clapper, a beret, the ever-present dark glasses, and a name tag announcing the presence of one "Cecil B. McNair." Already tucked away aboard the space vehicle was his soprano saxophone.

On the launchpad, lights painted the orbiter stark white against the garishly yellow external tank in the predawn of 3 February 1984. Inside the ready area, astronauts Brand, Gibson, McCandless, McNair, and Stewart finished their preflight breakfast, clad in light gray T-shirts sporting the Mission 41B insignia across the front: ovals within a larger oval, centered on the word *Challenger* and an illustration of the orbiter. Inside one oval is an illustration of a payload-assisted satellite being deployed. In the other, that of an astronaut making the first nontethered extravehicular flight in space. Eleven stars grace the dark blue of outer space, six in one oval, five in the other—all of it set against the orb of the earth below. It was to be the first flight for all of the crew members except Mission Commander Brand, who was about to embark on his third spaceflight. The pilot, Robert L. Gibson, was preparing the way for his wife, scheduled to fly later in the year.

A security specialist gave them the high sign, leading them out to board a converted motor home for the ride to the launchpad. An early morning patter of applause greeted them. In the white room, near the top of the mammoth gantry, they geared up, tugging on black or white skull caps before adjusting their helmets over them. As dawn broke, a slight fog played footsie with the orbiter, which sat proudly on Launchpad 39-A. Reporters and photographers glanced up from their vantage points across the still sloughs. As an occasional bird flitted by, its movement was reflected in the flat, liquid mirror of the water.[27]

Then the astronauts strapped in and began monitoring switches and computer screens. Waiting. Listening. The two-second-to-countdown window approached. At T-minus-two minutes and twenty seconds, fuel-cell ground supplies were terminated. The orbiter switched to internal power and onboard reactants. The feeding cap was removed and swung out of the way. At two minutes to launch, hydrogen replenishment was terminated. With one minute to go, the sound suppression and hydrogen burn systems were armed. At fifty seconds, flight instrumentation counters shifted to record mode. Thirty-eight seconds from launch, the automatic sequence started. At twenty-three seconds, the orbiter's onboard computers took control of the countdown.

"We have a go for main engine start! Six—five—we *have* main engine start!" Orange fire sprang from the main engines with a gargantuan roar. Smoke swirled. "Three—two—one—zero! We have solid-rocket booster and liftoff!" The orbiter's dull shine seemed alive as it moved off the launchpad, leaping upward on a solid finger of fire. "We have liftoff," the mantra-like voice from Shuttle Launch Control exulted. "The shuttle has cleared the tower!"[28]

Mission Control in Houston took over, verifying the mandatory roll maneuver that placed the orbiter in a position so the astronauts could see the ground during liftoff, in case of an emergency. Inside the shuttle, McNair was experiencing the same smooth elevator ride Guy Bluford remembered. First, there was the thrust, which became more and more powerful, until they knew they were well on their way into space. On the ground, the sound of it numbed the senses as the orbiter rode the smoking firetrail, looking like the tip of a flaming arrow pushed along by a shaft of smoke. The sound crackled like a monstrous popcorn popper. The crackling sound almost overwhelms, then slowly begins to subside, leaving the flaring cloud of smoke behind. One minute and twenty-three seconds after launch, the shuttle was traveling 2,300 feet per second and was nine miles down range. Two minutes and thirty-two seconds after launch, it was traveling at 4,700 feet per second and was forty-eight miles down range. The solid-rocket boosters jettisoned, to be followed later by the external tank, which descended into the Indian Ocean. After two orbital maneuvering burns, *Challenger* settled into its first orbit.[29]

McNair and the crew prepared to accomplish their mission objectives. Beneath them, the earth looked like a huge, blue, white, and brown semicircle, its cloud cover scattered in helter-skelter abandon.

Safely in orbit, the 41B crew performed standard checkouts of the payload and orbiter systems, then opened the payload bay doors. Radiators adjusted temperatures against the ever-changing cycle of day and night orbits of the earth.[30] Seven hours into orbit, Ron McNair began the routines necessary to launch the Western Union communications satellite *Westar VI*, with its payload-assist, solid-stage rocket designed to boost it another 22,300 miles up, where it would lodge in a geostationary orbit. When the sun shields over the satellite opened, the rotational sequence for deployment began. Restraints were removed. The satellite began spinning. As McNair and the crew watched, television cameras recorded the spinup. *Westar VI* glinted in the sunlight as McNair gave the final, electronic command. The satellite popped up, and up, spinning free of the orbiter. McNair and the crew watched it spin away. He'd made the deployment precisely on schedule.

"Tell those *Westar* folks they really have a pretty bird!" someone in the orbiter shouted.

McNair then busied himself with the Arriflex, filming Robert Stewart as he indulged in a bit of fitness exercise: jogging on the onboard treadmill. Ron was in his element. Up came the shot-sequencing clapper. Very professional in his approach to movie-making, the crew delighted in calling him by the nickname they'd conferred. "Cecil B. McNair" was on the job again! Capable of extreme wide-angle shots, the Arriflex had to be pointed away from Stewart in order to include him in the filmatic sequence.

At zero gravity, the crewmen seemed to drift through their chores. Things floated, tumbled, and slowly turned. A camera needed by Robert Stewart sidled serenely into his hands. Coming into daylight the next morning, the crew concentrated on filming the earth. The coastline of Baja California lay below. Over the United States, in the blue spaces between billowy, broken cloud cover, airliner contrails scrawled white signatures through the earth's atmosphere, disappearing into the clouds and then coming out again.[31]

The idea of earth's being an oasis hit Ron McNair as he savored its enormity and awesome magnificence. As he filmed, looking out the orbiter's windows, he thought about how warm the earth looked, how exquisite. It looked, he thought, like a fantastic world God had placed in the hands of mankind. It was man's responsibility "to allow earth to be the beautiful oasis that she is." More important, perhaps remembering the hatred and prejudice existing in the world in which he had grown up, McNair expressed a wish that earth's residents could "allow themselves to live more in the peace she generates."

The *Westar VI* satellite's failure to achieve orbit ended the idyll. Radar tracked it as the device trailed the orbiter in a strange orbit, 690 by 173 miles, well outside the higher orbit needed to make it effective. The satellite's payload-assist engine had fizzled when an exhaust nozzle burned through. Concern was immediate, for still in the payload bay resided the Indonesian satellite *Palapa B-2,* scheduled for deployment that same day. It was equipped with the same payload-assist engine.

As they waited for a decision on the deployment of the Indonesian satellite, the crew conducted other experiments. One involved launching a target for rendezvous experiments. A metallic balloon, ejected from a canister in the payload bay, was expected to inflate to a diameter of six feet. Instead, it too fizzled.

"It looks," Mission Commander Brand reported to Houston, "like the balloon blew up!" Success was achieved, however, by tracking the balloon's remains with radar for two or three hours, then verifying the accuracy of the tracking instruments.

At the beginning of the fourth day, Ron McNair was again on center stage. Indonesian authorities had decided to move ahead with the deployment of the *Palapa B-2* satellite. The *Westar* failure, they thought, was an unusual event. The payload-assisted module used for that deployment had been employed successfully eighteen times before. McNair again activated the satellite spin motor sequence and *Palapa* inched upward out of the payload bay, into the sunlight and away from *Challenger.* Watching intently, the crew could see the solid-fuel rocket booster fire. But it also fizzled, stranding *Palapa B-2* in a too-low, ineffective orbit.

On the fifth day out, McCandless and Stewart prepared to become human satellites. Prebreathing for an extended period through launch and entry helmets before putting on the meshed, one-piece spandex Liquid Cooling and Ventilation Garments, they cleared their bodies of nitrogen in order to prevent getting the "bends" while breathing pure oxygen in space.[32]

After suiting up, they entered the airlock. Next, McCandless donned the MMUs, which he had helped design, and readied himself for the first untethered foray from the orbiter.[33]

McCandless exited the payload bay airlock hatch first, floating free inside the bay. He gyrated, testing the controls, as the continent of Africa slid by below.

"How does it feel?" a voice sputtered on the intercom.

"That may have been a small step for Neil," McCandless replied, referring to Neil Armstrong's first words on the moon, "but it's a heckuva big leap for me!"

Gingerly backing out of the payload bay, he jetted out 150 feet away from *Challenger,* always keeping the orbiter in view. Then, his confidence building, he flew three hundred feet into cold space, looking like a small, man-shaped satellite in orbit above the spinning earth, tiny running lights flashing on the top and bottom of the backpack.

Back in the payload bay, Stewart set up and tested the Manipulator Foot Restraint (MFR), a little platform and tool carrier that attached to the end of the shuttle's robot arm, operated by Ron McNair. It thus became a kind of "cherry picker," which could transport an astronaut to a work site, holding him steady by his feet.

McCandless jetted back to the shuttle and gave the MMU to Stewart. "Enjoy it, have a ball!" he shouted.

McNair, Brand, and Gibson watched in utter fascination from inside the spacecraft as Stewart soared alone in the vast caverns of space 305 feet from the orbiter.[34]

The intercom crackled.

"Gentlemen, the president of the United States is on the line!"

"Commander Brand," Ronald Reagan began, "I'd like to say good morning to you and your crew! I'm talking to you from California. I don't know exactly where you are—I know you're up there someplace. You're all doing a fine job on this historic mission! I'd like to say hello to Bruce McCandless and Bob Stewart for giving us this historic footage of a walk in space. What's it like out there—maneuvering freely in space?"

"Well," McCandless replied, "we've had a great deal of training, sir, so it feels quite comfortable. The view is simply spectacular and panoramic!" McCandless said enthusiastically as the earth spun by. "We'll be preparing the way for many important operations on the coming space station, sir!"

The president congratulated them on a job well done, showing America's "commercial foreign space partners" that the mission could be accomplished.

"What do you and Hoot Gibson and Ron McNair do while Bruce and Bob are walking outside?" the president asked Brand.

"Well, we're pretty busy in here just keeping track of 'em!" Brand answered. "They have a lot of tests to go through—and the backpack is something that's rather futuristic. We're just monitoring them to make sure they do fine!"

"That's good," replied President Reagan. "How are the experiments on board the shuttle working out? I understand that you have one dealing with arthritis and other experiments on board that have to do with various types of materials processing."

"Well, Mister President," said Ron McNair, "the experiments are working out very well. We're very pleased with the results we're getting. We look forward to getting back on the ground to analyze and review them."

"Well, let me congratulate all of you. You're doing a fine job. Have a safe journey home and God bless all of you!"

"We really appreciate it!"

"All right! Good-bye!"[35]

Before the space walk was over, McCandless and Stewart tested a docking mechanism to be used in the upcoming repair of the *Solar Max* satellite, and docked with a practice target in the payload bay.

Then the crew rested for a day. This may have been the time that Ronald McNair broke out his saxophone, producing memories of his times in Jerry Mack's Bar and Restaurant, his uncle's place in Connecticut. He just let go, reared back, floating there in the glory of zero-G, whomping out a little jazz. A little "What the World Needs Now Is Love, Sweet Love," while the crew smiled in appreciation.

"Yes," remembered Charles Bolden, another African-American astronaut then in training, "although all the filmed records of his playing were inadvertently taped over in a rush to record another project, he did play several songs during that mission!"[36]

One photograph of the historic moment did survive. Ronald McNair, laid back in zero gravity comfort, his head resting on a white canvas bag jammed against a bulkhead, the collar of his dark blue shirt up, the fabric of his trousers attempting to flail, cheeks puffed out, fingers flying over the saxophone keys—the first man to play a saxophone in space!

On 9 February, McCandless and Stewart took another spacewalk, ostensibly a dress rehearsal for the coming repair of *Solar Max*. With McNair operating the robot arm, they were unable to complete the process, since, no matter how hard he tried, the robot arm's "wrist" refused to work. Instead, they practiced docking procedures and flew the MMU through various maneuvers, testing its ability to hold attitude and make small adjustments.

After another day of rest it was time to come home. Equipment was stowed and the payload doors closed. Preparations complete, the crew members strapped into their seats. At about sixty minutes from touchdown, weather at the Cape was clear, visibility thirty miles.

"Thank you for getting us that kind of weather," joked Brand.[37]

They turned the orbiter around against the direction of flight. The Orbital Maneuvering System engines fired, slowing down *Challenger*, which perceptibly dropped and turned nose-first again. Belly up, the orbiter slammed into the upper atmosphere at over sixteen thousand miles per hour. Deeper into the atmosphere it plunged as ionized gas surrounded it. The heat temporarily blocked all communications as the orbiter passed through the fifty-mile-high mark, still over three thousand miles from touchdown.

Challenger next executed a series of banked turns that helped slow the orbiter and permitted lining up with the runway. Streaking across the United States, the shuttle swept out over the Atlantic and circled in, its speed brakes deploying, delivering a double sonic boom as it slowed even more. Chase planes charged in behind the orbiter. Its landing gear is gravity-lowered, assisted by springs and hydraulic power. *Challenger* finally settled onto the three-mile-long runway amidst the swamps of the Kennedy Space Center as the chase planes pulled away, stopping, they say, "just a half-inch from the center line."[38]

Forty minutes after landing, the crew left *Challenger* to the close-out units, and NASA officials rolled out a red carpet in honor of the first shuttle landing at the Kennedy Space Center. "We are happy you brought it back where it belongs!" said the KSC director, Richard G. Smith.[39]

At the official greeting for the returned astronauts, McNair said

This is just one more step in the evaluation of our overall capa-
bility as a space transportation system, and there's a lot of growth
left. So we'll be seeing more and more as time goes on. Again,
we had a great time on 41B! I wish words existed to describe it.
If not, I think I'll make up some![40]

He and the rest of the *Challenger* crew had orbited the earth 127
times, traveled 2.87 million miles while orbiting 165 miles above the
planet—and it was all in a day's work to them.[41]

As usual, both before and after a flight, McNair called his family.
His mother in Lake City. His brothers in Atlanta. Return to his wife,
Cheryl, must have been particularly sweet, for in the coming July, their
daughter, Joy Cheray, would be born. The time was fast approaching
when they must choose a place to settle and raise their children.[42] They
talked about that.

But Ron McNair was at last a full-fledged astronaut. After all the
training and preparation, he had finally done it. He'd gone out there
and performed his duties; looked out the spacecraft's windows at a
magnificent earth; played his saxophone in space. Suddenly, he was in
great demand on the public-speaking circuit.

He went back to MIT to meet with high school students from Boston and Cambridge. He visited with old friends and studied with them.
But perhaps his greatest joy was realized as he shared his experiences
in space with the children, many of whom were black. He saw great
hope and opportunity for his race in them.

If Professor Tom Sandin, McNair's old A&T advisor, was impressed
by him before, he must have been doubly so as he watched McNair
become a consummate public speaker. Before McNair became an
astronaut, Sandin had catalogued him as "an average speaker; an ordinary student, but good." But then Sandin saw an accomplished platform
speaker, one capable of dashing off anecdotes that fit, and speaking
"in a polished manner!"[43]

Sandin recalled McNair's appearance before the Massachusetts
legislature. He'd met the governor, then spoken during a break in
legislative proceedings. "People were talking on the floor," Sandin recalled.

"Nobody paid attention. It was just a political thing." But Ron McNair spoke despite the lawmakers' inattention and, within minutes, the random conversation stopped. "You could have heard a pin drop!" chortled Sandin. The legislators sat riveted as Ron made an "eloquent plea for education." Laughter roared and applause dashed along the chamber as he made one of many points: "Monkeys and elephants will work all day for peanuts and look forward to tomorrow. Teachers, however, do not think much of the idea!"

Black minds and great talents, as well as hands able to control a spacecraft, reside in the inner cities, McNair told them. And they can do it with the "same dexterity with which they control a basketball!" That talent was not to be wasted. Good teachers should be maintained in American schools or quality of instruction would diminish, "education will suffer and our dreams will vanish," he cautioned.

The legislators rose as one, applauding and cheering in a standing ovation. McNair stepped back alongside his wife and mother, whose faces were full of pride.[44]

"When he was chosen, he was ready," Sandin reflected. That was the real essence of Ron McNair: "Definition of goal, determination of the path to reach that goal, and persistence until he reached it!"[45]

They renamed the main street in Lake City in McNair's honor. The South Carolina legislature bestowed its highest honor on him: The Order of the Palmetto. They gave him the key to the city in Greensboro, North Carolina.[46]

Ron McNair had seen God's handiwork from a vantage point few mortals have enjoyed—outer space. And he returned in quiet meditation to Cambridge, Massachusetts, to worship in the church in which he and Cheryl had been married so long ago. There would be more spaceflights, and Ronald Erwin McNair was ready for them.

During one of his visits to Lake City, his grandmother discovered just how ready he was.

"Ron," she said, "you talk about a lot of things. But what about God? What about the Lord in all of this?"

If she thought she'd tripped him up with that statement, she was wrong.

"I would not have entered the space shuttle," came the quietly solemn reply, "if I felt that God was not there with me!"[47]

CHAPTER 5

THE LAST
OF THE FIRST

Col. Frederick D. Gregory

Maybe some people would call Fred Gregory lucky. If you could call being assigned to Vietnam in 1966 "lucky." He flew the small H-43F helicopter; its primary missions were search and rescue, and fire suppression. But when the fight is furious, missions change in combat zones. More helicopters were needed. New ones were still in the re-supply pipeline. Until they arrived in sufficient numbers, Fred Gregory and his crew became an alternate resource. A supernumerary. A searcher for and rescuer of not just downed pilots, but also of American infantrymen mauled by the NVA and Viet Cong. That kind of mission upgrade made for increased adrenaline flow and required accomplished piloting skills.[1]

So, being a good helicopter pilot was a given. It had to do with longevity. Slipping up and down the green hillsides, flying a straight line—the way a sentinel moves—across the face of a mountain; minimizing chances of becoming a target. Controlling the fear, always on mental tiptoes. Ever mindful of the chilling "*tick, tick*" sound bullets fired from the ground made as they punched through a helicopter's metal skin. There were the war stories about flying helicopters in a combat zone. Fred and his crew, his copilot and two "PJs" (pararescue specialists), knew them all. They knew that most helicopter crewmen went home in a box or were wounded. They and other helicopter people considered themselves lucky to complete a normal tour of duty. They had heard the horrific recountings of how helicopter windshields suddenly turned red with the sucked-up blood of a crew member wounded by savage ground fire.[2] Each found solace in the fact that these unhappy warriors were mostly "search and destroy guys," not search and rescue folks like them. But these things were always on their minds. That's probably why Fred, when remembering those days, felt it necessary to say, "I never felt in danger of my life. We would go out and we would always have a high bird and other aircraft suppressing enemy fire."[3]

That's the kind of day it was when they got the call to pick up a marine fire team. They flew out over a jungle where parakeets, parrots, wild boar, and red deer watched curiously through green undergrowth as they pulsated by. Along the way, they might have seen army combat helicopters still burning on the edges of the battle zone. Circling to avoid the mayhem, they watched as artillery rounds walked across the jungle floor. When they reached the fire team's grid coordinates, Fred found he needed all his piloting skills to pick them up. He rested one wheel of the helicopter on a cliff and the other hung over the side, hovering interminably, holding the collective lever to counteract gravity.

A fairly small helicopter, the H-43F could comfortably accommodate only five or six additional people in its boxlike cargo bay. The marine fire team clambered aboard with full field packs; there were seven, now eight of them! Finding no room inside for their equipment, marines hung from an outside hoist. Fred worried that he was fast coming up on gross weight limits. The clambering stopped. The fire team was aboard.

"You looked back," Fred marveled, "and it was like a mass of men back there!" The excess weight was still a problem.

But he had done it. He'd held that helicopter reasonably still while more people than his little ship was ever designed to hold came aboard; constantly changing that center of gravity, while he hung the whole thing over the edge of a cliff. Kicking the bird around, he made for Da Nang.

The fun began as he set the bird down in front of a MASH unit. As the first marine rolled out of the little H-43F, a bemused medical corpsman watched. The corpsman thought it was the damnedest thing he'd ever seen. Disappearing momentarily, he returned in a flash, a buddy in tow, both come to see this newly arrived menagerie. Still more marines rolled out as additional corpsmen ambled out to see the show. The medics were doubled over in hysterical laughter.

"It was like one of those clown things in the movies," Fred recalled. Belly laugh time in Vietnam.

Not all of his missions were as light-hearted. Some were damned dangerous—and a hell of a lot tougher. The next day or so proved the point.

An O-1 observation plane crashed into a hill. The pilot died, but his guy-in-back survived. Fred kicked the H-43F into a hard turn and settled into a slow hover over the spot where the lone survivor stood, staring up through the foliage. There was no high bird that day. They were down there by themselves. A-1 SPADs were flying suppression missions. Firefights proliferated. Mortars crumped and AK-47s burped. Rockets flared and napalm scorched the earth.

The PJs released the jungle penetrator. Attached to the helicopter by a cable, it was designed so the person on the ground could climb on and be hoisted aboard. The compact penetrator plunged easily through the dense foliage. Following the instructions printed on it, a person could quickly adjust it. Problem was, the survivor was a "foreign guy who couldn't read English," and therefore, didn't understand how to work with the penetrator. The sounds of exploding ordnance grew louder. The guy on the ground tried to hold on to the cable and be pulled up. That didn't work. The firefights grew more raucous.

A PJ leaned far out of the helicopter, yelling and signing to the man, trying to get him to open the penetrator so he could sit on it. Baleful, uncomprehending stares were the only response.

The copilot yelled to the PJ, "Pull that penetrator up! We'll get *you* on it, lower *you* down and *you* help that asshole onto the cotton-picking thing!"

The whole scenario began to get to Fred. The firefights. The SPADs doing their suppression thing. Napalm roiling.

Fred recalled, "I was just sitting there. We're hovering at perhaps fifteen or twenty feet above the ground, and there was all kinds of activity going on. And I looked down at my legs and my legs were absolutely shaking; my legs were scared to death! And I reached over and hit my copilot and pointed to my legs and they were just shaking; there was nothing I could do about it!"

Later, they laughed about it. But they hauled the guy out and saved his life. The stress of it was there. Fred felt it, but what he remembered most was saving that man's life. It gave him a kind of satisfaction. "I couldn't worry," he later ruminated, "about the possibility of getting hurt!"[4]

What had happened to Fred was nothing to be ashamed about. It came with being a combat helicopter pilot. Every day. Up from Da Nang. Sitting on the northern tiers of South Vietnam. Dashing off to the rescue up around the DMZ; going into "burning fields to rescue guys in crashed helicopters." And he did it *more than five hundred* times, sometimes over the Gulf of Tonkin, at night, or in horrible weather.

Some say the luck of the draw weighs heavily in combat when it comes to ultimate survival. So do common sense, adequate preparation, a sense of humor, and good training. In the midst of carnage, a touch of the "milk of human kindness" doesn't hurt, either. Fred Gregory possessed all of the above, and the latter in particular. When his Vietnam tour was over, he reflected with great satisfaction on how "he'd helped save twenty-eight or twenty-nine lives over there!" And though he wasn't very high ranking (a first lieutenant), Fred knew the value of the men who flew with him, and that without them, the outcome of the deadly games they were tasked to play may have been quite different. Lots of people mouth the sentiments, but Fred truly believed that:

All the guys that I worked with, the crews that I worked with were just superb. . . . It was just such a pleasure working with those PJs. I thought they were probably some of the smartest guys in the air force![5]

Frederick Drew Gregory was born 7 January 1941 in Washington, D.C., the only child of Francis Anderson Gregory and Nora D. Gregory. As with most of the country, the nation's capital was stretched and torn by racism, prejudice, and segregation. The Gregorys lived in an integrated neighborhood. Two houses mattered in the area. The Gregorys', and the one belonging to Dr. and Mrs. Rivers, both professors at Howard University. Surrounded by a white community, the friends Fred made as he grew up were mostly Caucasian. School was the exception. There they separated. The white kids went to their school three blocks away, whereas Fred went to school across town near Howard University.[6]

He found himself a member of a family immersed in education. Its lineage could be traced back into northern Virginia and, on his father's side, to Madagascar several generations before. Nourished and raised by his mother and father, Fred was buoyed by a plethora of cousins. Both parents were secondary school teachers, and Fred's father ultimately became a public school administrator, eventually serving as assistant superintendent of schools in the District of Columbia.

As educators, his parents were highly regarded in the black community. Teaching, after all, was one of the few professional avenues available to blacks in those days. It was one of the few "traditional occupations" to which African Americans could aspire. Although revered, many blacks like the Gregorys felt personally unfulfilled. They knew that, were it not for the color of their skin, they could probably have soared to the top in their chosen professions. Fred's father, for example, was an electrical engineer, with a degree from prestigious MIT. His parents, and others like them, were caught in a great obfuscation created by the American mainstream, denying them access to progress.

Because their chances, despite all their education, were so limited, they were drawn to and became teachers in the black schools. As far as their students were concerned, they offered them a challenge that led to excellence of performance, and in this there was "no compromise." In the Gregorys' view, students were there to learn. To them, education included not only academics, but all those "other cultural activities which allowed students to experience all of what life was about."

As the decade of the eighties swept by, Fred Gregory still remembered his sixth-grade teacher, Mrs. Smith, who taught him and his classmates "that they, as a people, were at least equal to anyone else in the world." His fifth-grade teacher, Mrs. Chew; Mrs. Graves, his fourth-grade teacher; and his third-grade teacher, Mrs. Henderson, had all stressed excellence.

The message came through clearly, Gregory remembered in 1991. "It was one of those things that said: 'This is a separate school system, but this school system is at least as good, and we expect you to be at least as good.'"

Enrollment in college was the next step. Period. Being the best that one could be seemed to be the motivation in Fred Gregory's young world at school, in the home, and in the community.

Early in his life, church also figured prominently. Fred's paternal grandfather was minister of the People's Congregational Church. The Drews, his mother's family, had worshiped for years at the 19th Street Baptist Church.

At home, the rhetoric smacked of unstinting support. "We will prepare you to do whatever you like to do and will support your doing it," was a constant refrain. It was important, his parents said, that he realize "there are no barriers and obstacles to you." The name of the game was to "demonstrate that you can do exactly what anybody else can do—or better. Then you will be selected!" The object of the game was to "aim for a particular profession," and that choice was to be his alone. For example, Fred's father was an electrical engineer, but Fred felt no particular pressure to follow in his father's footsteps. His charge was to "learn all you can about everything—we support you!"

Not only did his parents support him, they protected him from the pressures of segregation by creating an environment in both the home and with other parents in the community that ensured that protection.

"Colored and white" signs were in evidence, but so all-encompassing were the protective cloaks thrown about Fred that they remained on the periphery of his life, like the flight of a gnat across a great room. He knew they were there, but parental intervention minimized the threat. On family trips by automobile from Washington to visit friends in the South, his parents would "drive straight through without stopping so we weren't exposed to the prejudices of the South."

By 1953, he found himself a member of a segregated Boy Scout troop. Gregory recalled that although the Scouts were integrated very early on at major events, his own troop in Washington remained segregated. But, when they were sent to the big Boy Scout Jamboree, "when they gathered the kids together, and we went out there, it was integrated!"

Scouting was part of his life from Cubs on up. But his earliest Scouting experiences were in segregated packs and troops. Again, his parents and other parents in the community stepped in to protect their offspring.

Fred's father and many of his father's friends recognized that although the black kids had a Boy Scout troop, they had no Boy Scout camp. Pooling their resources, they acquired land along Chesapeake Bay and built their sons a camp. They also organized clubs in which all of the kids could get together and meet each other, Fred said.

As laudable as the efforts of their parents were in protecting Fred and his friends from the barbs of segregation and racism, there was an entire world out there for them to explore. It was a grand enigma. After all, they felt "comfortable around white people," for they were their neighbors and playmates. Some could be counted as friends with something of a "discernible difference," residing partially in the fact that they didn't and couldn't go to school together. Instead, Fred went to school across town with his black friends. Added to these were his "social friends, his church friends, and his Boy Scout friends," none of whom were white.

For the most part, Fred's role models were decidedly black and in great supply throughout his young life. All he had to do was look around. His parents were successful educators. His grandfather was a successful minister, and his mother's brother, Charles Richard Drew, was a famous surgeon and pioneer in the production and preservation of blood plasma. His efforts saved the lives of many soldiers during World War II.

In 1941, the ugly arm of racism inserted itself. The government directed that the Red Cross *must* keep non-Caucasian blood separate. Although Dr. Drew and other scientists affirmed that the chemical differences in human blood depended only on blood type and not on race, the directive stood. Drew resigned his position as assistant director of blood procurement for the armed forces and devoted himself to research, surgery, and teaching.[7]

Thus did young Fred Gregory see a member of his family strike back at prejudice and segregation in the best way he could, while still maintaining its protective equilibrium.

Her name was Barbara Archer. Slightly "oriental" in appearance, she came, according to Fred Gregory, "from a community of people who look just like that. There's a pocket of them down in North Carolina." She was lovely enough to catch Fred's eye and mentally hogtie him when she was but a tender thirteen, and he at the ripe old age of fourteen.

They met at a party at his cousin's house. Barbara really steamed and curried him out to dry, it seems, for he called his cousin aside to tell her about his intentions as far as this Barbara Archer was concerned.

"I'm going to marry her," he said.

Apparently, Fred was able to keep his hormones in check for a couple of years at least; they didn't go on their first date until she was fifteen. They dated steadily during the last half of his high school years, and it soon became evident that the vision Fred had shared with his cousin was not simply idle conversation.

The relatively neat world in which black parents protected their offspring was turned upside down in the name of progress when, on 17 May 1954, the Supreme Court unanimously held that racial segregation in public schools was unconstitutional. Fred was in the eighth grade when District of Columbia schools began to integrate. He was transferred to Sousa High in his senior year, and would no longer go crosstown to old Bannecker and Mott, the schools he'd attended with his black friends. He would go to school with the white kids, some of whom were his neighbors—the same kids with whom he'd played baseball and football on the playground, but who had gone their separate ways when the school bell rang. Other than the playground connection, there had been no social connection. Though many knew Fred, maybe even thought of him as a mellow guy, after the order to integrate, they made it pretty obvious they didn't want him or anybody like him in their school.

They made that perfectly clear on the first day of school in the fall of 1954. Dissension against integration grew to what seemed almost insane proportions. Banding together, the white students became zealots, opposing the integration order until almost the entire student body was boycotting the school.

That was Fred Gregory's baptism by fire on the racial front lines. Astounded, he was caught up in it as though by a whirlwind. If ever he had wondered what those white people he had grown up around and played ball with really thought about going to school with him, or their positions on race, he knew then.

Similar things were going on in the rest of the country. For example, the governor of Mississippi loudly announced, as had his neighbor, the governor of Louisiana, that he intended to "lean on his state's police power" in order to get around the Supreme Court's decision on school desegregation. "I am," he blustered, "going to see this thing through to make certain that Negroes never enter the white schools!" Later, the Mississippi legislature passed a constitutional amendment empowering the state to abolish public schools should "no other way be found to keep blacks segregated."[8] The Alabama legislature quickly followed suit. In Virginia, Governor Thomas B. Stanley declared, "I shall use every legal means at my command to preserve segregated schools!" Texas also argued in favor of "continuation of separate but equal schools." And in White Sulphur Springs, West Virginia, just west of the Alleghenies and a few hundred miles southwest of Fred Gregory and his boycotted school in Washington, D.C., authorities "ordered 25 Negroes out of the white high school after 300 students went out on strike," and some 600 townspeople threatened at a mass meeting to "drag the Negroes out bodily if the board won't give in!" The order was necessary, said the school board, "because of overcrowding."[9]

When he reported to the classroom designated as his homeroom, Fred was shocked to find he was the only student present. The remainder of his classmates were all outside participating in the boycott. Only the teacher was in the classroom. They exchanged looks. Neither spoke. Fred walked to the windows and saw them all, resplendent in the sunlight, chortling and buzzing; sitting defiantly on a nearby grassy hill. "I'll always remember that," Fred recalled in 1992.

It was as if the teacher had been struck dumb as far as Fred was concerned. She may have said a word or two or three; but to this day, he doesn't remember for sure if she said anything. That wasn't important. What held his attention was the mob of protesting students on the hill.

Fortunately, the unrest was short lived. There were few blacks at Sousa, certainly not enough to pose a threat to white students, and a quiet routine soon emerged.

So, Fred did well at Sousa. The next thing he knew, he was asked to be the "Captain of the Hall Patrol." There were "incidents," but he simply rolled with the punches. Although he felt that he was not "accepted socially," Fred said he enjoyed his stint at Sousa.

Throughout high school, Fred found himself drawn to things military. Partially because it was the thing to do ("boys were expected to be part of it"), he joined the junior ROTC program. And, because he lived relatively close to Andrews Air Force Base, Maryland, his interest in aircraft and flying was continuously stoked. He wanted, he recalled later, "to be part of it, to fly, to participate in the military in some way."[10]

During the midfifties, several things happened that made it seem possible to reach out and touch that dream. At Andrews, Fred had an opportunity to talk with a real, live member of the air force acrobatic flying team, the Thunderbirds.

"How can I get to fly jets like you do?" he asked the pilot.

"Well," said the flyer, "there's a school being built—the Air Force Academy, in Colorado Springs. Maybe you can get in."

Fred filed away the information for future reference, although he told his father about the new academy before doing so. Following family tradition, Fred enrolled at Amherst College after graduating from high school. His grandfather had graduated from the school in 1900. But Fred still yearned for the air force, something he discussed with his father from time to time.

After Fred matriculated at Amherst, his father, sensing his son's discontent, began making the rounds of black congressmen in Washington, seeking an appointment to the Air Force Academy for Fred. He struck paydirt with Harlem's Adam Clayton Powell.

Powell agreed to appoint Fred, adding, "But I already have one boy in the wings right now and his name's Chuck Bush." Fred would be his next appointee.

Although he'd never really thought about it, Fred had been close to black men who were deeply involved in the air force and in flying. Benjamin O. Davis, Jr., who later retired as a three-star general and commanded the country's first all-black fighter squadron in World War II, was a frequent visitor to his parents' home. In fact, Fred was literally surrounded by the Tuskegee Airmen Davis had commanded. They, too, were friends of the family. Young Fred was so involved in other areas of his life that he "never knew what they'd done—they were just there." He'd even flown and taxied in aircraft with them. The significance of their story continued to escape him.

The academy appointment became reality and, in a rush of excitement, Fred prepared to travel to Colorado to join the class of 1964. His enthusiasm was tempered by the realization that he was going to be "the only black in the class." This knowledge left him with a couple of choices: he could go out to Colorado and let the fact of his minority "aloneness" bother the hell out of him, or he could rely on his past positive contacts with whites, the fact that the military had integrated already, and that there had been three blacks in the class of 1963 (Roger Sims, Chuck Bush, and Ike Payne)—and *they* had made it! He therefore took the position that any problems posed by his solitary presence in the "larger body of seven hundred classmates would be seen as minuscule."

He admitted that "there were some social problems, but those didn't bother me." He stacked up well academically, militarily, and athletically, and maintained his cool when faced with racist attitudes. For example, the Air Officer Commanding told a racial joke in Fred's first squadron during a meeting. The tenor of the joke made Fred recoil inside, but he said nothing. About an hour later, the officer called Fred in and apologized for telling the joke, saying, "I didn't realize you were black [probably alluding to Fred's light complexion]. I am very, very sorry about that. I'll make sure nothing like that ever happens again." The Air Officer Commanding, Fred recalled, was from the South and, true to his word, nothing like that ever occurred again. "From that point on," Fred said with a chuckle, "we just became the Class of 1964!"

Barbara and Fred were married after he was graduated from the academy. On their way to their first air force assignment, they experienced their first incident of blatant racism, while driving from Ohio to San Antonio. No motel along the way would accept them as guests.

Fred had been so sheltered from racism by his parents, community, and, finally, the changed racial climate within the air force itself, that prejudice other blacks accepted as part of the status quo scared Fred so much that he called his father and asked for advice and help. Fred and Barbara were in Tennessee at the time, and the elder Gregory called friends there who secured the young couple lodging. After staying the night, the friends told them that Holiday Inn was the only motel chain that accommodated people of all races at the time. They stayed in Holiday Inns for ten years after that, "just because of the protection they afforded my wife and me!"

Gregory wanted to be a professor of military history at the Air Force Academy. Or perhaps an engineer. But marriage intervened. He chose helicopters because he knew the resulting assignments would probably please his bride. After earning his chopper wings, Gregory transitioned to fixed-wing aircraft. Then came Vietnam and more than five hundred combat rescue missions. After his return, he went to test pilot school and became an operational test pilot, flying both fighters and helicopters.

Things remained fairly steady until 1977, when Gregory became disenchanted with the test pilot game, thinking that "one night I'd wake up and say, 'Okay, that's it!' " That's when the NASA announcements about the selection of new astronauts hit the airwaves. "Well," Gregory said later, "I thought *that* would be a good idea!" Especially since NASA hadn't selected any astronauts since the midsixties. His decision to apply was almost a knee-jerk reaction. There was no long, drawn-out plan. It was, "Okay, I've done this, let's try something else!"

Gregory probably felt pretty smug about being a black in the military, a pilot considering the possibility of becoming an astronaut. It was at about that time he learned more about the accomplishments of the Tuskegee Airmen. As noted, he'd been rather blasé about them, even though he'd known some of them practically all his life. That changed when Gregory got a call "from a gentleman who said, 'There's an astronaut program I think you should apply for. The organization I represent is the Tuskegee Airmen.' " After that, Gregory slowly began to get the picture. Looking back on his awakening, he said, "I honestly thought that I was the *beginning* of this thing. I listened with great interest and I found out that I wasn't the beginning, I was the continuation!"

He had been the "first one" so often insofar as integration was concerned that it came as something of a shock to learn that blacks before him had been at the cutting edge of fields other than teaching, the law, medicine, and funeral direction.

Suddenly, applying for the astronaut program was something he had to do. Approaching the process in his usual thorough manner, he realized that since he had gone to the Navy Test Pilot School at Patuxent, Maryland, he was an unknown quantity in the air force test pilot community. Hedging his bets, he submitted two applications: one through official air force channels, another as a civilian. Fred was so set on becoming an astronaut that he was willing to resign should his civilian application be accepted.

According to Gregory, ex-astronaut John Young, then serving as chief of the Astronaut Office, called Lt. Gen. Tom Stafford to ask, "Who is this air force officer applying as a civilian?" The extra trouble seemed warranted to Gregory. "As I suspected," he theorized, "I was not selected through the air force, but my credentials were interesting enough as a civilian for consideration." But the air force claimed him anyway, so his resignation was not required.

Which is how Col. Fred Gregory wound up in Houston, along with Guy Bluford and Ron McNair, as America's first black astronauts.

At first, Gregory thought being an astronaut simply meant "flying in space." But like Bluford and McNair, he discovered that learning about spaceflight was what generated real excitement. "Working in areas that very few people know about." Handling information. Meeting people. Speaking on the road to youngsters across the nation.

Actual spaceflight promised to be anticlimactic, little more than a drill after the hours of study and overlearning, testing, special assignments, and survival training—not to mention the support he lent to other shuttle missions.

Anticlimax or not, Fred Gregory wanted his turn in space. He watched with approval as first Guy Bluford, then Ron McNair, rode the shuttle into the heavens. He cheered their achievements, knowing in his heart there were other "firsts" awaiting him.

TOWARD PINNACLES: FRED GREGORY AND FLIGHT 51B

The eighties promised excitement and a plethora of NASA shuttle flights. The period not only saw the successful launching and flying of the *Challenger* orbiter, but the introduction of the new *Discovery* and *Atlantis* orbiters. After Ron McNair's maiden flight, over a year would pass before another African American was assigned a mission. During that period, two missions utilizing *Challenger* were flown, while *Discovery* went into space four times. Thirty-five astronauts and mission specialists, five of whom were women, went into orbit.[11] Their accomplishments were notable. Repair of the *Solar Max* satellite. An increase in the number of satellites carried aloft on the same mission. Greater accuracy in the accomplishment of long-term weather prediction. The first space walk by an American woman, Kathy Sullivan, who demonstrated the ability to refuel satellites in space. Capturing and returning satellites to earth. Placing military payloads in orbit, including a signal intelligence spy satellite that monitored Soviet electronic messages from a 22,300-mile-high orbit above the Russian steppes.[12]

Yet, despite the promise of the eighties, women and minority men in the astronaut ranks were confronted by silent sentinels of prejudice and bigotry. Despite these pressures minorities and women scaled veritable pinnacles of achievement—and did it with considerable élan.

So prominent were the pinnacles on which African-American astronauts stood, their commitment to excellence was recognized when NASA scheduled four of them for shuttle missions in less than a year. Fred Gregory was slated to become the first African American to pilot a shuttle on 29 April 1985 aboard *Challenger*. Guy Bluford was tapped for his second trip into space on 30 October 1985, also aboard *Challenger*. Charles F. Bolden, Jr., was chosen to pilot *Columbia* into space on 12 January 1986. Finally, Ron McNair would again ride *Challenger* into the heavens on 28 January 1986.

In fact, with Bluford's scheduled flight in October, *Challenger* logged a record nine missions in just two years and seven months. Examinations of its landing images clearly showed the effects of constant use and weathering.[13]

It was in this orbiter that Fred Gregory prepared to fly as pilot with *Spacelab 3* aboard. *Challenger* had been grounded for six months for correction of hardware problems, inspection of tile-damaged areas on its fuselage, and resolution of confusion as to exactly what its payload should be. Thus, preparations for the flight of Mission 51B consumed much of 1984 and spilled over into the following year.[14]

While Gregory and his crew awaited the *Challenger* flight to which they were assigned, Ron McNair traveled up and down the eastern seaboard, speaking to and challenging youngsters everywhere he stopped. In February 1984 he was in Boston, speaking to MIT students and local high school students about "being a winner and hanging it over the edge."

At a reunion with friends in Boston during April 1984, McNair hauled out his saxophone and "wailed a smoking line of riffs in accompaniment to a taped recording of Grover Washington."

On 30 March 1984, his alma mater, North Carolina A&T State University, honored McNair at a "Welcome Home" celebration. John Forbis, mayor of Greensboro, awarded him the key to the city, after which McNair charmed the assembly with his newfound speaking abilities.[15]

Spacelab 3 was finally fitted into *Challenger's* payload bay on 27 March 1985. By 10 April, the solid-rocket boosters and external tank were mated. *Challenger* was rolled out to Launchpad 39-A five days later. Twenty-four hours before launch, the live payload was installed so the animals could get used to their new environment. On launch day, the crew sat down to breakfast, wearing gold and silver T-shirts, continuing the motifs of their *Spacelab 2* gold and silver team assignments. They were driven to the launchpad after obligatory waves to bystanders.

After they were strapped in, the countdown continued uninterrupted to T-minus-four minutes. A front-end processor in the launch-processing systems failed, causing a hold for over two hours.[16] Bob Overmyer, the marine colonel commanding the shuttle, and Gregory, the pilot, fidgeted as Don L. Lind, William Thornton, and Taylor G. Wang—the Gold Team—and Norman Thagard and Lodewijk van den Berg—the Silver Team—checked procedures and chatted. They were ready to go, to "burn paint," as the astronauts say, referring to the way heat from the launch sears new paint on the launch structure.[17]

Gregory, as well as others in the crew, was caught up in the emotion of the launch. He felt an anxiety devoid of fear, for fear itself had ostensibly been handled by NASA training, which instilled confidence in both the crew's ability and in the hardware they were about to ride into space.

Confidence abounded. There were many things to be done. Mental synapses were flashing. Possible risks were buried away—unreachable.

"I was so confident," Gregory said, "that when I got on board, and there were any breaks, I just shut my eyes and drifted off."

They had to "nudge" him to wake him up a bit. It was the constant practice. The repetitive training for emergency. He knew his job. Pilot. Responsible for most systems on board. Constantly dogging all those gauges and switches and displays—looking for that failure that, happily, never came. To Gregory, this ascent into space was "extremely boring" because of acquired confidence born of training. At least, that was so on the ground in those simulators, anticipating those failures, never looking out the windows, just "looking at everything inside."[18]

But all that changed when the main engines lit and the solid-rocket boosters fired, rattling and roaring to liftoff at 11:02:18 EDT, 29 April 1985. Spectators gasped at the roiling smoke mushrooming around the structure of the launchpad, gushing from its sides like some strange, primeval flower. *Challenger* soared into the morning sunlight as Fred Gregory found himself suddenly relieved of the doldrums.

Son of a gun really rattles! he thought exultantly.

Not only was he awed, he found himself looking out that window he'd thought so mundane during simulator practice.

"Go back to your instruments," cautioned Bob Overmyer, the shuttle commander.[19]

The horizon came into view and at forty-two thousand feet, *Challenger* raced through cloud cover as if it weren't there. Mach 8, throttle down. They were really traveling! A camera whirred over Gregory's left shoulder, recording scenes he dearly wanted to see. He could only sneak a glance from time to time as they fired up the eastern coast of the United States, like an Indy racer in the sky. Chesapeake Bay, a little slice of home for Gregory, lay sparkling, the Potomac River twisting like a wide, fat snake into the big bay. The Hamptons and Delaware. Long Island and Manhattan. And then there was old Cape Cod. All this within scant minutes. In real time. They were moving along like the proverbial "bat out of hell." Then the solid-rocket boosters and external tank separated.[20]

Two normal orbital maneuvering burns later, *Challenger* settled into orbit 190 miles above the earth, its horizons staring back at them in curvaceous splendor, testifying that it is, indeed, round.

Suddenly, nobody walked around anymore. They floated and swam in space. As Guy Bluford had discovered, nobody can prepare you for zero-G. Training helps, but it's really inadequate.

"You train when you get there," Gregory explained. It's disorienting at first. The sense of up and down is lost for several days until you figure which way is "up" and which is "down." And just when you think you're about to handle it, "your best buddy comes floating by," and your brain says, "Hey, this isn't right! Let's talk about this for a little while!"

As Gregory observed, "It's like being put, as a kid, in a dark closet with the door shut. You get in there and, at first, you're totally disoriented. You don't know where you are. You feel around, and you might feel mom's dress; some shoes on the floor. You begin to gain comfort and confidence, both in where you are and the warmness and feelings around you. So, as you would adapt in this closet, in a dark closet, we adapt to this new environment. It takes about a day and a half, [you have to] get rid of the idea that the floor is down, the ceiling's up, and the walls are on the side. You begin to say: 'My feet are down, and to heck with what I'm looking at!'"[21]

In a way, it was a special kind of fun, though. For example, Gregory began tossing around in space a plastic container of juice and a pen. Just for fun. Called himself a juggler. Another crew member assumed the fetal position and did wheelies in the air. Something about angles. Just for the fun of it.[22]

It was time to go to work. The Gold Team was told to power up the *Spacelab* in the laboratory mode. The Silver Team went to sleep, thus ensuring continuation of the scientific experiments around the clock.

Four hours into the mission, they deployed the minisatellite (NUSAT) from its "getaway special" (GAS) canister. A second satellite (GLOMR) failed to launch as microswitches on the lid of its canister failed to work.

After a weightless "swim" down the nineteen-foot tunnel to the *Spacelab,* work began for the Gold Team about six in the evening. Because of glitches, some experiments seemed doomed. The Very Wide-Field Camera failed. ATMOS, a sensor designed to record the composition of trace elements in the upper atmosphere, worked, but slowly. A short in a crystal growth sample cell blocked full operation.[23]

But then, the sheer beauty of outer space swept them up in nocturnal arms as *Challenger* approached the earth's night side. The sun waned. Angled shadows sculpted definitive lines against tree lines athwart the sides of mountains. Lazy rivers meandered. Gregory looked toward space and saw a black sky. In contrast, what was left of the sunlight bounced deftly off the planet, creating colors that seemed to vibrate. Black space turned into shades of blue, going small and smaller, until the color disappeared between "the dark of space on one side and the dark of earth on the other side." A kind of sparkle caught the peripheral sight in time to see a wee bit of sunlight glow on *Challenger*'s tail.[24] Gregory was deeply moved:

[Space] amplified the spiritual feelings that I had. When you're isolated in one location, you tend to forget that greatness around you. You tend to believe that things happen just normally and naturally. But when you're in space and you're looking down at earth and you see this perfect globe beneath you and you see the organization and nonchaos, you have to feel, as I did, that there was one great Being—one great force that made this happen.[25]

Even the nonbeliever, confronted with such a sight, might agree that God probably *is* somewhere out there influencing all manner of things as only He can. Then the sun twinkled, arcing off *Challenger's* tail, while space went blacker than black. One caught breath later, way out on the farthest horizon, scintillating shades of blue melded, shimmered, and faded into gray near the earth's surface.

Challenger was completely nightside. Gregory and the rest of the crew looked out toward the stars, toward the very center of the universe. Marshalled stars seemed to march along the back ends of space. Finding guiding stars was no longer a problem. They leapt out at them. A turn of the head, and the earth churned by in shades of dark and light gray. Topside the planet sits the light gray of atmosphere, blurring rising stars until "they finally exit and pop on, like light bulbs." Crisp lights of cities far below stab at them through silken space.[26] Awed, Gregory later said that

it seemed that there had to be a plan, and that the plan had to emerge from something. It gives great comfort to realize that [the] person who created this was also looking over you and making sure everything was going to work out right. The earth is the most beautiful thing [to see]. We look at maps and we see the United States, North America, and Africa as something drawn on a piece of paper. The same land forms. You don't see the boundaries. Your concepts of neighborhoods expand significantly.[27]

And, as if that weren't enough, they were startled by the beauty of *aurora australis,* the southern hemisphere's version of the northern lights, nature's electromagnetic light show hard by the south pole, consisting of particles shot from the sun and diverted towards the earth's magnetic poles, colliding with gases in the atmosphere, changing their electrical charge so they glow like the inside of a fluorescent tube. Curved bands of light danced about the glow. Beams of light shot toward the middle of the sky, constantly changing color. White. Shades of green. A wan paleness turning bright, then deep red, until the aurora seemed to cover the entire sky "with shifting curtains of light like draperies waving in the wind." Conducting an observation experiment, Dr. Don L. Lind noted, as *Challenger* flew through the upper reaches of the aurora, "There were discrete areas—really quite spectacular stuff!"[28]

The wonder of it all overwhelmed Fred Gregory. The sudden knowledge, for example, that it's really a simple matter of ten or fifteen minutes between the United States and Africa by spaceship. About the time it takes to visit a friend. And if that's so, he began to reason, then the people in North America and the people in Senegal are essentially very close together. More than that, he thought, the Atlantic Ocean is really no barrier at all. A really small body of water, actually. He turned for the last time that night to watch the dancing aurora australis, and it all became clear: "You feel as though you are a member of a *community* that's not just [part of] the District of Columbia or Houston, it's of the *community of the world!*"[29]

Stockholm and Moscow passed beneath them. Then they flew over the entire, wide panoply of the super-electric United States. Australia. China, occupying more than one-fifth of the continent of eastern Asia. The flat low plains of Manchuria eased by, gradually sloping up to the great heights of the Khingan Mountains. The high Mongolian desert. And off the coast of Africa, these almost magical observations have more than a kernel of truth for Gregory as they pass over his ancestral home, Madagascar. And he would do it again, on another space mission, passing over his ancestors' island some seventy-eight times.[30] He could see the city of Mahaja and the red-hued Betsiboka River, coursing through stands of mango trees.

Like Alex Haley visiting Kunta Kinte's country, Gregory later visited Madagascar as a representative of the United States in June 1990. He recalls that he felt at home. He and his wife met the people, saw the president of Madagascar, and took a spin by the queen's palace.

Lessons learned from the flight of Mission 51B and subsequent flights served only to heighten those convictions. He is as sure now as he was then that all the people of the world are of one society. As a species, we have myriad things in common. An awed journalist from the island's *Midi Société* made the leap when he looked around and found a "perfect lookalike for the Colonel Frederick Gregory."

"And it's true!" he marveled.[31]

On the second day of the mission, William E. Thornton, Ph.D, the Gold Team mission specialist in charge of life sciences, discovered he had a problem. As he began to change the food bars in the cages for his animal charges (a squirrel monkey and twenty-four rats), a pull on the food trays yielded "a stream of dust-like food particles into the module." Additionally, it looked as if "Monkey One wasn't moving or eating well," a sure sign of space sickness. But when Thornton opened the outer doors to the cage, checking out Monkey One's condition— out popped "crumbs, food pellets and feces floating in the air." Air currents were designed to push wastes like these to the bottom of the cages, but movement of the animals interrupted the airflow. Of course, feces floating in the air posed a health hazard to the crew, so tape was strategically placed over cracks around the cages and the airflow was turned off, thus solving the problem. Later, it was proved that it was not feces after all. A second astronaut stood by "with a vacuum cleaner to scoop up any stray matter."[32]

This was a minor development compared to the problems Fred Gregory had with the on-board waste collection system, a device we here on earth affectionately regard as "the toilet." For a fairly long period, the system was renamed the "Gregory Waste Collection System" in his honor because of the problems he had experienced. In fact, other crew members blanched a bit whenever he approached the device to answer Mother Nature's call.

"Oh, my goodness," someone was sure to sing out, "He's getting on it!"

"Will it be working when he leaves?" another wiseacre would crack.

Fred's duel with the toilet as he flew around the world (to be dubbed the "Gregory Failure") was to happen on other flights. Finally, he lost his temper and manhandled the thing.

"I physically broke it!" he recalled, a smile gracing his face, "I— I overpowered it and broke it!"

That was apparently what was needed. "They delved into it and found out what actually happened," he said. "It turned out there was a faulty part in the WCS design." Vindication at last. "I'm not the least bit sensitive about it!" he added, saying he's happy he doesn't have to "suffer that indignity again."

The scientific teams, despite some anomalies with experiments and hardware, would probably agree with Dr. Taylor C. Wang, who encountered problems with his modules, but found ways to fix them, as he said: "I think we got what we came for. Maybe asking for a bonus is being greedy." Of fifteen investigations, fourteen yielded impressive data.[33]

On day seven, deactivation of *Spacelab 3* began and the ship was battened down for reentry. Strapped into their seats, Overmyer and Gregory performed a relaxed return into the earth's atmosphere, the generated heat creating the usual red glow outside the windows. Facing them was the last special sunrise of the mission and its brilliance washed away the red glow. They brought *Challenger* up from the Antarctic Circle northward over the Pacific. Screaming in over Los Angeles at Mach 4, burglar alarms announced their arrival. Four hypersonic S-turns for energy management later, *Challenger* landed on Runway 17 at Edwards Air Force Base.[34]

On 17 June 1985, *Discovery* was launched with six crew and Prince Sultan Salman al-Saud of Saudi Arabia aboard as a passenger. *Challenger* was back in space on 29 July 1985 for another *Spacelab* mission. Up for seven days, problems caused serious consideration of an abort of the mission. Orbit was achieved, however, and the mission completed. The NASA launch tempo increased. *Discovery* was launched on 27 August; *Atlantis* on 3 October 1985. *Challenger* was in space again on 30 October, with Guy Bluford aboard as leader of the Red Shift, *Spacelab D.*[35] *Challenger* looked good after this mission, even though externally the orbiter looked as if it had "gone through the mill." The shuttle had logged nine missions (a record) in a little over two years. In 1986, *Challenger* was scheduled for no fewer than five trips into space with a variety of payloads. It arrived at the Kennedy Space Center on 11 November 1985 for its next launch from Complex 39.[36]

It had been a time of pinnacles for the African-American astronauts. Bluford. McNair. Gregory. Two mission specialists and a pilot.

Then all eyes turned to the first flight of *Columbia* in more than three years. Modified, brought up to par with the later shuttles. Carrying a commercial satellite for launch. An almost-automatic materials science lab. Thirteen getaway specials. A special camera to photograph Halley's Comet. Infrared test images of target areas on earth. Even a congressman on board.[37]

The pilot: Col. Charles F. Bolden, Jr., U.S. Marine Corps. African American.

Pinnacles.

CHAPTER 6

Col. Charles F. Bolden, Jr.

ANCHORS AWEIGH AND *SEMPER FI!*

*They were the biggest, baddest, most tenacious and
hard-headed young men I had ever seen. (They) called the
corps the "crotch," and they bitched about it all the time.
But if anyone outside the corps criticized it, they'd be all over
them like stink on shit. They loved the corps
even when they wanted out.*
—*John de St. Jorre,
quoting a black captain at the
Washington Marine Barracks in* The Marines

The man represents a sort of double-whammy. Annapolis. A full colonel
and Marine Corps fighter pilot. Grumman A-6A *Intruder* jockey. Vietnam
veteran. Astronaut. Shuttle pilot. Shuttle commander.

Black. African-American black.

"Charles F. Bolden, Jr., looks like a typical astronaut. He is trim, has
the instinctive grace of an athlete, is quick to smile, and exhibits a demeanor that suggests he meets life head on." That was the considered
judgment of Baltimore columnist Albert Schlstedt, Jr.[1]

145

Born 19 August 1946, Bolden began life in Columbia, the capital and center of the state of South Carolina. Astride the confluences of the Broad and Saluda Rivers in the middle of rolling sand hills, it has been the state capital since 1786. A place where, in 1860, slave markets flourished until more than half the state's population was slaves. A similar ratio exists today, for there has been little population mobility. Surveys show that of one hundred residents, ninety-nine were probably born in South Carolina, most descended from the blacks and whites who "arrived in the area centuries ago." Of these, almost 30 percent are black, challenging the percentages in the state population of Mississippi, the only other state with more blacks per acre.

Satisfying an apparent need to preserve attachment to the state, it is common for South Carolina families to have lived in the same areas, towns, and homes for generations.[2] The Bolden family was no exception. The astronaut's father, Charles F. Bolden, Sr., was born in Columbia in 1917. Early on, he traveled summers to New York, visiting his father who had moved there. While attending high school in Columbia, he met and fell in love with a young lady named Ethel. Dating was sporadic. After a season in New York working in a Chinese restaurant garnering enough money for college, he returned to the South, enrolling in all-black Johnson C. Smith University in Charlotte, North Carolina. His Ethel was there, too. Their dates became more involved. They completed their bachelor's degrees in 1940, were married, and became educators, teaching in the black schools of Columbia. World War II intervened, interrupting the senior Bolden's career. After service as an enlisted man in France and Italy, he returned to South Carolina.

Two sons were born to the couple: Charles Frank, Jr., and Warren Maurice. Both were good looking. Both were smart. One was apparently on "automatic pilot" as far as his personal focus was concerned. The other was a bit scattered. The younger of the two, Maurice, failed to complete even a year of college, running with "the wrong crowd." When he was drafted into the army, his entrance test scores were so good authorities suggested West Point as a possible option. But Maurice wanted no part of that idea. "Nah," he said, "I don't want to do it. I just want to serve my two years and get out!"

Disenchantment followed; the army discharged him for drug abuse.

On the other hand, Charles, Jr., seemed to know where he was going. At three years of age, he'd settled on Alexis Iona Walker ("everybody calls her 'Jackie'") as the love of his life. The daughter of close family friends, their friendship and ultimately serious attraction seemed the most natural of things. As far as Charles's father was concerned, there may have been a bit more involved in his affection for Alexis's family. Charles later recalled that his father "had always kind of admired *her* mother from afar" when they were in high school.[3]

Charles loved both his parents, but he was very close to his father, who was not only a confidant, but his football coach as well. The two were inseparable, especially during football season, overseeing team conditioning together. Nursing the secret ambition of one day becoming a first-string quarterback ("I was a *mediocre* quarterback, at least!"), Charles, in the absence of the injured starting quarterback, guided his team to victory in the 1963 state championships. It may have been a purely accidental thing, but he will remember the glory of it until the day he dies.

Finding the love of his life at age three and quarterbacking and winning a state football championship were only beginnings for young Charles, Jr. It was church every Sunday; a decision to deep-six the Presbyterians and adopt the Episcopalians on his own recognizance. ("Mother didn't care [where I went] as long as I was going to church.") Baseball and basketball. Summer jobs. Lifeguard at the swimming pool. Guardian of the public clothing while people swam. There was one other thing he *really* wanted more, and that was an appointment to the U.S. Naval Academy. The glamor and regimen captivated him, and he did something about reaching that goal, applying repeatedly for admission. "I knew I was not eligible for an appointment until I became a senior," he said, "but I wanted to plant the seed so there'd be no questions" about how seriously he wanted to go.

Charles wrote to his senators and congressman, campaigning for an appointment. Albert Watson. Olin D. Johnston. Strom Thurmond, the senator who'd run unsuccessfully for president as the candidate of the short-lived "Dixiecrat Party" in 1948 and who, Charles observed, once "strongly favored racial segregation." In his senior year, he pulled out all the responses he'd gotten, including one from Vice President Lyndon B. Johnson. After reviewing them, it was evident that, to a man, the three South Carolina politicians viewed his ambitions with a jaundiced eye, his request coming in the middle of the civil rights revolution. "At this particular time [1963–64]," they replied, "it's just not politically feasible to nominate somebody like you to the Naval Academy." Oozing largesse, Olin Johnston offered him an appointment to the Merchant Marine Academy, a career in which Charles was not the least bit interested.

Then an assassin gunned down President Kennedy in 1963, and Bolden's hopes were dashed when he learned he was ineligible for a presidential appointment. With Johnson in the White House, Charles thought he had lost his sole champion. But he wrote the president anyway, telling him what had happened and that "I just [didn't] feel that I was going to get an appointment out of South Carolina."

Strange things sometimes happen when the president of the United States is ostensibly on your side. Suddenly, a retired judge (L. Howard Bennett, of Pensacola, Florida) began "combing the nation for young blacks interested in going to the service academies." Apparently by coincidence, the judge came by Bolden's high school and spoke with the principal. "Three of us went in and talked with Judge Bennett and the principal."

It was sweet, but baffling. To this day, Charles has never found out exactly how his appointment to the Naval Academy came about.[4] One thing is certain, it *had* to hinge on his letter to President Johnson and the interview with Judge Bennett. Not long after, a recruiter in the garb of a navy chief petty officer knocked on Charles's front door.

"Okay," growled the chief, looking at him with steely eyes as only a navy chief can, "we have word that you're interested in the Naval Academy. My job is to come out here and interview you and see whether you're worth it!"

Shortly thereafter, Charles was offered a slot in the Class of 1969. It meant waiting an extra year—something Charles didn't want to do. He'd already been accepted by Yale and the University of Pennsylvania, not to mention the navy's ROTC program. A week later, the navy advised him that an opening in the Class of 1968 had become available through Congressman William L. Dawson, a black legislator from Chicago, who agreed to appoint Charles.

So everything was moved up a year. Charles went to Annapolis by way of Chicago, and the astute gentlemen from the state of South Carolina watched in utter fascination as the great civil rights revolution unfolded before their very eyes.

*   *   *

Annapolis. They call it "the seat of the very soul of the United States Navy."[5] It is the place Charles Bolden, Jr., went in 1964 to learn and master those things all Annapolis graduates are expected to learn: "skills, honor, integrity and that sense of duty, responsibility and accountability which is the hallmark of Annapolis, of which the Naval Academy is justifiably proud." To gaze reverently upon and absorb the meanings of the monuments and plaques scattered about the place. A memorial to a fellow named Michelson, who figured out how to measure the speed of light. The crypt of naval hero John Paul Jones, who uttered the phrase, "I have not yet begun to fight." At every turn is captured weaponry on display from past naval engagements. It is a place where the plebe is expected to learn and memorize the formal statement of the academy mission, splendidly engraved on the walls of mammoth Bancroft Hall:

> To develop midshipmen morally, mentally, physically, and to imbue them with the highest ideals of duty, honor and loyalty in order to provide graduates who are dedicated to a career of naval service and have potential for future development in mind and character to assume the highest responsibilities of command, citizenship and government.

But make no mistake about it, the Naval Academy is tough. Part college, it has earned worldwide respect because of the excellence of its engineering and science programs; its majors in political science, languages, history, English, and management. Its military instruction and training.[6] It is so tough, Charles almost quit during his plebe year.[7]

Realistically, he was a bit "ahead of the curve," so to speak, for not that many black men were graduates of the Naval Academy when Charles showed up. Not until 1974 were blacks actively recruited for the Brigade of Midshipmen. Even then, with the blessing of the highest naval authorities, the fact of it was considered highly controversial, loudly discussed before God and the country.

The alumni magazine *Shipmate* and the Naval Institute's *Proceedings* discussed the issue in print. "Eleven percent of the population was black," therefore "the expectation could be that the typical Annapolis class would have 150 blacks. Fifty in 1975. Seventy-three in 1976. One hundred twelve in 1977." A special office for minority recruitment was established. It was recognized that traditional recruiting efforts failed to get into inner city areas, where able black young men could be found. The academy superintendent at the time, VAdm. William P. Mack, endorsed the idea. The navy will do it, he observed, "because it is right. By every ethical, moral standard you can name."[8]

So Charles's road may have been a bit rough at first, holding forth along with the forty-two-hundred-strong Brigade of Midshipmen in Bancroft Hall. Out on Tecumseh Court, aligned by company and regiment on the yellow tiles. Learning to be an "Officer of the Navy." And what *is* an officer of the navy? Charles learned that from an utterance laid out by John Paul Jones in something called *Qualification of A Naval Officer:*

> It is by no means enough that an officer of the Navy should be a capable mariner. He should be as well a gentleman of liberal education, refined manners, punctilious courtesy and the nicest sense of personal honor. . . . the soul of tact, patience, justice, firmness and charity. No meritorious act of a subordinate should escape his attention or be left to pass without its reward, even if the reward is only a word of approval.[9]

The advice struck home. Some thought Charles mirrored the advice.

John Riley Love, then a marine major and Charles's first company officer, said he was impressed with Charles's quick intelligence, maturity, and ambitious approach. He was a positive person. "Most importantly," Love added, "he established himself as a 'noncolor person' who did not use the color of his skin or his race as a crutch when something went wrong." As a result, he became a "popular, smart guy, [who] worked hard, portraying a very fine person."

Nor was Charles afraid to get involved. As a case in point, there was a Christmas party held just before the midshipmen left for the holidays. A Santa Claus was needed and Charles volunteered. "It was quite a sight," chuckled Love, "to see him all dressed up as Santa Claus in that red suit and white beard—because Charlie never was a very large person." Certainly not large enough to be a convincing Santa Claus. "He brought the house down!" Love recalled. "But that's the way he was. He *volunteered* to do it because it needed to be done."[10]

Always neat and affable, Charles made quite an impression on his shipmates in the 2d Battalion, 11th Company. He is remembered in his yearbook as a gentleman who "brought with him a never-ending supply of confidence and humor (earning) him the respect and admiration of all who knew him (and there were few who didn't)."

There is also the matter of what Charles calls "his tactical call sign—the nickname all midshipmen come by. ("You pick it or they give it to you. If you're lucky, *you* get to pick it!") Michael James Cummings and Jerry Wayne Crawford, members of his brigade, were respectively known as "The Horse" and "The Monk."

Charlie was known simply as "Poop."[11]

Most Americans simply accept the literal meaning of the word: "To be exhausted; weary." Of course, there is also a scatological meaning that even the lexicographers have left alone (so far, at least). But Charles will have none of that. According to him, the nickname is derived

> From when I was younger and I was at an Episcopal church camp and—and there was a character named "Alley Oop"—I don't know if it was a cartoon character or what—and we were being raucous one night and the priest in charge told us to be quiet. As he walked out, I yelled, "I'm still Alley Poop!" It almost got me thrown out of camp, but the name followed me all the way through life.[12]

As graduation from Annapolis drew closer, each midshipman had to decide the direction his career would take. Bolden was no exception. What was new in Bolden's era was the fact that, within certain parameters, they had a choice. In the "old days," midshipmen were rather routinely looked upon as the navy's future "ship drivers." But Bolden and his classmates were offered a wide array of choices: naval aviation, nuclear submarines, surface ships, nuclear power school, engineering, metallurgy, naval architecture, and oceanography.[13]

Of course, there was also the Marine Corps. A choice limited at that time to just over 12 percent of any graduating class. Getting into the marines was highly competitive, so class standing became an important factor. "Marine Air" was even more involved, since there would be no flight training before a solid six months of ground training. *Nobody* just walked into the Marine Corps and became a marine officer merely because they'd graduated from a military service academy—not even Annapolis![14]

A mindset centering on joining the marines was the least of Bolden's worries when he first arrived at the Naval Academy. He "had no desire or any plans whatsoever to go into the Marine Corps," Bolden recalled. "In fact, it was one thing I knew I was *not* gonna do!"

Until, that is, he met Major Love, his first company officer. "Love was," Bolden explained, "a typical marine. Very hard, but infinitely fair."

Oddly, John Riley Love said nothing to Bolden about *becoming* a marine. Instead, he just concentrated on being a marine himself. He and the other Marine Corps officers at Annapolis were just "people-people, without exception." Charles was impressed. He wanted to be like John Riley Love. Become a marine officer. Act like he acted. Talk like Love and the rest of the marine officers talked. Walk that marine walk.[15]

The marines seemed a special place to him. "The place," observes John de St. Jorre, "where little guys often surprise big guys, where sons catch up to their fathers; where a nobody becomes a somebody." And, as John Riley Love noted, Charles was a little guy.

But maybe it was none of that. Perhaps it was something more basic and defining. That *Semper Fi* thing. The motto that is always percolating in the back of every marine's mind. But *Semper Fi* is more than a motto. It is that indescribable something that makes marines a bit different from other people who call themselves military.[16] It is a most sanguine connection, like the old Indian custom of melding blood, giving each man license "to walk in the company of brave men, each knowing that one day, on any appointed day, one of them may be asked to pay the ultimate price." And it wouldn't be about dying; it would be about doing a job for one's country. There is a certain nobility in that. Maybe that's what Charles saw in Major Love that motivated him to cast his lot with the U.S. Marine Corps.

Three days after his graduation from the Naval Academy, Charles and Alexis (the girl everybody called "Jackie" and whom he had known since he was three) decided to get married.

"It was," he remembered, "a typical military wedding at the chapel. With swords, uniforms, and all that stuff!"[17]

"All that stuff" was pure pomp and romance as the ushers prepared for the arch of swords ceremony after the exchange of vows, first directing the wedding guests outdoors and athwart the chapel steps. The bridal party located itself on either side of the outer doors as other guests lined the steps and walkway. The ushers hooked on their swords, marched down the chapel steps, and formed up, facing each other in two equal rows.

A hush fell. Conversations were muffled. An errant laugh sounded peculiarly like a Christmas bauble breaking.

"Officers, draw swords!" the head usher ordered. Metal hissed as the swords were drawn in one continuous motion and raised into the air, tips touching, to form the wedding arch.

"The arch is formed!" the best man whispered to Charles and Jackie.

Smiling, they stepped into the daylight and passed gingerly under the metallic arch as sunlight glinted on sword points like tiny, glittering stars. They paused for a moment.

"Officers, return—" began the head usher as the swords go to present arms for a moment. And then, "Swords!" The swords slid in unison into their scabbards, except for the final three or four inches of their length, at which time the officers thrust them home with a single "click."[18]

It was done.

The Marine Corps, Charlie's service of choice, awaited him. So did a new enlightenment.

Basic School is a bit different from marine Officer Candidate School (OCS), where they take a "wet-behind-the-ears person off the street with no prior experience and make him into a Marine Corps officer." A second lieutenant. A rifle platoon commander. Charles was no rookie. He was an Annapolis man. No matter, it was the Basic School for him. Six months. Infantry-oriented. Exposure to all of the Marine Corps's occupational skills so as to enable him to select one to pursue. Class standings dictated what you got. When it was over, he knew how to lead troops. "You learned the basic thing about Marine Corps training, and that is that it teaches you first how to follow—so you can lead people!"

Second in his Basic School class, he was guaranteed Marine Air. He took the slot, he reminisced, "as a whim," because he "had no intention of going to flight school." He was still probing, searching for something exciting and meaningful. Flight school might just fill the bill.

Pensacola Naval Air Station. Saufley Field. Basic flying in the T-34 Beechcraft they called *Mentor*. Class standing was still everything, continuing to influence what one would eventually do. A jet pilot or a helicopter pilot or fly a C-130—whatever the Marine Corps had.

Jackie made him study hard, and Charles finished number one in his class. He chose to transition into jets and they moved to Meridian, Mississippi. There he learned the basics of flying jet planes. Formation flying. Gunnery, air-to-ground and air-to-air. Carrier qualifications. Going aboard "the boat" and doing his first carrier landings ("You get a little scared the first time!") at Kingsville, Texas. Advanced jet training in the F9F *Cougar*. Instruments. Advanced formation flying and gunnery. More gunnery. Back to the boat for more carrier landings—except that Charles didn't have to do that. Instead, he went off to learn how to fly and fight in the A-6A *Intruder*.[19]

In May 1970, they called him a naval aviator. By June 1972, he was assigned to a marine air attack, all-weather squadron—VMA(AW)-533 at Nam Phong, Thailand, flying *Intruder* sorties into Cambodia, North and South Vietnam, and Laos.[20]

The Grummen A-6A *Intruder*. High subsonic performance. No individual defense system. A forerunner of the 1990s breed of strike aircraft, it relied on guile, cover of night, speed, and ordnance that numbs the enemy's senses. Single airplane sorties. Letting down a hundred miles from the target; drilling through the air two hundred feet above the treetops; flying under the enemy's ever-watchful radar. Electronic systems guiding, warning, directing. Finding targets in any weather.[21] Bolden, the pilot, and as often as not, the man Charles can only remember as "Bullet"—his bombardier-navigator. Trail and road interdiction, flinging man and weaponry through the night sky, wheeling daggerlike against the early dawn at mission's end. The missions came and went until Charlie had flown almost a hundred. Then, one night, he came to know how opaque and "now you see it, now you don't" a strike fighter pilot's life could be. All of it could be over and done in the blinking of an eye. It seemed innocent enough, roaring into beautiful, lush green valleys in the middle of the night. But down among the greenery lay flak emplacements and multicalibered guns, manned by people who had vowed to try to kill his bombardier-navigator and him the very next time they (or anybody else like them) had the temerity to show up.

THE GREENING OF CHARLIE: VIETNAM TO FIRST FLIGHT

Bolden and his bombardier-navigator (BN) had drawn a night strike. They listened attentively during the evening general briefing, picking up the latest-known intelligence regarding the strike area. The nature of the threat. Locations and types of known radars and gun emplacements. Numbers and types of enemy aircraft that could be expected to sortie. There probably wouldn't be a problem with the latter, since the *Intruders* mainly flew where there were few, if any, MIGs.

The name of the game was to get that A-6 *Intruder* in under the enemy radar, attack, and get the hell out. That may sound simple; it wasn't. Night interdiction and road reconnaissance is serious stuff against people armed to the teeth and waiting to take you out.

Poring over their maps, Bolden and his BN carefully planned their attack route, taking into account the data about known defenses. After choosing navigational checkpoints, distances, and heading, and calculating times for each leg of the flight, they loaded the results into their on-board computer.

Soon it was time to take the *Intruder* hunting. They would hit the primary target first, then maybe the controller would steer them to another target so they could raise a little more hell. Bolden fired up the sleek, round-nosed, raked-wing A-6, while arming crews pulled the red safety clips from the bombs. The roaring jet brought them alert as their hearts pounded; their senses sharpened. Bolden felt a slight sweating of the palms as he got clearance for takeoff. Once airborne, a complete transformation occurred in their *Intruder,* making it an awesome mechanical bird that was faster than a bullet as it swept them toward the stars.

Airspeed stabilized. The night drew deeper and darker as the A-6 howled along, despite its external ordnance burden. The crew could see no lights below, but from the many daytime sorties they'd flown, they knew how lush and beautiful the countryside was. In the eerie darkness, they somehow became detached from reality. Only they and the *Intruder* seemed alive, the red lights of its gauges and sweeping radar screen the only link to the world below.

Miles from the primary target, Bolden began descending for ultra low-level flight. Bullet lined up the run-in heading. Slashing along two hundred feet above the earth, they skimmed treetops, fooling enemy radars into believing they weren't there at all. From time to time, they'd see reflections of a bashful moon, hiding behind scudding clouds, flashing off a rice paddy. Suddenly, from the corner of his eye, Bolden saw quick flashes on the ground below that were almost, but not quite, like king-sized fireflies winking on and off, only faster. But it was nothing quite so innocent. One lucky shot from an AK-47 could take them out. Ignoring that possibility, they attacked the primary straight on, delivering the *Snake Eye* bombload right on target. As soon as they were clear, the controller gave them new coordinates for a bit of road reconnaissance. The real game was about to begin.

"Okay, Bullet, ol' buddy," Bolden breathed, tuning the radar with one hand while adjusting the images on his scope. "We're coming up on the place." Small-arms fire multiplied. From the corner of his eye, Bolden saw staccato flashes of machine guns opening up. He concentrated on keeping low, jinking randomly to avoid the guns.

Antiaircraft gunners opened up with big-caliber stuff, lighting up the night sky. Tracers arced by, scorching the darkness. The ferocity of it all was startling. Charles later described the scene:

> All of a sudden, the whole world lit up and it was different than all the other times. I mean, we were always lit up, but this time [those] guys were *really* shooting at us. You *knew* they were shooting at you and there was nothing to do except keep going—just keep going!

Rows of tracers leapt up—reaching, flaring, grasping for the ship. Despite all the strikes he'd flown, it was more awesome than Bolden had ever imagined it could be.

"Holy shit, Bullet! Look!"

Bullet sat up in his seat, raising his head from the boot of the radar scope for a moment. As he looked around, his eyes widened.

"Gawd! I don't wanna see!" Bullet gasped, then buried his face in the boot again.

On and on they raced above the darkened ground. White-hot metal spewed at them from all directions. Their remaining bombs were almost ready for release.

"Your pickle is hot," Bullet breathed.

Bullet had the target. He was on it, into the attack mode. He flipped several switches and the computer segued into the attack solution as Bolden watched the release marker on his scope. A flip of the finger and suddenly it disappeared. The bombs were jettisoned, singing a death song in the fetid air. Bolden hauled back on the stick and the *Intruder* chandelled away so they wouldn't become victims of their own exploding ordnance.

There should've been rejoicing, but more trouble was brewing. A *Firecan* gun-control radar locked them up and huge tracers lolled up in quatrain. They jettisoned chaff and the enemy ammo went astray. That wasn't the end of it. The enemy *knew* they were still up there. The sky lit up. It was extraordinary:

Every once in a while they'd do what they called barrage fire. Just [light] up the sky. Put up a wall of antiaircraft radar and small-arms fire and everything and hope they'd hit you when you flew through it. Barrage fire. That's what we encountered. Best thing to do was nothing; just fly straight ahead. Ducking. Dodging. Listening.

Listening for the *Firecan*'s bleep. "There was a *Beeeep!* Another that went *Brrrt!* And another that went warbling, like *Loodle! Loodle! Loodle! . . .* That one meant somebody had locked on and was getting ready to shoot you. You *don't* wanna hear *that one!*"[22]

They made it back in one piece—amazed they hadn't been shot down. Not a single bullet hole or shell fragment scarred the body of their *Intruder*.

Charles Bolden went up in harm's way a hundred times during his Vietnam tour. Then it was back to the United States and two years in Los Angeles as a marine recruiting officer, and another three years at El Toro Marine Corps Air Station, California. Then he began dreaming even bigger dreams.[23]

Bolden still doubted himself, despite his obvious success at Annapolis and as a marine combat pilot. Being a marine officer recruiter and performing other varied duties was mundane stacked up against the excitement promised in NASA advertisements for space shuttle astronauts in the late 1970s. Bolden experienced a mounting thrill when the Marine Corps asked for administrative action forms from qualified personnel wishing to apply. A huge door was opening, but Bolden didn't know if he ought to walk on through.

An intense personal battled raged within him. He heard imaginary voices. One seemed to tell him he'd better get busy and apply. The other wondered quietly if they would even accept him. The latter voice won—for the moment. "I chickened out," he said later. "I figured I'd *never* be selected, so I felt why waste my time and their time? They weren't interested in anybody like me."

In 1979, when Bolden was about to graduate from the navy's test pilot school at Patuxent River, Maryland, he met Fred Gregory, the first black graduate of that school and one of three African Americans already selected by NASA to become shuttle astronauts. Ron McNair was also in the area, and Bolden knew about Guy Bluford. There were others he'd known at the Naval Academy who'd made the grade as well.

In the face of all these successes, Bolden decided he'd pick up his pencil and apply the next time NASA advertised. His confidence grew, but didn't presage action until he got a handle on what had been going on inside himself: "If they [Ron, Fred, and Guy] had *not* been there, I never would have applied. I needed role models!"[24]

NASA's Dr. Curtis Graves remembered how important role models were to Bolden. "Charles was pulled along by other blacks," said Graves. "At [Patuxent], Fred's picture is on the wall. Charlie didn't have to prove that blacks could do it—Fred had already done it. Charlie cried—walking in their footsteps!"[25]

NASA selected Bolden in May 1980, and in August 1981, he became qualified for assignment as space-shuttle pilot.

Bolden's experiences as he entered the astronaut's world were similar to those of all new candidates. "During the first year," he explained, "you're trying NASA out and NASA's trying you out. Classes for the first six months. After that, technical assignments. Working with somebody else in the office—with the engineers—just to get your feet on the ground."[26]

Almost six years passed before he could fly the shuttle as a pilot. Meanwhile, he saw duty as safety officer, as technical assistant to the director of flight crew operations, and a long list of other jobs at space centers around the country. The technical assignments were challenging. He helped "develop a material (to be) used in orbit to make repairs to the tiles." The plan called for an astronaut to make a space walk with something like a caulking gun and replace broken tiles. It proved impractical. Next, it was into SAIL, where Bolden helped test computer software, working with Autoland, the automatic landing system.

By late 1985, Bolden knew he would be pilot on an upcoming flight, Mission 61C. All the study and practice, the time spent learning systems and routines from the ground up, was about to pay off. About two weeks before the flight was scheduled to go, he got his first chance to get into the shuttle. The crew, led by Robert L. Gibson, was something of a "mixed bag," with people who'd flown before and people like Charles, who hadn't. The mission specialists were Franklin R. Chang-Diaz, George "Pinky" Nelson, and Steven A. Hawley. Robert J. Cenker was the payload specialist and Congressman C. William Nelson was going along for the ride.

"I was pretty excited," exclaimed Bolden. "I don't think I had any undue concern. You're trained. We all felt very comfortable, confident. But I was concerned about being able to do my job if something unusual came up."

So Bolden spent most of his time lying in the pilot's seat that first time. Looking around the cockpit. Making sure he knew where all the checklists were.[27]

They wondered if they would ever launch. Delay followed delay. Slated for 18 December, the launch was pushed to the nineteenth for more work on the refurbished *Columbia*. On the nineteenth, countdown descended to fourteen seconds before the launch was scrubbed and reset for 4 January because of the Christmas holiday break. That launch was pushed back to 6 January so the astronauts could spend more simulator time after the holidays. That countdown ran to T-minus-thirty-one seconds. Again, the launch was scrubbed, this time because of a computer error and the failure of a propellant valve to close. Adverse weather at emergency landing sites stopped the launch on 7 January.[28] Mission 61C finally got off the ground on 12 January 1985 at 6:55 A.M. The rocket's blast seared the early morning darkness like an errant, upside-down comet.

It was the first time Bolden had felt the full seven million pounds of thrust under his butt. He had thought himself prepared, collected. But the awakening was rude. He remembered the experience as "interesting," feeling "like when you're a teenager, stepping off a curb or getting off from a stop light or a stop sign." It was not unlike, he thought, being in a commercial airplane, when the pilot releases the brakes and goes to full power. Lying on your back, it's a different kind of feeling:

> When the main engines ignite, you don't really feel the vehicle strain[ing] against the holdings and everything. You can tell that the main engine's ignited, but I didn't even get the sensation of what they call the "twang"—where the vehicle kinda pitches nose down and then comes back up as a result of the engines being pointed off center. [And] when the solids ignite, you hear them, you feel them—and you sink back in your seat as it lifts off, so you know you're going somewhere![29]

Bolden noticed the initial vibration most of all. It lasted for the first couple of minutes or so, until the solid-rocket boosters separated from the vehicle. During the "roll program," when the shuttle is essentially upside-down, he recalled seeing the sunlight, then the vehicle was beyond most of earth's atmosphere and things got very smooth. He was surprised to feel the orbiter accelerate when the main engines were throttled down during the period of maximum dynamic pressure, the solid-rocket boosters still burning and providing most of the thrusting. The main engines throttled up again for another surprise acceleration because, Bolden explained, "you wouldn't expect that you'd feel it because you're getting five million pounds of thrust out of the two solid-rocket boosters and just over a million [pounds of thrust] out of the main engine!"

It was *Columbia*'s first mission in over three years. The orbiter had been extensively modified to bring it up to par with the newer shuttles. Two commercial satellites were launched during the six-day flight, which covered over two million miles in orbit. Bolden helped hold the orbiter in precise position as the satellites rotated up and out into space. A Material Science Laboratory 2, which ran nearly automatically, was aboard, as were thirteen getaway specials, some containing telescopes for an experiment designed to survey regions of ultraviolet emissions in the galaxy. Also scheduled was using a special camera to photograph Halley's Comet.[30]

Several thoughts occurred to Bolden while they circled in orbit. One was how little actual "piloting" the pilot does on the shuttle. In actuality, he said, "the pilot is the copilot" and the commander is the first pilot. The pair work closely together. The commander is the boss and lands the shuttle when it returns to earth. The pilot "helps to fly some, on orbit" when there is any manual flying to do. The commander might let the pilot fly for about thirty seconds once they get back into the atmosphere after the shuttle goes subsonic, but then the commander takes over again and lands the orbiter.

"The total amount of flying you do is about three minutes out of however many days the flight lasts. The pilot puts the landing gear down," said Bolden.[31]

He was constantly amazed how quickly the shuttle passed over the entire United States. "In about ten minutes! I've never been in an airplane that could do that!" The weightlessness he took in stride.

The crew had considerable time during the flight to observe the earth. They watched as Thailand, the city of Rangoon, Burma, and Southeast Asia passed by below. The atmosphere seemed unusually clear. The west coast of Australia. Across the Indian subcontinent and over the Himalayas at five miles a second. The coral reefs off New Caledonia. Cameras whirred.[32]

Bolden was intensely fascinated with the continent of Africa, and he took loads of still photographs. Never having been there, he was doubly fascinated with Nigeria, since his wife, Jackie, had gone there as part of a college program.

About two nights into the flight, an experience, frightening at first, caught the crew completely off guard. In the final analysis, it served to further explain Fred Gregory's mysterious affair with the waste management system. According to Charles:

We were awakened by this alarm that told us we had a *cabin leak!* That's a terrifying sound. It's a klaxon. You know the sound . . . it only means one thing: there's a hole in the vehicle somewhere and the air is leaking out. So, we were asleep, and this thing went off. Right away, we knew it was real because you could hear the nitrogen rushing into the cabin. That may be what Fred told [you] about. Well, [the nitrogen] comes through a little hole right above your head when you're sitting there. So we heard this *p-s-s-h-h-h-s-t!* [and] we knew that something was leaking. It turned out [that] what we had done was somebody had left the toilet on. When you do that, you're essentially pumping air out of the cabin to flush all the stuff. It really doesn't flush, but that's what creates the suction that pulls it all down! And if you leave it running long enough, it'll draw the cabin down to the point where it sets off an alarm that says the cabin pressure is low. And that's what happened.[33]

NASA decided to bring the astronauts home a day early on 16 January in order to prepare for another mission to further observe Halley's Comet, since attempts to get long-exposure photographs of the comet fizzled because an image intensifier failed. But clouds and rain blanketed, delaying their return. On the seventeenth, *Columbia* again prepared to land, but again weather caused cancellation. Finally, on the eighteenth, *Columbia* came in for a night landing at Edwards Air Force Base in California, completing ninety-six orbits of the earth.[34]

Jackie, Bolden's long-suffering childhood sweetheart and wife, took another of those long sighs of relief. Charles had made it back safely. He knew how she felt about his going out there and the empathy was great:

She enjoys the work, the association with the people. I think she tolerates my going into space. She's very happy working up to the flight, and she's very happy probably during the course of the flight. She's *not* very happy and comfortable at all during the ascent. I think (all the wives) worry during reentry (also) because they're very much aware that those are the two times that, if something's going to happen, that's when most problems *will* happen![35]

Nobody knew it at the time, but the long delays in getting *Columbia* to launch and to land, as well as some of the anomalies experienced during the flight, perhaps presaged the bad luck that would soon bedevil the shuttle program. Not even the astronauts knew the extent of the jeopardy to which they had been and were being exposed. The people who did know "were well-intentioned" to be sure, but had somehow convinced themselves that the astronauts knew; understood—because after all, "it happened so often."[36]

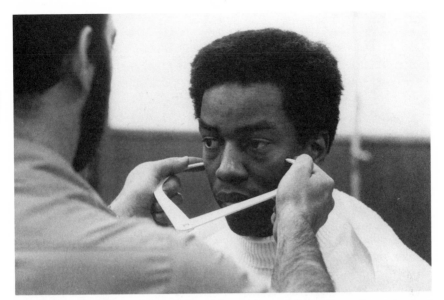

Guy Bluford is measured for a helmet visor as he and thirty-four other astronaut candidates undergo initial orientations and training at the Johnson Space Center in late January 1978.

The crew of STS-8, the first mission on which an African-American astronaut ventured into space. The astronauts are (clockwise from left): Daniel C. Brandenstein, Dale A. Gardner, William E. Thornton, Guion S. Bluford, and Richard M. Truly.

Astronauts Vance D. Brand and Ron McNair board a NASA T-38 jet trainer prior to an exercise in preparation for Mission 41B.

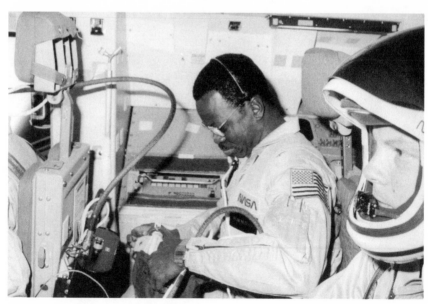

Ron McNair unbuckles his straps aboard the space shuttle *Challenger* ten minutes after Mission 41B's launch on 3 February 1984.

McNair plays his saxophone during a break from his mission specialist duties aboard *Challenger*.

Five astronauts and two payload specialists were aboard *Challenger* on its tragic final mission. All lost their lives. The crewmembers were (front row, from left): Michael J. Smith, Francis R. Scobee, and Ronald E. McNair; and (top row, from left) Ellison S. Onizuka, Sharon Christa McAuliffe, Gregory Jarvis, and Judith A. Resnik. McAuliffe and Jarvis were the payload specialists.

Mission operations director Eugene F. Krans (left) discusses the situation with astronaut Fred Gregory (center) and Richard O. Covey at the spacecraft communicator console in Mission Control shortly after learning that something had gone wrong with *Challenger*'s launch on 28 January 1986.

Cheryl McNair speaks at the memorial service for her late husband, astronaut Ron McNair, at the Massachusetts Institute of Technology. *Photo by Calvin Campbell, MIT.*

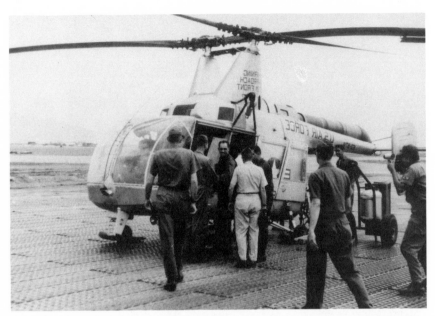

Fred Gregory prepares to board an H-43 helicopter for a mission in Vietnam. *Courtesy Fred Gregory.*

Fred Gregory (right) and his crew on the flight deck of a space-shuttle trainer during preparation for mission STS-33.

Charles Bolden in the pilot's seat on *Columbia*'s flight deck just prior to reentering the earth's atmosphere.

Charles Bolden (inverted in dark suit) and his fellow astronauts on Mission 61C undergo zero-gravity training aboard NASA's specially equipped KC-135 aircraft.

Astronaut Mae C. Jemison undergoes water survival training.

Mae Jemison appears to be clicking her heels as she moves around *Endeavour*'s science module in zero-gravity.

Astronauts Bernard Harris (center) and Hans Schlegel (right) perform a physiological test at the "Anthrorack" aboard *Columbia* during mission STS-55 in May 1993.

Bernard Harris listens to a briefing before heading out for the field training portion of a survival course taught at Vance Air Force Base, Oklahoma.

CHAPTER 7

COUNTDOWN TO GLORY: THE *CHALLENGER* TRAGEDY

As for the likeness of the living creatures, their appearance
was like burning coals of fire, and like the appearance of torches.
Fire was going back and forth among the living creatures;
the fire was bright, and out of the fire went lightning.
—*Ezekiel 1:13,* The Holy Bible

Nobody suspected that America's spectacularly successful space technology was about to turn killer. Although there were setbacks in the shuttle program, remedies were found for the glitches. NASA simply called them "mishaps, delays, and interruptions." Television networks stopped live coverage of launches. No longer hot news, newspapers followed their example, relegating NASA shuttle launches and landings to inside pages.[1] It seemed logical in a way. After all, some parts of that technology had gotten mankind to the moon and back and propelled other men into space. Astronauts had been lost, to be sure, but on the ground, never in space.

The crew designated for Mission 51L in 1985 was special. A year before, on 27 August 1984, President Ronald Reagan announced that the "first private citizen to fly in space would be an American teacher, as part of the Space Flight Participant Program, opening shuttle experiences to a wider public through education and communication." Eleven thousand teachers applied. On 19 July 1985, Sharon Christa McAuliffe of Concord, New Hampshire, won the chance after a careful review of the applications.[2]

The crew was an American microcosm. It included an African American, Ron McNair, who'd flown on *Challenger*'s fourth mission; an Asian American, air force colonel Ellison S. Onizuka, who cut his teeth in space on *Discovery;* and two women, Dr. Judith A. Resnik, the second American woman in space, and Christa McAuliffe. The mission commander was a retired air force test pilot, Maj. Francis R. (Dick) Scobee, who had piloted *Challenger* on its fifth mission. Navy commander Michael J. Smith was the pilot. Flight 51L was his first shuttle mission. Then there was the Hughes Company payload specialist, Greg Jarvis, who would finally get to fly after having been bumped by congressmen on two previous flights. Their experience level helped NASA hedge its bets. They trained mightily for a year. By all odds, the mission seemed headed for unqualified success.[3]

But weird omens were in the air.

Rescheduled launches plagued the mission, which slipped from July 1985 to November 1985 to late January 1986. There were payload changes and changes to the orbiter itself for the crew to contend with. Several elements had to be cannibalized from other orbiters not yet close to a scheduled flight. On 16 December 1985, the launchpad assignment was changed from 35-A to 35-B. Then came a series of launch aborts on 22, 24, and 25 January because of constant delays in launching STS-61C, which carried equipment needed on *Challenger*.

Unacceptable weather was predicted for the twenty-sixth, not only at Kennedy Space Center, but at contingency landing sites around the world. The countdown was stopped. On 27 January, fueling of the mammoth external tank began a half-hour after midnight. The countdown moved ahead. At 5:07 A.M., the crew was awakened, served breakfast, and they were strapped in their seats by four minutes to eight. An hour and fourteen minutes later, the closeout ground crew reported problems. A balky hatch. A stuck bolt. A dead battery. High winds whipped the Cape as other crews reported battling ice all through the night. Eighty minutes later, the hatch handle was secured, but cross-winds at the return landing site seriously exceeded safe levels, should it be required. The crew left the vehicle.[4]

During the night, an Arctic cold front barreled across central Florida, dropping the temperature well below freezing. Citrus growers braced against the big chill, trying to protect crops from temperatures they feared would be as damaging as the killer frosts of 1983 and 1985. Six people died as cars slid off roads from New York to Georgia. Wind-chill factors around the Great Lakes dropped to 60° below zero. The next day, schools closed because of the cold in Georgia, Alabama, Tennessee, South Carolina, and from Pennsylvania to Vermont. In Miami, the temperature sank below 30°; the coldest recorded in that city in forty-five years.[5]

Out on the Cape, NASA management stirred itself to "review the possible effects of the cold on the launch planned for the next day." The weather was clear, but launch crews reported finding ice on the upper sections of the launchpad, 150 feet off the ground, by ten that night. They pumped antifreeze through some fluid lines and let water spigots drip to keep the pad from freezing. A half-million gallons of supercold liquid oxygen was drained from *Challenger*'s fuel tanks. The countdown clock was recycled and the countdown continued throughout the long night.

The decision to proceed was confirmed after looking at all the evidence. The weather was expected to be fine on Tuesday. Visibility unlimited. Extreme cold with clear skies.

"We'll go tomorrow," announced launch director Robert Sieck, "we think tomorrow is our best shot—that's what we're going to do."[6]

But something untoward permeated the atmosphere. Ron McNair felt it that night when he called his father, Carl McNair, Sr., who later said:

I feel that he must have had some sort of premonition. The day before the flight, he spoke with me on the telephone and it seemed like he didn't want to put that telephone down. He spoke with me a long, long time. "I hope they get this thing off the ground so I can get back there and finish raising my children." That was the most important thing he said to me.[7]

It seemed that at some subconscious level, the rest of the crew also knew things weren't all right. On 8 January they had all posed for a fateful photograph high up on Launchpad 39-B at the entrance to *Challenger*. In retrospect, there is something about that picture. Something in their eyes makes it seem they were looking beyond the camera, past the lens and all of us. They held their helmets as the cameraman had coached them. Onizuka looked relaxed, his mouth slightly parted. Mike Smith appears resolute, McNair's smile is tight; perhaps he was thinking of the conversation with his father. The commander, Dick Scobee, also looks resolute. His right hand firmly grasps his helmet, a smile teases his face, but it seems feigned. Resnik is smiling a lovely smile, long hair framing her face, as if to say, "No matter what, it's really no big deal!" Gratitude tinges Greg Jarvis's smile. He'd finally made it aboard a space shuttle! Under the thinning hair, his eyes seem a bit mischievous, as if he'd outfoxed them all and this was the culmination, the high point of his life. Finally, there is Christa McAuliffe, with the widest, biggest, shiniest smile of all. Trusting. Full of faith in the NASA system and its technology. Christa, who told Bruce Desilva, a reporter from the *Hartford Courant,* that she "was unafraid," that "if I thought I was risking my life by going into space, I wouldn't be doing it." And furthermore, "If NASA thought it was dangerous, they wouldn't be sending an average citizen." Questioned again as launch time drew closer, Christa seemed "impatient about the potential dangers" of spaceflight. "I am too excited to have the jitters!" she exclaimed.[8]

After a relaxed breakfast, the crew got the usual weather check and suited up in the now-famous, blue flight coveralls for the trip to the orbiter. During the weather briefing, NASA management told the crew about the ice on the launchpad. But they weren't told anything about the possible effects the extremely low temperatures might have on the shuttle. They weren't told of concerns expressed by solid-rocket booster (SRB) engineers about the problems with O-rings in several previous flights, or about conversations between the SRBs' manufacturer and NASA management as they considered the option of delaying the mission until the weather warmed up.

So they walked to the waiting van, Dick Scobee in the lead, followed by a waving and smiling Resnik. Ron McNair was next, walking jauntily, as if about to launch into karate exercises. Then came Smith and McAuliffe; Onizuka and Jarvis. By 8:03 A.M., they were at

Launchpad 39-B. Thirty-three minutes later they were strapped into their seats aboard *Challenger,* Scobee and Smith on the flight deck, with Resnik, the flight engineer, and Onizuka centered between them. McNair, McAuliffe, and Jarvis sat on the middeck. Resnik ground through the pre-flight with Scobee and Smith. The rest of the crew waited on their backs as the countdown marched ahead. Nine minutes before scheduled launch came a planned hold. After the launchpad was checked for ice buildup by two separate teams, Mission Control announced the decision to go.[9]

The countdown to glory resumed.

Thousands waited on the ground for the flight taking America's first teacher in space. Across the country, millions of school children and their teachers felt a bit giddy anticipating the coming launch and the two live classes to be taught by McAuliffe via communications satellites: "The Ultimate Field Trip" and "Where We've Been, Where We're Going, Why?"[10]

Members of a touring band from Ron McNair's alma mater, MIT, scheduled to appear at Astronaut High School in neighboring Titusville that night, were driving along a nearby causeway, watching for the shuttle launch. Suddenly, cars began pulling over and they knew liftoff was getting close.[11]

Guy Bluford was at home. "We had gotten very comfortable with shuttle launches," he recalled later. "By the time *Challenger* flew, shuttle launches had become rather routine. The whole office was not supporting this one flight. We were all spread out, doing other things."[12] Charles Bolden and his crew were still debriefing after their flight and had taken a break in order to watch the launch on television in a nearby conference room. Oddly, the room wasn't anywhere near full.[13] Out in California, astronaut-to-be Mae Jemison was getting ready to go to work.[14] Fred Gregory was in the Mission Control Center working as lead capsule communicator (CAPCOM), "supervising Dick Covey, who was working his first launch," and coordinating the gathering of weather data—winds aloft, cloud levels, etc. After that, Gregory sat watching the monitor beyond the flight director's position as the countdown continued.[15]

At 6.6 seconds before launch, the liquid-fueled main engines ignited in sequence, running up to full thrust. At 11:38 A.M. EST, *Challenger* slowly lifted from the launchpad into the cold, clear sky, the Atlantic Ocean looking like a mammoth blue cyclorama. Resnik euphorically yelled, "Allriiight!"

"Here we go!" Smith shouted at T-plus-one in response to the motion and movement of the vehicle.

The crew couldn't see it, nor could anyone else, but a few seconds after liftoff, a puff of grayish black smoke *whooshed* from the aft field joint of the right-hand solid-rocket booster. Smith egged *Challenger* on with "Go, you mother!" at T-plus-seven seconds and Resnik hollered "Hot shit!" at T-plus-fifteen. Scobee agreed with them both, saying "Ohhhkaaaay!" One second later—puffs and puffs of increasingly blacker, deadlier, more ominous smoke trailed alongside the orbiter, mixing with the rocket plumes and the atmosphere. Nobody knew it, but the grease, joint insulation, and rubber O-rings in the joint seal were being burned and eroded by hot gases blowing by. Forty seconds into the flight, forward velocity hit Mach 1 as they slammed through nineteen thousand feet of altitude. In Mission Control, the launch still appeared normal. The main engines were throttled down and at fifty-two seconds were throttled up again to 104 percent of thrust. Smith's exuberance knew no bounds.

"Feel that mother go!" he yelled.

"*Wooooooooooo!*" somebody else exhaled.[16]

A bus driver down on a causeway watched the liftoff with interest. An old-time shuttle watcher, he'd seen lots and lots of launches and he didn't crack a smile. Instead, he shook his head in dismay.

"Don't look right to me," he groused, before settling back in his leathered and worn seat.[17]

At T-plus-fifty-eight seconds, as the solid-rocket boosters were increasing their thrust, a small finger of fire flickered on the back of the right-hand SRB. A second later, it blossomed, growing into a continuous, well-defined plume. As it grew in size, the rushing slipstream and the "upper ring attaching the solid-rocket booster to the external tank directed the flame onto the surface of the external tank." Automatic control systems tried to counter the changes in the shuttle's attitude. At T-plus-sixty-four seconds, the shape and color of the fiery plume changed, mixing with hydrogen leaking from the external tank. At T-plus-seventy-two seconds, the external tank pulled away. Massive amounts of liquid hydrogen escaped. The now-rotating, right solid-rocket booster hit the lower part of the liquid oxygen tank. White vapors signaled the failures. In milliseconds, while still moving at Mach 1.92 at 46,000 feet, *Challenger* was totally enveloped in the explosive burn. At T-plus-seventy-three seconds, pilot Smith said, "Uh-oh."

Then silence. A mammoth fireball. The twin solid-rocket boosters went crazy, roaming the skies at will, until an air force range officer pushed a button and blew them up to prevent them from landing in a populated area. The orbiter broke into several sections, finally emerging from the fireball.

At Mission Control, the last readings from the shuttle froze on the screens with an "S" beside the numbers to indicate a static situation. They gave no hint of trouble.[18]

Inside Mission Control, Fred Gregory, the CAPCOM, had just turned away from the data readouts on the CRT in front of him. His gaze settled on the television monitor recording the shuttle's progress and his world went topsy-turvy. The flight director's face turned ashen as the monitor faithfully displayed the exploding shuttle. Gregory's breath caught in his throat.

I saw the explosion. At first, I kind of intellectualized it. I said, "That's solid-rocket booster separation." And then I said, "Boy, they certainly have improved the cameras, because I've never seen it so close before." And then, perhaps within a second or so, I realized that wasn't right, and I almost keyed my mike to say, "Godspeed, *Challenger!*"—but I didn't. I knew at that point that something horrible had happened.

He tried to tell himself the astronauts aboard *Challenger* had a chance. That, by some miracle, they had survived that holocaust ten miles above the earth. But inside, he knew. There was absolutely no chance. Words failed him. The horror of it overwhelmed him. The world around him shifted into slow motion. He felt detached from reality. Later, he would remember listening on the communication net. Listening to the public affairs officer (PAO) still talking and talking. Talking as if the mission was progressing normally. Talking on and on for several seconds, despite the horrific vision on the television monitor of the shattered, stricken *Challenger,* spinning and disintegrating as it traveled across the wide sky. It was the built-in delay of six to ten seconds before available data is displayed on the CRT. The PAO was still reading, his eyes glued to the CRT and the data it presented. Suddenly the data stopped, but the PAO continued to talk for a few seconds after that. The aural and visual impact made the setting surreal.

Suddenly, everybody in Mission Control realized what had happened.[19]

Cheering stopped in classrooms across the country. Noisemakers brought in for celebrations were slowly put down as shock and grief began to register on faces. Teachers were as stunned as their students. Words stumbled. Tears streaked cheeks.

Grief bent the families of the stricken astronauts like tall grass in a mighty wind.

Ron McNair's father and brothers had gone to Atlanta before the launch. They had seen a launch before and planned to go back to the Cape for the landing. Arriving home, his father turned on the television and fell asleep. Stirring long minutes later, his eyes opened to see the interminable taped replay of the accident on the television screen. "I thought," he recalled, "that it was one, big, horrible dream. But the networks showed the tape over and over again. And I realized that dreams don't repeat like that." Grief overwhelmed him. Perhaps somewhere in his psyche, he could still see his son's infectious smile and dancing eyes; hear, from some great distance, that saxophone sound that only Ron could make. Tears flowed freely. His eyes grew puffier, the circles under them darker. The age lines seemed deeper, and his lips tightened under the pencil-thin mustache. Carl, Sr., almost forced the words out: "He was one of the most important people in my life."[20]

Charles Bolden and his orbiter crew sat in the conference room of Building 4 at the Houston Space Center, watching the liftoff. Then came the explosion.

I didn't let myself think that what had happened, happened. I—I—guess—I really wanted to convince myself that the solids had really—had separated early—and I knew that was bad. But at least, there was a possibility that—that you'd see the orbiter come flying out of that thing and, you know, *somehow* they'd manage to—to get somewhere, or ditch. But it didn't take very long. They lost data. We were listening. We have all kinds of loops up on the table and that's kind of hard to—You *knew* what had happened!

When Charles Bolden talks about the accident, his voice breaks and wet tears gather in the corners of his eyes. Annapolis and the marine in him well up as if to dare him to become too emotional about this thing. But he can't help it. He does anyway. Because he and Ron McNair were close friends. Both born in South Carolina. More than that, they were fraternity brothers. McNair was an undergraduate Omega; Bolden pledged after coming to Houston. The memories came flooding back like multicolored ground cover in bloom. Flying together down to Cocoa, Florida, during their pledge period. McNair kind of like his big brother. Respect for his unbelievable brilliance; his determination to become a citizen of the world, despite the odds. Because of that, there was nobody with whom he refused to associate. He was earthy, not stuck on himself. "Ron was just as comfortable out on the block as he would be here in the center director's office," said Bolden.

Then Bolden remembered things they'd done together. Like down in Cocoa, in the projects. At a fraternity fish fry. Ron down there selling and smelling of fish, like everybody else. His karate talent. Going over to Houston's Third Ward, picking up kids and bringing them over to the space center gym. Working with them outside—practicing karate under the trees.

A sixth-degree black belt, McNair knew karate inside and out. He wanted his son, Reggie, to know the sport, too. And maybe that vision was one his wife, Cheryl, was to later recall—how he wanted his children to do well and always function as a family. Although his time as an astronaut was limited, she smiled later at the thought of how he used to put his little son into a basket and take him with him to karate practice. To watch and learn while his father taught the discipline of karate. Ron was the center of his family's world.

That was why Bolden rushed to the side of McNair's wife and family. To comfort and console, to provide necessary casualty assistance. There was insurance to discuss. Coordination with accountants and tax preparers. Funeral arrangements to be made. Public appearances.[21]

Out on the causeway, graduate student Charles Marge, a member of the MIT touring band, began taking pictures as soon as dawn arrived. He'd run up a nearby hill for a different angle shot when the explosion came. He missed the actual explosion, but his friends saw it. They watched in horror as the orange-colored plume emanated from the shuttle. Then Marge heard the people there on the causeway.

"An-h-h-h-h!" they soughed. "The teacher! The teacher!" Then someone mentioned Ron McNair. That he was on this flight. They couldn't believe it. "I just heard him talk at MIT," a guy said. The setting turned almost mystical for Marge:

> The strangest thing—it was a crystal clear day with no wind. And that cloud hung in the sky all day. It slowly diffused, it was white with a little gray, and every time we looked up all day, there was this cloud in the sky. And it was *that* cloud because there was nothing else in the sky at all.[22]

Except for the debris and pieces of *Challenger* raining into the Atlantic for what seemed an eternity.

CHAPTER 8

MIT Photo

REQUIEM

For those who knew Dr. Ronald E. McNair, there was the feeling that they and black America had lost a special angel. "Dad," said one of Professor Feld's sons, a college senior, "he's gone back to heaven."
—Dudley Clendinen, "Seven Lives, the Last Crew of the Challenger," New York Times, *5 February 1986*

Six weeks passed before searchers located *Challenger*'s crew module where it had crashed into the Atlantic at almost two thousand miles per hour. The obligation to mourn and dedicate could not wait. The need was too pressing.

At 4:00 P.M., Sunday, 2 February 1986, a special memorial service was held in Boston at the church to which Ron McNair belonged. The Rev. Dr. Leroy Attles remembered that "McNair was unpretentious in any way," and that he "had lost a good friend."[1]

At 3:00 P.M. the same day, in his hometown of Lake City, South

Carolina, a memorial service was held at the Wesley United Methodist Church. Governor Richard "Dick" Riley was there. The keynote speaker was the Rev. Jesse Jackson, like McNair an alumnus of North Carolina A&T. The address was vintage Jesse Jackson.

They had come, Jackson said, to celebrate the life and the legacy of Dr. Ron McNair. He had made his life's statement. Now he was gone to glory. Those left behind should put it in God's hands:

> On Sunday, the superbowl of football, a day of technological success, excellence and physical prowess. A day of ecstasy—high noon. Then, on Tuesday, in the twinkling of an eye, in world view, our sun was eclipsed at high noon. The superbowl of technology had failed. There was agony, the gnashing of teeth; trauma and despair. Our tin God was shattered. The bodies of our friends were dismembered. Our hearts were shattered. As Ezekiel said long ago, observing separated bones at the end of hupman extremities and limitations with no ability to rearrange them, "Lord God, *Thou* knowest!"

On that day, Jackson said, African Americans were at that point. Only God knew. Hearts were broken. Dreams had been reduced to nightmares. People felt robbed as the young, brave, courageous, and talented astronauts were snatched away without warning. Death alone is certain. But there were lessons to be learned in the tragedy:

> Is there honey in the rock? I submit to you that there are treasures. America is curious; in search of new frontiers together. On this journey were two women, a Jew, a Black, an Asian and White males. At its best, America tries to grow together, explore together, live together, die together. It was a rainbow in the sky. Progress always comes after sacrifice. Beyond sacrifice is discovery and greatness. Great dreams worth living for are worth dying for.

McNair had not been honored the preceding week, Reverend Jackson intimated, "because we didn't know who he was." He then drew an analogy: "If the innkeeper had known who Jesus was, as he lay restless in His mother's womb, as she stood before him in labor, asking, 'Is there room in the inn?'—he would have given her his bed. But he didn't know who He was." Every child, therefore, has a little of Ron McNair in him. Every child has a little astronaut in him. Ultimately, through education, "from the lowlands of South Carolina, to A&T, to MIT, and on to NASA, the genius of Dr. McNair was uncovered."

Flying high, Jackson pressed on. "He was a rejected stone, and transformed into a cornerstone. He was a scientist, with a profound God-consciousness. He was a prayer-deacon. He knew the finitude of modern technology, and yet, was startled by the infinity of God. He knew the universe was measured in light years."

Therefore, Jackson continued, McNair "was startled by the infinity of God. When he heard Him say, 'How great Thou art,' he had a deeper understanding." McNair, Jackson said, understood the rapture of the psalmist (Psalm 8:3–5):

> When I consider Thy heavens, the work of Thy fingers,
> The moon and the stars, which Thou has ordained;
> What is man, that Thou are mindful of him?
> And the son of man, that Thou visitest him?
> For Thou has made him a little lower than the angels,
> And hast crowned him with glory and honor.

Forcefully grasping the lectern, his knuckles glistening, Jackson raced to the finish line: "Dr. McNair was determined to be upward bound and heaven bound. Now our friend belongs to the ages. He is an Omega chapter. He took the wings of the morning, and now his soul is at rest with Thee."

Then the choir sang:

> Oh, Lord, my God, when I in awesome wonder
> Consider all the things Thy hands hath made;
> I see the sun, I hear the rolling thunder,
> Thy power throughout the Universe displayed.
> Then sings my soul, my savior God to Thee,
> How great Thou art; how great Thou art![2]

Dr. Donald Edwards, retired professor of physics at North Carolina A&T, McNair's first alma mater, recalled how strong Ron's wife,

Cheryl, was at the service. How, when an overzealous photographer kept edging closer for the ultimate shot, she never flinched. And how that photographer would not be denied, getting so close she was almost in Cheryl's face. How like Ron, he thought. How unpretentious. How unflappable.[3]

Across the country, teachers and students alike were still feeling the effects of the accident. Psychologists warned parents and teachers to play it gently with the children. The memory of the accident could scar them for life. "They were pretty stunned about it," remembered high-school teacher Bob Allen in northern California, "but they understood what was going on. They asked questions afterward and were pretty calm about it." Some teachers of high-school sophomores and juniors asked their students to write down their thoughts and feelings. They hoped the students would eventually assemble their notes and "send a letter to the families of those involved in this."

A teacher named Sweigert was "particularly upset" by McAuliffe's death. "It's more than me being involved in science," he said. "I think the fact that this was a teacher was something that had us all pretty excited. It was something a lot of teachers could identify with."[4]

Perhaps one of the more moving memorials to the last flight of *Challenger* came from poet-teacher Perie Longo of Santa Barbara, California. Under the auspices of the California Poets-in-the-Schools Program, she asked her sixth grade students at the Hollister School to put their feelings about the accident into poetic form.[5]

Struck by the irony of all those perfect flights before the accident, young Stacy Leabhard began her poem, *Gone,* with this first stanza:

> They said, "It's too perfect—
> Nothing will go wrong!"
> But it went wrong.
> They said, "What went wrong?"

And Danny Gonzalez wrote:

A Pilot's Point

> My stomach is queasy
> as if this is my last meal

but I am determined
It is the calm
before the storm
    Goodbye
    LIFT OFF
My heart is intense as
I go now
a starchild to be reborn.

And then Longo, an accomplished poet and author of *Milking The Earth,* wrote:

Analyzing the Data (After the *Challenger*)

I open the door for the cat
who won't leave me alone
four dawns after the explosion
to grass gold singing high
in natal light and last week's
funny dream
    Computer breakdown . . .
    inside the disk insert
    7 white plastic astronauts
    bonded together pop up
    when I insert my finger
    and explode
Later, time is a figure of speech,
I invite children into my dream
gone haywire on a blue sky screen
people clawing
at the relentless dragon
whose scales and fire we ride

An unexpected letter arrives
from the teacher whose voice
rushes through waves
to reach for the stars
    a sock retrieved and metal shoe
    that tried to race past time
Looking up I kick a hole in the grass

which sings this morning
there are no worksheets for lessons
that drift in from space in the rain
in the fire in the wind in the sea
in the heart a new constellation
in the sky after smoke from the funny dream
clears[6]

On 5 February 1986, plans moved ahead at the Massachusetts Institute of Technology for a memorial service honoring Ron McNair. The afternoon of 12 February, more than four hundred people gathered in Kresge Auditorium. Twin potted plants stood like sentinels beside the brightly lit podium on the darkened stage. A portrait of a smiling Ron McNair was projected onto a large screen. Low-key chatter wafted through the air, coming to an abrupt halt as Clarence G. Williams, special assistant to the MIT president, presented the opening remarks. Reverend Leroy Attles—the pastor of Ron's church; the keeper of the flame that had drawn Cheryl Moore and Ron McNair together in that church; the grieving minister who mourned the loss of a friend—gave the invocation. After a musical selection by the MIT gospel choir, friends of Ron McNair came forward to speak, one by one.

First was Paul E. Gray, president of MIT, who began with a quote from poet Stephen Spender: "I think continually of those who were truly great. Born of the sun, they traveled a short while towards the sun, and left the vivid air signed with their honour."

Gray and the four hundred had come there to remember and comfort each other in their remembrance of Ron McNair, one who was "truly born of the sun." Although McNair's time on the earth was short, that time "was one of stellar achievement, bright promise, clear vision and disarming and gracious generosity." A son of MIT, he stood out. A self-starting high achiever. A goal-setter extraordinaire, who not only met his goals, but exceeded them. Instinctively, Gray said, Ron understood that

He represented, for a whole generation of younger people at MIT and around the nation, a symbol, a shining example of what dedication and risk-taking and hard work and faith and self-confidence could achieve. The nation is diminished because of that terrible moment in this flight of *Challenger*.

What then remained, Gray noted, was "the task of communicating his dream—his wisdom—to the generations to come." Necessary, because McNair's example was an engine of sorts, with the power to ennoble, inspire, and "cause people to achieve impossible goals. His was the contribution of the great teacher—a contribution that persists from generation to generation, and we are his acolytes."[7]

A number of McNair's friends followed Dr. Gray to the podium. Dr. Shirley A. Jackson, research physicist at AT&T Bell Laboratories, the first black woman to receive a Ph.D. from MIT. Ron McNair's thesis advisor, Professor Michael S. Feld, director of MIT's spectroscopy laboratory. The University of Maryland's Dr. S. James Gates, from the department of physics and astronomy. Dr. William W. Quivers, Jr., of the physics department at Wellesley College. Dr. John B. Turner, MIT's associate provost and associate dean of the graduate school. Dr. Michael E. Fant, president of the Black Alumni of MIT (BAMIT), and Gregory C. Chisolm, a graduate student in MIT's department of mechanical engineering. Jackson, Gates, Quivers, and Fant were all graduate students with McNair at MIT. Williams and Turner first met McNair when he arrived at the school.

And, although not listed in the program, Cheryl McNair took the stage. She seemed small, almost lost on the wide stage behind the tall lectern. She wore glasses she did not normally wear in public and her hair cascaded to her shoulders. The elevated microphone, sitting high on an extension from the lectern, seemed to float in the air in front of her, while over her right shoulder, the smiling projection of her late husband looked down at her and out over the four hundred.

Cheryl McNair thanked everyone for coming, for the love and consideration that had drawn them all. She conveyed Ron's thanks and the exhilaration she knew he would feel at being so honored.

Dr. Donald Edwards sat in the audience, as did members of the McNair family. Edwards was so moved that he thought, I don't care what these other people do, I'm going to stand up and give her an ovation when she's finished. And then Cheryl read again the now-famous words her husband had uttered and written:

Truly, there is no more beautiful sight than to see the earth from space beyond. This planet is an exquisite oasis. Warmth emanates from the earth when you look at her from space. I could no more look at the earth and see anything bad than I could look at a smiling little girl or boy and see a bank robber. It's impossible to see anything but goodness. My wish is that we would allow this planet to be the beautiful oasis that she is, and allow ourselves to live more in the peace that she generates.

Before Dr. Edwards could think about it, the entire audience sprang to its feet and applause crescendoed. Years later, he still chuckled at the memory with deep satisfaction.[8]

Six weeks later, searchers found the wreckage of the crew module strewn along the sea bottom in about ninety feet of water off the Florida coast. Nearby, they found parts of the orbiter's forward fuselage. From what the experts could determine, "it was conceded that some, if not all of the crew members, may have been alive until the moment the cabin section hit the water, although they were almost certainly unconscious."[9]

By June, Paul Gray was able to tell MIT's 1986 graduating class that the governing board had voted to name the building housing MIT's Center for Space Research after Ron McNair. "The McNair Building," said Gray, "will stand as a permanent reminder to future generations at MIT of the grace and significance of extraordinary achievement tempered by an uncommon wisdom and an abiding love of humankind." Looking proudly over the sea of graduates, he added, "I could wish no better model for you."[10]

On 10 December, MIT spent an entire day celebrating the dedication of the McNair Building. From 10:00 A.M. until noon, there was the Ronald E. McNair Dedication Symposium, "The Space Frontier: Hanging It Over the Edge," taking its cue from an earlier appearance by McNair after his first spaceflight. At that time, he had shared with students his ideas on how to be a winner: "Stepping past our place of comfort to walk over to the edge of our abilities and then move beyond that edge." Distinguished speakers talked of the ultimate goals of space travel. Of how fragile and unpredictable science is, calling for an increased responsibility in realizing ultimate human aspiration and "prospects as a species." Of the future of astronomy in space; of seeing perhaps "ten or fifteen billion light years ago, when the universe began." Of experiencing the space frontier through an astronaut's eyes, verifying what McNair had seen while out in space.

Dedication ceremonies commenced at 2:30 P.M., in the Edgerton Lecture Hall. Colonel Charles Bolden was the keynote speaker. He told the audience that in the future he envisioned young men and women coming to MIT and clamoring, "I want to go where Ron McNair went. I want to go where Ron McNair dared! I want to go where Ron McNair chose to start his life taking risks! Young men and women will come from all over the country, all over the world!" Bolden observed that it had been a risk for McNair to leave South Carolina to study in North Carolina, and it was a greater risk to leave there to study at MIT.

Applause erupted when Bolden said, "MIT didn't make Ron. Ron McNair was made before he came to MIT. But we will allow you, we will allow you to share in the pride!"

When the applause faded, Bolden quoted Horace Mann: "Be ashamed to die until you've won some victory for humanity." Ron McNair had won lots of victories for humanity, and that was what would bring young men and women to MIT, Bolden concluded.

MIT president Paul Gray again honored the memory of McNair. A multidimensioned man. Musician. Athlete. Rich in spiritual life. An intellect. Husband and father. An advocate of hard work; of achievement, promise, vision, self-confidence. Integrity. Wisdom. Judgment. Generosity. A builder of bridges between people, using his talents to reach people of all races and cultures, while retaining his own cultural identity. "Ron McNair was, as Charles Bolden pointed out, 'a real, live hero.'"

Cheryl McNair then captivated the audience, thanking those present for "the consideration, respect and love it took to motivate an entire community to come together to do just such a dedication." Showing that "both she and her husband loved MIT," she presented a MIT insignia letter "T" to President Gray, which had been retrieved from the floor of the Atlantic Ocean after the crash. Ron McNair had put it aboard the ill-fated shuttle with the intention of returning it to the university as a special remembrance of the flight.[11]

Escorted by David S. Saxon, chairman of the MIT Corporation, Cheryl and the couple's two children, four-year-old Reginald, and two-year-old Joy, walked slowly to the lobby of the new McNair Building. The McNair family—Ron's mother and father, Pearl and Carl McNair, Sr.; his brothers and sisters, Carl Jr., Eric, Mary, and Linda; his uncles, Clifton and Paul; and Cheryl's parents, Harold and Vertell Moore—followed. There, Cheryl, Reginald, and Joy opened the draperies covering the brand new inscription:

RONALD E. McNAIR BUILDING

NAMED IN MEMORY OF

RONALD ERWIN McNAIR, Ph.D. 1977

Scientist Astronaut Alumnus

My wish is that we would allow this planet
to be the beautiful oasis that she is,
and allow ourselves to live more in the
peace that she generates.

Three hundred people watched the dedication over closed-circuit television from the Edgerton Building.[12]

The requiem for Ron McNair was almost complete. Except for others who had known him at more relaxed moments, like old Elihu Lumpkin, a construction worker back in Hartford, who still sat on the bar stools in Jerry Mack's Bar and Restaurant. "He was just a regular guy," Lumpkin told Kim S. Hirsh, a staff reporter for the *New Haven Register*. "He'd be sitting here lookin' like the rest of us!"[13] And there was John Thompson, a brick mason, also something of a philosopher, who said, "For us black people the loss was compounded. We don't have too many of them—this man was a scientist and an educator. It'll take many a kid to fill his shoes, and many a man to walk where he walked." Thompson said he hoped Ron McNair would be remembered as a pioneer, for "Any man can achieve if he just applies himself!" His gnarled hands gently picked up and raised a glass of beer to his lips for a slow sip, and then he asserted, "We'll probably see more Ron McNairs—but he left a big impression on people. I know he left a big impression on people here!"[14]

Then everyone looked around at Uncle Jerry, sitting there, a big picture of his nephew in his blue flight suit, standing upright on the bar next to him, inscribed at the top in big, block letters: "Uncle Jerry." He'd like to forget last January twenty-eighth, he said. "I'm not going to do anything. I would like to put it in the back of my mind and make it stay there. But I know it won't."[15]

CHAPTER 9

STASIS

"He stood there almost in stunned silence," said presidential spokesman Larry Speakes of Ronald Reagan when the president watched television replays of the shuttle accident. "You could read the concern, the sorrow, and the anxiety on his face as he watched." Shaken, the president ordered an immediate investigation, promising that "there will be no further shuttle flights until space officials are absolutely certain as a human being can be that such missions are safe."

For the first time in history, a State of the Union speech was delayed so the president could speak to the nation. Flags flew at half staff on 29 January 1986, a day for mourning and remembering. "The astronauts wanted to serve, and they have done it for all Americans," said the president. For all its success, America was still a neophyte in space:

We've grown used to wonders in this century. It's hard to dazzle us. But for twenty-five years, the United States space program has been doing just that. We've grown used to the idea of space and perhaps we forget that we've only just begun. We're still pioneers. They, the members of the *Challenger* crew, were pioneers.

Then Reagan spoke to the thousands of children who had been watching and waiting to hear from Christa McAuliffe. "I know it's hard to understand, but sometimes painful things like this happen. It's all part of the process of exploration and discovery. It's a part of taking a chance and expanding man's horizons." The future, the president added, did not belong to the fainthearted, but to the brave. "The *Challenger* crew was pulling us into the future and we'll continue to follow them."[1]

If the president had any doubts about the continuation of the space program, they were probably dispelled when Vice President George Bush returned from the launch site at Cape Canaveral, where the wife of *Challenger* commander Dick Scobee approached him.

"Please," she said, "don't let this stop the space program!" Only hours had passed since the accident. Bush also reported that the families of the stricken astronauts had expressed a wish to grieve together at Houston's Johnson Space Center. It was a decision apparently welcomed by the president. Not only was it a chance to demonstrate the country's continued commitment to space exploration, it was a chance to show that the entire U.S. government cared. On 31 January 1986, President Reagan and his wife, Nancy, flew to Houston to participate in a memorial service honoring the seven astronauts.[2]

The distinguished committee appointed by the president to investigate the accident swung into action. Chaired by former Secretary of State William P. Rogers, the committee included a score of prominent Americans. Among them were astronauts Neil Armstrong and Sally Ride, and Brig. Gen. Charles Yeager.

A complete review of available data was ordered, to include all reports and records. A number of tests were performed in support of written materials. The availability of telemetric and photographic data, plus analysis of debris recovered from the Atlantic Ocean, pointed early on to the possible conclusion that the trouble triggering the chain of circumstances leading to the explosion began with the right-hand solid-rocket booster.[3] Enhanced photographic evidence further supported the preliminary conclusion.

The committee's investigative work was supplemented by members of the astronaut corps working on special assignment. Colonel Guy Bluford worked with a group whose primary function was to study existing procedures and design requirements. Because he had worked with *Spacelab*, Bluford concentrated on that system's design and requirements to determine "if we were safely doing what we think we should."[4] Over the next year and a half, Col. Charles Bolden was to wear several hats. The first was as a member of a working group that concentrated on mission operations, by tracking training concepts and procedures.

Hardware wasn't the issue, it was *how* things were done. Securing accurate documentation of how missions were planned, describing how flight and ground crew training was structured. Were any of these things a factor in the accident? After six months, when the Rogers Commission began preparing its final report, Bolden moved on to begin a year-long stint as technical assistant to the Johnson Space Center director.[5] Fred Gregory remained in CAPCOM until summer, going on to NASA as chief of operational safety, where he helped organize that program.[6] Astronaut-aspirant Mae Jemison in Los Angeles had her security-clearance checks postponed and saw the selection process shut down. She continued to hope.[7]

Retrieval and analysis of the recovered *Challenger* wreckage helped solidify the coming conclusions as to what *really* happened. On 6 June 1986, the commission published its final report, concluding that:

> In view of the findings the commission [found] that the cause of the *Challenger* accident was the failure of the pressure seal in the aft field joint of the right solid-rocket motor. The failure was due to a faulty design unacceptably sensitive to a number of factors. These factors were the effects of temperature, physical dimensions, the character of materials, the effects of reusability, processing, and reaction to dynamic loading.[8]

Hidden in all of that were serious administrative and procedural errors that, "rocked NASA to its core and seriously threatened the agency and the very future of the American manned space program." Within NASA, "the pressure to launch was always high," as was the pressure of astronaut training. Perhaps most damaging of all was the apparent reluctance on the part of NASA launch and flight staff to communicate adequately with outside contractors. The glaring example was their ignoring urgent warnings from the designers and builders of the solid-rocket boosters (Morton-Thiokol) to consider delaying the *Challenger 10* launch until the weather improved.

Beyond that, the evidence suggested that the suspect O-rings had been a problem for years. The solid-rocket boosters used on previous flights showed evidence of damage to the O-rings, to the point where they had nearly burned through. This was especially so on STS-8, the celebrated mission on which Guy Bluford rode. Ostensibly, a disaster similar to the *Challenger* accident had been narrowly averted.[9]

It seems the astronauts didn't really know how serious the O-ring problem was. It was a kind of rumor; a darkling thing that somehow didn't really exist. As Frederick Gregory has since put it: "The criterion was, if it doesn't fail, it's okay." He recalled that "my commander, Bob Overmyer, was pretty upset when he did see that a lot of erosion had taken place!" A kind of mute acceptance of fate seemed to have evolved: "That was another era. We were hanging out. We had accepted a very high risk deal. All of us bought into that."[10]

Charles Bolden is not quite as accepting. In his view, the accident never should have happened, because it was avoidable. "We screwed up," as far as the O-rings were concerned, he said, adding that it was up to NASA to make sure an accident like that never occurred again. Guy Bluford's first flight wasn't the only one on which O-ring degeneration had been noted. According to Bolden:

Fred's first flight was almost as bad. Fred's flight was about as bad as you could get and survive—you know—without getting burned. And my first flight was not all that red hot. But, at the time, none of us knew about that. And there are people in management who probably didn't know about it, I would imagine. It's really hard to describe to people, because they will think you're saying somebody conspired to do this. And that's not the case at all. We had people who were very well-intentioned, and they worried day and night, but they convinced themselves that we knew and understood what was going on because it happened so often.

Ideally, Bolden continued, if the O-ring problem had been "a one-time thing," it very well might have gotten everyone's attention and the problem might have been fixed. "But we were comfortable that we understood it, and we didn't do anything about it."[11]

Guy Bluford also took that middle road. When asked what his family thought of the risks involved, he said, "They became more aware that there was a fair amount of hazard associated, aware that the business I was in had some degree of risk to it."[12]

As a group, the astronauts weren't silent about the fact that they had not been told about the O-ring problem. Once upon a time, it had been routine for astronauts to be involved with contractors in the development of the hardware they were to use, but those days had long since passed. The commission recommended that their relationship be reestablished, and several current and former astronauts were assigned to "influential posts" at key locations within NASA for that purpose.

On 15 August 1986, President Reagan gave NASA the approval to order a sixth orbiter. Tests were run on a redesigned SRB field joint. Fits and starts described the NASA space program until a launch date for *Discovery* was set for February 1988. The wreckage of *Challenger* was buried and sealed in deserted underground silos at Cape Canaveral Air Force Station.[13]

The two-year stasis in which NASA had found itself was nearing an end. Again, the agency began to look to the stars as several thousand workers at the Houston Space Center paused on 28 January 1987, one year after the *Challenger* accident, and recalled the words of President Reagan in a speech there on 31 January 1986:

The future is not free—the story of all human progress is one of struggle against all odds. We learned again that this America, which Abraham Lincoln called the last, best hope of man on Earth, was built on heroism and noble sacrifice. It was built by men and women like our seven star voyagers, who answered a call beyond duty, who gave more than was expected or required, and who gave it little thought of worldly reward.[14]

In California, Mae C. Jemison, bidding to become America's first black woman into space, underwent a kind of stasis herself. Not only had her application to NASA been placed in limbo and the routine background checks stopped, she was now getting telephone calls from her concerned family:

> My mother called, asking if I was sure I really wanted to [become an astronaut]. My father said he understood and things like this happen. My sister called and said she was a little nervous. I said, "Whoa, guys! This is it. I'm going to do it. And yeah, I'm really sad [about the accident], I'm really sorry, but I'm going to do it!"[15]

Innately quiet, except when it counted, Jemison hadn't discussed her application to NASA with her coworkers at the Cigna Health Plan. The calls, for all her bravado, did give her pause. She'd met Ron McNair once and thought highly of him. She had been watching television that morning and observed the demise of the seven astronauts as she was getting ready for work:

> All I could think is, you've got to be kidding! No way! And then they showed the video and I thought, yeah, it looked like it exploded. I remember thinking there must be some kind of rescue attempt or some kind of rescue that's going to happen. I remember hearing them saying that they were to drop frogmen into the area to take a look, but that they couldn't go in until the pieces stopped falling.

She thought there was no way McNair could be dead. It was a huge mistake. It wasn't fair. It wasn't right. Despite her personal denials, the television verified that everyone was dead. It was the first time in her life a public event like that had affected her so. She called in late for work. Her patients were rescheduled. She sat very still for an hour, listening.

Something deep within her psyche flared. Something about the relative unfairness in the way the media focused on Christa McAuliffe when "there were other people on the Shuttle"—an African American, an Asian American, another woman, and two white men. Journalists might have called McAuliffe the "newspeg" of the disaster story; the pretty, young teacher killed on this *Challenger* flight was the "hook." But for Jemison, the way it was reported was an aggravation, another failure of an American society that would not allow equal weight to be given to all parts of a story.

It wasn't fair, Jemison thought, to talk so much about Christa and appear (at first, anyway) to forget about Ron and Ellison, Dick and Michael, Gregory or Judith.[16]

The thought rankled, but Mae pressed on with her application. She was finally selected by NASA as an astronaut candidate in June 1987.

The *Challenger* accident dealt NASA and its schedules a severe blow. The year 1986 was to have been the most ambitious since the moon landings. Fifteen flights had been planned, plus four additional ones for *Challenger*. Telescopes carried aloft to look at Halley's Comet. A probe to Jupiter. A craft from Europe, designed to sling itself around Jupiter so it could observe the poles of the sun. The Hubble telescope. In 1987, there were to be nineteen more flights, six of them by *Challenger*.[17]

Despite the obvious need to get the United States back into the space business, progress seemed inordinately slow. But, as Charles Bolden noted, the resolve was to be smart. The Rogers Commission's report recommended that the O-rings in the solid-rocket boosters and, indeed, the "whole rocket motor design" be evaluated. The manufacturer, Morton-Thiokol of Utah, spent thousands of hours doing just that, resulting in several major design changes.[18]

Searing and burning itself into the human consciousness, the accident was an event not very many Americans alive at the time would ever forget. People like Valerie K. Sorosiak, then living in Charlotte, North Carolina, with her family. She had been busy dressing and getting breakfast for her three children—Rebecca, five; Eric, three; and one-year-old Jessica. She knew about the launch and wanted to watch it, but because of her busy involvement with her children, she'd missed the actual launch. Jessica reclined in her arms as Valerie, tuning into a replay, turned on the television.

All day, she tried to answer the children's questions as she "sat in shock, unable to leave the television with its continuous coverage." She needed to find an answer to the elusive, "Why?"

It didn't come until early the next morning. It had to do with the need to share the grief of the nation. To do something, she picked up a pen and wrote

The Challenger

We watched with wonder in our eyes
Excitement took our breath away
Those silver wings reached toward the skies
The *Challenger* left Earth today.

Its trail of fire—an awesome sight
Its brilliance in the blue sky shown
Earthbound dreams soared into flight
Free to explore the vast unknown.

As *Challenger* raced out toward heaven
Our thoughts and prayers were turned
To that very special crew of seven
Our love and pride they'd earned.

In just an instant hearts stood still
Our minds refuse to comprehend
That midst this morning's winter chill
The *Challenger* met its end.

The shock and horror slowly grew
Burning tears stung our eyes
In our hearts and minds we knew
That fireball claimed seven lives.

We grieve the loss of precious lives
But they didn't die in vain
By making sure their dream survives
Humanity will gain!

For Christa, Judy and Ellison
Ron, Dick, Mike and Gregory
Another journey's just begun—
Their souls embrace eternity.[19]

On Saturday, 10 January 1987, the city of Jackson, Mississippi renamed the theater of their Russell C. Davis Planetarium the Ronald E. McNair Space Theater.[20]

CHAPTER 10

STAR GRAZING

It was over two years before the singsong countdown cadence was again heard from NASA's launch control. Shuttle flights finally recommenced on 29 September 1988 with the launch of *Discovery*. Thirty-one astronauts rode those seven million pounds of thrust as they flung brilliant fingers of fire into the sky after the likes of *Atlantis, Columbia,* and *Discovery* again through most of 1989.[1]

No African-American astronaut would fly until 22 November 1989, when Col. Fred Gregory, serving as spacecraft commander, took the orbiter *Discovery* aloft. On board were the pilot, John Blaha, and three mission specialists, Manley Carter, F. Story Musgrave, and Kathryn Thornton. Theirs was a Department of Defense mission, and the orbiter carried military and other "secondary payloads." The five-day flight concluded with a landing at Edwards Air Force Base on 27 November 1989.[2]

On 24 April 1990, Col. Charles Bolden again went into space, this time as pilot aboard *Discovery* (STS-31). The five-day mission's primary objective was orbiting the $2-billion Hubble Space Telescope. Loren Shriver commanded the flight. Mission specialists Bruce

McCandless and Steve Hawley were the Hubble Space Telescope experts. Kathy Sullivan and McCandless were set to take a walk in space if a problem should arise with the telescope during deployment.

Named in honor of astronomer Edwin P. Hubble, the telescope is as tall as a four-story building and has a ninety-four-inch primary mirror. The largest telescope ever placed above the earth's atmosphere, it was designed to test Hubble's theory of an "ever-expanding universe" through scientific studies never before possible. Astronomers would be able to see targets in space seven times better than they ever could; expanding some 350 times the area of observable space. Highly significant is the fact that it could be maintained by shuttlecraft after initial deployment into space.[3]

It was dark when the astronauts were driven out to the launchpad. There is something special about the orbiter on a launch day, Charles Bolden observed. "It somehow seems alive," strangely malleable. After entering through the side hatch, the astronauts were strapped into their seats minutes later.

"T-minus-twenty seconds and counting," droned Launch Control. T-minus-15, 14, 13—T-minus-10, 9, 8, 7, 6, 5, 4—

Bolden and the rest of the crew heard the deep growl denoting readiness for takeoff. "We have gone for main engine start. We have liftoff of *Discovery!*"

It felt like a normal airplane ride. The orbiter's a giant, but it's gentle. The ride's not usually violent, but for this mission the crew members wore bright-orange pressurized suits and bounced around inside as the motion set up a vibrational patter.

Launch Control's chatter knew no bounds. "Another mission is on as seven million pounds of thrust hurl the shuttle skyward. The shuttle clears the launch tower, turns out over the Atlantic and quickly accelerates!"

Shallow cloud cover hung over the launchpad as the mighty spacecraft roared toward, then through it, flashing out topside on a flaring tower of fire, trailing long smoke plumes in the November air.

Mach 1, Mach 2, Mach 3!" a voice from Launch Control enthused. "At the two-minute mark shuttle is traveling over three thousand miles per hour and has reached an altitude of twenty-eight miles!"[4]

This was no ordinary ascent. With the Hubble Space Telescope aboard, they had to go for a direct orbital insertion at the desired altitude. It was a record for the shuttle; a record for a circular orbit in any spacecraft that didn't go to the moon. There was no orbital maneuver burn; they went for orbital insertion at 331 miles above the earth. The previous altitude record for a shuttle was 250 miles. If they had been able to do what the Hubble people wanted, they'd have gone even higher. But they couldn't. They had used half their propellant getting there, and the remainder was needed to get home. The cargo bay doors, carrying the radiators needed to maintain even temperatures in the constant day/night cycle of earth orbit, were opened.[5]

On their first day in space, the crew checked out the Remote Manipulator System, which they would use to lift and maneuver the mammoth Hubble Space Telescope up and out of the cargo bay. They also limbered up special tools they might need if an extravehicular spacewalk was needed to fully extend the telescope's solar arrays. Two of the astronauts conducted prebreathing tests of the spacesuits they would wear should an EVA be necessary.

On flight day two, the crew was given a go for deployment on the telescope. When the release opportunity arrived, Steve Hawley manned the RMS controls. He grappled with the telescope, chiding it, slowly moving it up. Loren Shriver, the mission commander, maneuvered the orbiter holding altitude while the telescope was in motion so close to the ship. Earth loomed in the background as, finally, the telescope was unberthed and deployed in its own orbit, the sun glinting on its surfaces. Far below the long, brown topography of the Andes and Chile, the blue-green waters of the Pacific arched away into infinity under bits and pieces of white cloud.

The telescope's solar array panels began to deploy. One deployed nicely; the other balked on the first attempt. On the second attempt, only partial deployment was achieved. After an in-suit, prebreathing period, Sullivan and McCandless entered the airlock for a contingency spacewalk. But the balky solar array cooperated, and Sullivan and McCandless didn't have to go. The Hubble Space Telescope will remain out there for fifteen to twenty years. Every five years or so, an orbiter will be sent up to replace any failed hardware.

With the space telescope in position, the astronauts began conducting other experiments, including a University of Alabama protein crystal-growth project.

Sullivan took photographs of Baja for her father.[6] Bolden and Shriver conducted an orbiter systems check to ensure things would go smoothly the day before landing.

Finally, the outer doors were closed. Shriver and Bolden slowed the ship down several hundred miles per hour and put it in a tail-first position by firing the two orbital maneuvering system engines. Once slowed, they turned *Discovery* back to a nose-forward position. Reentry began about eighty miles out. They were still moving about 17,500 miles per hour, literally grating against earth's atmosphere. Tiles began to glow red hot. *Discovery* became a meteor, hurtling deeper into earth's atmosphere toward home. Then it became a glider, its wing ailerons helping to make a series of turns that dissipated even more energy, slowing the orbiter to just over two hundred miles per hour for touchdown. An air force chase plane drew alongside as Bolden lowered the landing gear.

"They're down," the chase pilot conferred by radio, "pick up your feet. Five, four, three, two, one, touchdown!"

Twin puffs of smoke billowed out as the main landing gear settled on the runway, the nose wheel following ten seconds later.

"Welcome home, *Discovery!* Beautiful. Beautiful," a voice chimed over the radio.[7]

In June, Bolden visited Annapolis, Maryland, and the Parole Elementary School. He told the kids about the mission and explained why the Hubble telescope was up there in the first place.

"Air, like water, bends light," he said. "That's why we put the telescope *outside* the earth's atmosphere. It enables us to see things farther away than ever before."

Bolden showed them slides of Mexico, the Pacific Ocean, and Brazil, all taken through the eyes of the telescope, and pointed out the extreme detail possible.

"The photos are so clear, it's like being in an airplane! What Hubble showed us was that where we thought there was only one star, there were actually two. It has already made a major contribution."

In neighboring Truxton Park, Bolden intrigued a gathering of about fifty youngsters by pulling a nickel out of his pocket and telling them that if he could stand on the moon with that coin, "The Hubble Space Telescope could read from the earth the words, 'In God We Trust.' " That's clarity of vision, and he applied that idea to their lives and their futures.

The telescope story illustrated, Bolden said, how the youngsters should keep their sights on their goals.

The earth's atmosphere distorts images of stars the same way water distorts the location of a penny at the bottom of a pond. Reach for the coin and you may not touch it the first time. But once those lenses are focused (the same way those youngsters should focus on their goals, Bolden told them), the Hubble Space Telescope will allow scientists to see things in space, better than ever.[8]

On 24 November 1991, the air at the Kennedy Space Center was charged with excitement. *Atlantis* sat on the launchpad, looking sleek, able, and ready for mission STS-44. Another DOD mission, its major goal was orbiting the Defense Support Program (DSP) missile-warning satellite. Originally scheduled for blastoff on 19 November, problems were discovered with the upper stage rockets designed to lift the satellite into a 22,300-mile geostationary orbit. Five days were required to replace the unit. Set now for launch a little after 6:30 A.M. on the twenty-fourth, a leaky liquid oxygen valve was discovered in the external tank. Countdown went on hold while the leak was stopped. Then a satellite meandered into the programmed flight path and another hold was ordered to prevent a collision during launch.

Already aboard, the crew waited. Fred Gregory was the mission commander. His pilot was Terence T. "Tom" Hendricks. Three mission specialists were aboard: Mario Runco, Jr., James S. Voss, and F. Story Musgrave. The payload specialist was Thomas J. Hennen.[9] After many weeks and months, Gregory had completed his commander's routine. Determining mission goals. Gathering written biographies of his crew. Formulating his ideas of how the mission should be run. Getting the crew together to "basically let them know what my rules are— how I like to run things." They all talked about the mission. No tasks were assigned at first. The idea was to simply "flow with the idea of the flight" and its ultimate goals.

Now they lay strapped in their seats, waiting for the launch director to clear them. After the hold to avoid a collision with the passing satellite, the launch crew had replenished the oxygen lost as a result of the leaky valves in the external tank. Then there was a planned hold at T-minus-nine minutes, which was stretched an additional ten minutes. Finally, they heard launch director Robert Sieck doing his final prelaunch team poll. He got to the waiting *Atlantis* crew. Were they ready?

"*Atlantis* is ready, Bob," came Fred Gregory's reassuring voice. "We're ready to burn paint!"

"Copy that," Sieck responded, smiling to himself at the thoroughness of Gregory and his crew, noting all the fresh paint on the pad during one of the preflight walkdowns. "I think we've put this off long enough, Fred. So if the next nine minutes go okay, you'll get to do that!"

At 6:44 P.M. the engines ignited and paint burned as huge clouds of smoke billowed from Launchpad 39-A. *Atlantis* rose like a flare through the clear Florida night. On the ground below, smoke oozed like a sticky fog, glowing in the illumination of floodlights.[10]

Mission specialist James Voss had settled in to really enjoy the ride, but then he looked over at Musgrave.

"Story," he began, "how are you doing?"

"I'm scared to death," Musgrave said tightly. "The older I get, the more scared I get!"

Maybe that was justified. Even though it had begun without any problems, it was, after all, his fourth shuttle flight.

Atlantis scribed its fiery path across the sky like a falling star going home and moved into its first orbit. The crew went into "orbit ops" like the well-trained people they were, preparing the DSP satellite for space. About an hour and a half before deployment, Gregory began maneuvering *Atlantis* into the deploy attitude. At twenty minutes past midnight, Voss and Runco sent the electronic commands that caused the canvas covers to pull back from the DSP's sensors. They watched as the lines pulling back the covers began to "float like jellyfish" in cold space, then were drawn into "cup-shaped receptacles, like being drawn down a drain."

Thirteen minutes later, the crew released the latches that clamped the satellite in the payload bay. The satellite popped up about a foot. Two minutes later, Voss put the inertial upper-stage tilt table in motion, the stack of the DSP swiveling twenty-nine degrees above the payload bay. The satellite was transferred to its own internal power. On the ground, the flight director polled flight control stations for their go for deployment. The *Atlantis* crew was ready.

"*Atlantis!*" crackled CAPCOM's voice. "Houston. You are go for deploy?"

"Roger, Houston! We are go for deploy. We have released the umbilicals! Good release!"

The crew raised the tilt table to 58.5 degrees. It took over three minutes to complete the movement. And then the stack of the huge satellite began to rise from its berth, looking for all the world like the leaning tower of Pisa over the top of the crew compartment.

The staff of Houston Control Center held their breath.

Springs flexed, angling the satellite off the support cradle that had held it. Houston breathed again. So did Voss.

"Good deploy, Houston! On time. DSP *Liberty* is on its way!"

Everybody looked at old Voss. He'd coined a new name for the satellite. *Liberty.* It stuck as the crew christened the DSP before it drifted off into space, quickly disappearing into the darkness.

Gregory applied a short burst of the orbiter's thrusters to pull it away to ensure separation from the satellite. Fifteen minutes later, Gregory did a seventeen-second separation burn, placing *Atlantis* forty-five miles above and behind DSP *Liberty*. One hour after deployment, the satellite's first internal burn fired, raising its orbit to "geostationary altitude." A little over six hours later, the second satellite rocket fired, finalizing its geostationary orbit.

The second day of the mission began with the voice of *Star Trek*'s Captain Jean-Luc Picard sending greetings to the crew and also defining the remaining goals of the mission:

Space—the final frontier. This is the voyage of the Space Shuttle *Atlantis*. Its ten-day mission, to explore new methods of remote sensing and observations of the planet Earth, to seek out new data on radiation in space and a new understanding of the effects of microgravity on the human body, to boldly go where two hundred and fifty-five men and women have gone before!

Thus defined, crew duties were both medical and military in nature. A series of medical tests called the Extended Duration Orbiter Project was designed to combat the effects of prolonged weightlessness. The military tasks helped determine what could be seen from space and the way humans find and look at selected targets.

That afternoon, the Russian *Mir* space station angled towards them, twinkling starlight. From twenty-five miles away, it zoomed by incredibly fast. The next day Cosmonaut Sergei Krikalev sent greetings to the *Atlantis* crew, which were returned in kind.

As *Atlantis* cruised over the Pacific on the fourth flight day, typhoon *Yuri* captured the astronauts' attention. The biggest storm they'd ever seen, it stretched twelve hundred miles in diameter, with winds gusting to 180 miles per hour. The walls of its eye were deep and sheer. Gregory was awed by the size of it when he realized that, even traveling at five miles per second, it took *Atlantis* all of three minutes to pass over the storm.

Thanksgiving Day dawned. There was no holiday for the crew; experiments continued as planned. Minor hardware anomalies were addressed. Everyone looked forward to Thanksgiving dinner in space. It was to be the only meal during the flight when the entire crew would eat together on the middeck. Preparations were under way, but before the meal could be served, there was cause for alarm.

A Russian *Kosmos 851* rocket, launched 27 August 1976, and still orbiting the earth, threatened to collide with *Atlantis,* or at least come closer to the shuttle than safety regulations allowed. Flight rules required avoidance maneuvers if "another spacecraft or debris pass within 2.7 nautical miles of the orbiter, or 1.1 nautical miles to the side or below it." *Atlantis* would come too close on its present trajectory.

Now it was Gregory's show. Performing only the second collision avoidance maneuver in the history of the shuttle program, he did a reaction control system burn for seven seconds, changing *Atlantis*'s course, passing *Kosmos 851* 24.2 nautical miles ahead, 2.4 nautical miles below, and 20.7 nautical miles north of the Russian rocket. It might seem nerve-racking to the uninitiated, but Gregory asserted in a postflight briefing that "it's much safer than driving on the freeway."[11]

After Thanksgiving dinner with most of the fixings, the crew broadcast greetings to friends and family. Said Commander Gregory as the television transmission began:

> We wanted to say happy Thanksgiving to everyone in America from the Space Shuttle *Atlantis* and the crew of STS-44. We ate our Thanksgiving dinner just about an hour ago. Our meal was prepared by Jim Voss and Tom Hennen while the rest of us were busy. They were slaving over the oven and in the kitchen for an hour and prepared a scrumptious meal of turkey and gravy, some noodles, fresh cranberry sauce and some pumpkin delights—all the fixings of a traditional Thanksgiving. The only thing absent was family and friends, but you're with us in our hearts.

Although scheduled for a ten-day mission, the seventh flight day proved unlucky and they were to be brought home early—a Minimal Duration Mission (MDM). It was a shame, too, because the crew was getting excited about the Auburn football game, due to be played that afternoon.

The Inertial Measurement Units (IMUs) that measure changes in the shuttle's orientation were the cause of the problem. Inside their containers, each IMU contained things the layman might call gewgaws, but which NASA people call "a system of gyroscopes and acceler-ometers which sense changes in position and velocity of the shuttle."

The name of the game was to have at least two working in good order at all times. While one IMU could give enough data to land a shuttle, two made for greater accuracy. Three were employed in or-der to provide redundancy and safety. The second IMU had been turned off as a power-saving device because of the scheduled ten-day flight. Turned on for a routine check, its electronics went wild.

"It's like driving a car with a headlight burned out and making sure you don't stay out on the highway for long after dark. You still have enough headlight to guide you, but you don't want to take chances!"

Gregory got out his malfunction procedures book, eager to find a solution to the problem. Not much could be done. CAPCOM sug-gested a test. Gregory ran it. Finally, CAPCOM ran out of ideas on the IMU and declared that the unit had failed. Another failed IMU, and the problem would be as big as the proverbial "boogy bear" some folks talk about. In midmorning, Mission Control advised Gregory that the mission would indeed be shortened. They were to land at Edwards, but desert winds threatened a delay. That afternoon, the winds died and the deorbit burn was set to start at twenty-eight minutes after four. The payload doors closed a little before 2:00 P.M. and the two remaining IMUs were aligned. It was go for the deorbit burn at a little after four. Gregory fired the twin orbital maneuvering sys-tem engines. The orbiter slowed. The long descent began.

"Houston, *Atlantis,*" Gregory called. "How do you read?"

"Loud and clear, Fred."

"Okay—just wondering if you were there."

"We're still here," CAPCOM said with a laugh.

Entry interface. Boxing with the atmosphere. Ruddying up the tiles. Mission Control still didn't know on which Edwards runway they wanted Gregory to land. Maybe they'd test Runway 05, never before used for a shuttle landing.

"We're still going for zero-five, but we'll keep you advised," said CAPCOM.

Gregory seemed supremely relaxed at this juncture. Perhaps a lesser man might not have been. Maybe it was what he likes to call his approach to being a commander. "I knew that if something did break down, I could handle it, so I spent a lot of time talking to the crew, looking out the window, and doing that 'commander image' stuff. Still, I was anxious."

If he was anxious, it didn't show. Shuttle commanders usually don't joke during descent. But perhaps it was the "commander image" stuff.

"About the only thing missing on orbit is a person who can clean the front window!" Gregory joked.

"Well, maybe next time we'll have to arrange for an EVA to do that, Fred!" the CAPCOM responded.

There was an extended silence.

"Houston, *Atlantis!* It looks like we could turn for a downwind landing at Hawaii!"

"No—don't land there! Keep coming!" laughed the CAPCOM.

"Ha! Ha!—it's only fifty thousand feet at Mach 24.1! The clouds look like we're about a thousand feet above them in a T-38."

Winds were go for landing on Runway 05 at Edwards. Gregory was to roll the orbiter as far as he could without applying the brakes, to test the hardness of Runway 05. *Atlantis* boomed into the United States just south of Santa Barbara. The steep descent was completed as Gregory sat the orbiter down, twin clouds of dust erupting as the main gear let down. It was the longest rollout in shuttle history. Gregory let the ship roll until he was nearly at the end of the marked runway.

"Okay," he advised CAPCOM, "here's fifteen knots—putting on some brakes—wheels stop."

"Roger, wheels stop—good job, Fred. Welcome home, *Atlantis,* and congratulations on a great flight!"[12]

As 24 March 1991 dawned, Charles Bolden was poised to go into space again, this time as commander of *Atlantis* for mission STS-45. A *Spacelab* mission, it was one of the most important scientific flights by NASA up to that time. It was, in fact, "A Mission to Planet Earth," having as its goal the monitoring of the health of the earth and its atmosphere.

They called the mission ATLAS (Atmospheric Laboratory for Applications in Science).[13] Others had conducted medical research and investigated the stars and planets, but this mission was different, and it excited Bolden:

> We're actually going to take the orbiter for eight days and look into and across the atmosphere; try to get data for scientists and say: "Okay, at this altitude in our atmosphere, the makeup of carbon dioxide is this much, and carbon monoxide is this much, and there is this much oxygen and this much ozone." We're going to map the areas of earth over which we fly. We're going to try to give them definitive data about how the ozone layer is doing, so that atmospheric scientists can construct an accurate model of our atmosphere![14]

Having been there when the Hubble Space Telescope was placed into orbit, Bolden couldn't think of any mission he would have loved to have been involved with more than this one. It showed. That he was designated mission commander was a signal honor and demonstrated NASA's faith in his skills and abilities.

Four scientific disciplines were involved, utilizing scientific instrumentation from France, Belgium, Germany, and the United States. In atmospheric science, the relative abundance of two kinds of hydrogen in the upper atmosphere would be measured; trace gases in the atmosphere, out to ninety-three miles, would be recorded through spectral readings of sunlight as the sun set and rose. Spectrometers, overlapping specific areas of the atmosphere, would observe day glow and night glow out to 371 miles above the surface of the earth. Distribution of ozone, water, and chlorine monoxide would be measured. In solar science, the total amount of energy coming from the sun and the amount of that striking the atmosphere would be measured. The solar output in different wavelengths would be measured and ultraviolet light particularized, since it helps create the ozone that protects the earth's surface from UV. In space plasma physics, the crew would observe auroras and air glow, using low-light television cameras, and experiment with particle accelerators, generating an electron beam in the creation of artificial auroras to learn more about the process that makes them happen. Finally, in ultraviolet astronomy, they would use FAUST, the

Far Ultraviolet Space Telescope, to record wide-field imaging of faint ultraviolet sources surrounding galaxies and the remnants of supernovas.[15]

And so, shuttle commander Charles Bolden and pilot Brian Duffy; mission specialists Kathryn D. Sullivan, David C. Leetsma, and Michael Foale; and payload specialists Byron K. Lichtenberg and Dirk D. Frimout lay strapped in their seats, suffering the delays inherent in countdown to launch. That is, until the superintendent of range safety burst in on the communications loop.

"Okay," he said, "range is go. You are clear to launch!"

The fiery feet of rocket fires stomped on Launchpad 39-A, kicking *Atlantis* into the sky. Dialogue was up and running inside the spacecraft. Duffy sang out the mach numbers and altitude. Bolden "would try to throw something in every once in a while." People in the mid-deck "seemed to be aware of what was going on." It comforted Bolden to know that everybody was "alert and ready to get going."

There were some white knuckles for a while. Mission specialist Mike Foale discovered that the ride up "was a lot easier than [he] thought it was going to be." Anxiety seemed to float away as a result. Once in orbit, Foale observed at the postflight briefing, it was really "like going to a tropical island. Bright, bright, blue colors, black sky, the bright sun." Leetsma thought the external tank might blow up as it jettisoned, spewing residual hydrogen still in the huge tank as the main engines cut off. But that was a normal fear, he discovered later.

While the crew conducted its assigned experiments, to include the firing of an electron beam into the dancing auroras of the southern lights over the south pole, creating artificial auroras ("that beam really did look like one of the phasers in *Star Trek!*"), school children around the world talked with the astronauts through ham radio operators. SAREX, the Shuttle Amateur Radio Experiment, "a hand-held receiver and window-mounted antenna," allowed them to speak to amateur radio operators on the ground. Bolden had not been initially excited about the idea. As commander, he "related it to some of the other payloads that I've flown that are a lot of fun for the crew, but tend to be very time-consuming."[16] Perhaps it was that marine training, demanding constant focus on the job at hand. But the reality of it changed his mind:

One of the things that I was most happy with was the fact that as we talked to parents, teachers, and youngsters themselves, for at least nine days, kids across the world were turned on to science. SAREX put us in touch with the American public and the public around the world, especially school kids. You could just tell that they were standing in line, chomping at the bit to get their questions asked. They were very well prepared [and] asked questions that showed that somebody had taught them something.[17]

Mission STS-45 returned to earth on 2 April, eleven minutes after the sun rose over the Kennedy Space Center. It was a good mission. As Charles Bolden recalled, it was "beyond anybody's wildest imagination!" Said pilot Brian Duffy of Bolden, "We were very effective [as a crew] and that has to do almost solely because of the leadership we had from Charlie Bolden. I think Charlie could take any crew and make it run very smoothly, turn it into a well-oiled machine." Belgian payload specialist Frimout added with a smile, "Flying with Charlie is really something special!"[18]

Annapolis would have been proud. The marines would simply murmur, "*Semper Fi!*" John Riley Love, the marine officer who had inspired Bolden, would probably have burst a button.

Fred Gregory's crews were as enthusiastic about him.

"What a wonderful human being," said John Blaha, a member of Gregory's STS-44 crew. A great leader. Former air force test pilot. A commander who molds his crews into "a very professional, smooth-functioning team." Quiet. Self-assured. Knows how to distribute responsibilities.[19] The environs of the Air Force Academy might just sheer and shake a bit with pride when he flies.

They also speak of the skill and effectiveness of Guy Bluford, the first black American into space. As a mission specialist, Bluford led many scientific teams on *Spacelab* missions. Skillful. Knowledgeable. Dependable.

He flew again on 28 April 1991 aboard *Discovery* (STS-39), on what was apparently a follow-on to earlier environmental flights. Gathering more data about auroras, the earth's limb, and celestial activity, utilizing all the sophisticated instrumentation to achieve it. One hundred thirty-four orbits and 199 hours later, they came back to earth and home on 6 May 1991.[20]

By then, African-American male astronauts had spent almost fifteen years performing space-related duties. If not among the stars themselves, they were closer than the majority of mankind living in this century would ever be.

A new orbiter came on line in 1992. They called it *Endeavour*. People looked curiously at it. Squeaky new. Thermal blankets unblemished. Heat tiles perfectly black and unbaked. Waiting in the wings was a new astronaut. Mae Carol Jemison, M.D., a mission specialist. Some people looked curiously at her as she prepared to go into space.

They'd been doing that as far back as medical school, when Jemison mentioned she wanted to become an astronaut. Some flaky guy laughed his ass off. Thought that was the funniest damned thing he'd ever heard.[21]

CHAPTER 11

THE FIRST AFRICAN-AMERICAN WOMAN IN SPACE

Mae C. Jemison, M.D.

Mae Jemison was born in Decatur, Alabama, on 17 October 1956, although she considers Chicago her hometown.[1] She doesn't remember much about Decatur. She lived there until she was just three years old. Her recollections are of familial, fun things. Walking barefoot on the sidewalks of Decatur. Helping her mother, walking her brother, Charles, and sister, Ada, to school. Visiting Aunt Hannah, the great-great aunt she really liked. Doing things with her mother. Beyond that, she found many things that fascinated her, both in Decatur and after the family moved to Chicago:

> I was interested in just about anything you could name. I was involved with a long list of [things]. I was involved in dancing. I was involved with artwork. I was involved with climbing. I liked reading [and] just about anything you could name. I was willing to climb trees—anything you could name.[2]

Willingness to experiment—trying to do things, to stretch—came from her parents, Dorothy and Charlie Jemison. Her mother, an elementary school teacher, taught at the Beethoven School in Chicago for more than twenty years. Her father, as often as not, held down two jobs. For thirty years he was supervisor of maintenance for United Charities of Chicago and, a roofer and carpenter by trade, actively pursued contracting and construction work. Their children were the centerpiece of the Jemisons' lives, and they tried to make each of the children feel special, that they could do anything.

It was a matter of recognizing individual talent, being there to support its development, then standing back to let it flower. It came from their own personal philosophy: "Forward thinking; never having it in their minds that their children could not do." And even if they had some little reservation about something their children thought they could do, they'd still let that child decide.

That is how Mae Jemison developed a lifelong fascination with space travel. While growing up on Chicago's South Side, she read books about space. She learned about what was beautiful in the world through art classes. She learned to use space through dance, an art form she loved and seriously considered as a career.

After graduating at the age of sixteen from Chicago's Morgan Park High School in 1973, college beckoned. Mae scored high on the Preliminary Scholastic Aptitude Tests and submitted applications for various scholarships. Bell Laboratories ultimately sponsored her for a National Achievement Scholarship.

At first, Mae chose MIT, then balked at the idea. She said her first thought was that "MIT doesn't have a really good football team!" More important, when she advised the school of her National Achievement Scholarship, the admissions department proposed reducing the amount of MIT's scholarship support and advocated a work-study program as a requirement. Fireworks erupted at that point.

"We think *everybody* should work!" sniffed an MIT representative.

"Well, what about kids whose parents can afford to pay their whole bill?" Mae wanted to know. "*They* don't have to work! That's not equal!"

"Well," came the somewhat haughty reply, "that's what we do!"

"I thought that was pretty tacky," Jemison said in retrospect. Upon the advice of her sister Ada ("Don't go to a school that's going to require you to do work-study even if you're bringing in your own money"), Mae reversed her field, called Stanford, and found out she was still welcome there. A few days later, she received a letter verifying her acceptance. It made her happy because

> Stanford was really my first choice, and it's one of the best things that could have happened. Because Stanford was outstanding academically, in terms of science and liberal arts and just about everything, it allowed me to become involved in and develop my personality, skills, talents, and interests. Probably wouldn't have been able to develop [those things] if I had gone to a completely technical school![3]

The Stanford bus picked up Mae at San Francisco International Airport and, long minutes later, delivered her to her dormitory in Florence Moore Hall and Alondra House. As she hit the pavement, a female voice pierced the warm California air.

"Hey, Mae!"

Jemison looked about. Since this was the first time in her life she'd ever been to California, it blew her mind that anybody knew her name. So she looked again and saw a white girl, about five feet ten, standing there smiling widely at her.

"Hi! I'm your roommate! I'm Janet Waggoner!" the girl gushed.

"Yeah. Well, I'm—"

"Oh, I know who you are! C'mon, let me help you with your stuff!"

It turned out that Jemison was exactly one inch shorter than Janet (which was okay because they were matched by height). In fact, they sort of hummed when in each other's presence. They got along well, ending up, in Jemison's words, "having a great, great friendship!" They've stayed in touch over the years.[4]

In the main, Stanford was a great learning experience. Mae's biggest problem was with certain of the engineering professors who, by their very *attitudes* seemed to want to discourage her matriculation as an engineering student. It wasn't an *active* thing, as in, "You should *not* be in engineering," but that passive thing with which so many African Americans have had to deal for years. Physical cues. Mannerisms. Excessively lofty gazes that look over, through, and around blacks, as if they simply weren't there.

At first, you wonder whether this is simply an eccentricity. As Jemison finally noted, it had nothing to do with that:

I felt totally invisible. At times, they would look through me. My questions would be handled in a condescending way, and even be ignored, or not answered. It was a new experience for me because I had been used to teachers and professors showing active interest in my quest for knowledge. Additionally, they did show active interest, at least they seemed to, in other students.[5]

Jemison didn't want, nor was she looking for, coddling. She wouldn't have accepted it even if it had been proffered. But these people acted as if she didn't exist. They acted like "they were going to ignore you and make you go away!" For all of her coming successes, Mae would never forget those professors of engineering and science at Stanford who treated her that way.

She hastened to add that she did not mean to indict the entire program. There were certainly professors who were "very fine, very good." There was no time to cry in her beer, so to speak. Instead, she looked to herself. She immersed herself in extracurricular activities and professorial research. She sought involvement, whether she was made to feel welcome or not. Finally, she felt that "you can try so much and, after a while, you end up saying, well, I'll let that go. I'm not going to worry about that."

So she pushed herself and her energies into other arenas. A second major in African studies. Political science. She found professors who were receptive to working with her and she excelled in those classes. Her rapport was good in dance and theatre, as well. Directing. Choreographing dance. Performing.

Her centerpiece production experience while at Stanford was choreographing the entire production of *Pearlie*. She did the whole thing. Found the money to produce it, helped hang the lights, designed the costumes, and recorded the music. Under the auspices of the Palo Alto Community Theatre, it was called *Out of Shadows*, and was performed at Stanford. The music she chose was the hot jazz stuff of the day. *Westchester Lady* by Bob James. *Gula Matari* by Quincy Jones. Jones's *Everything Must Change*, sung a capella. Stevie Wonder. Lots of music. It was Mae's last dance and drama work at Stanford, and she put into it everything she had. Something inside warned her that she probably would not have a chance to put much time into dance again.

Perhaps it was her lifelong interest in space and astronomy. In eighth grade and during her freshman year in high school, she could be found in the library, reading all the astronomy books she could get her hands on. In grade school, she seemed interested in how the universe and life began. "The theories and possibilities excited me," Mae said. Space exploration and being able to go into space, explore it, and discover what was out there were big items on her personal agenda. But the need went even deeper. It was about space as a place to conduct research; to be used as a laboratory. It wasn't about "being an astronaut" when she was young, for there weren't such things then. Yearning to travel into space, like they did in *Star Trek,* was.

All of that was primarily dream stuff until her senior year at Stanford, when an old friend, Sam Denard, then a graduate student at Stanford, happened by, excitedly relating tales about the NASA mission specialist program. They talked for hours about space. After he graduated, they ran into each other in the university bookstore. Sam was still all agog.

"Mae! Let me tell you about NASA!"

"What?"

"I have the perfect thing! You need to apply to NASA to be an astronaut *right now!* They're bringing in mission specialists. You don't have to be an air force pilot or in the military. They really want to refocus the thing."

"Really?"

"Yep! I'm getting ready to go work for NASA now. Think about it, Mae."

She thought about it and filed it away in her mind as a good idea. But her skills were not yet complete. There were other things she wanted to do.

When she was graduated from Stanford in 1977, Mae had completed the requirements for a bachelor of science degree in chemical engineering and also fulfilled the requirements for a degree in African and Afro-American studies. She also noted at the time that NASA had released the names of astronauts selected for the shuttle program. There were three black men and several women among them. The need to become involved in space exploration suddenly gripped her.

In September 1977, Mae enrolled in medical school at Cornell University. She wanted to enhance her chances of achieving her ultimate goal, getting into biomedical engineering research. The direction in which she was headed seemed to fit her style of following her own "internal motivation," of doing things because "I wanted to do it and it was going to be fun."

Perhaps that is what helped drive her to apply for and accept a grant from International Traveler's Institute for Health Studies in rural Kenya as a medical student. It might have been Tanzania, but because of a mixup, she settled on the Kenya trip. She was to work with the African Medical Research and Education Foundation (previously known as the "Flying Doctors"), which was involved in projects concerning health, community health survey, and health care strategies in that country.

In many respects, it was a dream come true. She knew lots about Africa because ever

> Since I was a little girl in grade school, my sixth grade teacher had us study the African continent, and this was something that you didn't (ordinarily) do in school. We studied China, the Third World, Latin America. And so we found out about other parts of the nonwhite, Third World.[6]

Mae felt very comfortable about her pending trip to Africa, and prided herself on the things she knew about the continent, even before she'd ever been there. That, for example, Tanzania was a combination of Tanganyika and Zanzibar. She'd learned that when she was eleven years old. She'd taken African studies at Stanford; studied Swahili, the language of the African coastal people who were admixtures of Arab and Bantu. She'd even "started wearing a natural back in the third grade—which was when Miriam Makeeba first came over." Mae was very proud and aware of her blackness and African extraction. Therefore, going to Africa was something she was totally prepared for, even though reared in America.

There was still a certain amount of culture shock with which she had to contend. That began when the plane zoomed into the air and out over the wide Atlantic Ocean. She'd been to Jamaica and Cuba, but never this far away from home. First, there was Europe. New faces. New architecture. New languages. Overnight in Zurich. The next day found her crossing over the Mediterranean, looking out her window to see the great Sahara Desert stretching away as far as she could see. That it *really was* there came as a shock. It was a kind of "validation of something deep inside me," she remembered, to look down and see the huge desert. She knew its geography. Now it was a verified fact for her. Her plane circled Nairobi. Landing was imminent. She was enthusiastic, but not overwhelmed:

> I knew there was going to be a sharp contrast. There would be urban areas and there would be bush. . . . Because of that knowledge, it wasn't as shocking. I feel very comfortable in that world. I feel very comfortable in most Third World countries.[7]

But she was headed to a place where she could see the southern light of the moon. Africa, where things appear upside down.[8] And black though she was, although her roots sprang from some part of the land sliding by beneath her, she was something new to the people who'd never been out of Africa. She was an American who, by virtue of birth, had seen different skies, felt different winds. A modern black woman grown accustomed to other ways and other faces.

Despite her preparation and personal feeling of comfort, Mae was relieved to discover that for the first time she could "relax and be a little less concerned about race" in her day-to-day life. She found she could go anywhere and get her hair "cornrowed." Unlimbering her incomplete Swahili, she found she could sit and talk to people, and she soon realized she didn't have to worry about how people responded to her being black, except for the occasional "American thing" exuded by potential troublemakers.[9]

Mae recalled feeling a sense of security because black people were running things. A certain warmth, if only because the color of the faces around her were the same. The white faces she was used to became the exception, the freakish thing. Here, white people's eyes stretched wide because of a screaming inner alarm at the great welling up of sheer loneliness that oppressed them, the unreasoning fright[10]—things Mae had known all her life and had learned to live with in America, where "people you run into are always sizing you up by race first," and where the rhetoric of color-blindness is popular, "but the society is not."[11] An odd feeling, this. In one sense, she had come home, but not quite, for her home was America the place to which she must return.

But for a time, the warmth, the color, the comfort, and the strangeness of Africa south of the equator sufficed. Her shadow fell to the south, at night, the wide sky mockingly presented an Orion seemingly asleep on his head, and the stars were unfamiliar.

As close to the equator as she was, the weather didn't change much. But not many kilometers away, when June comes, winter approaches and chilly south winds blow purposefully across the high savannahs.[12] So Mae did her health surveys and then came home to write a report about community health and community health strategies in Kenya.

Her student activities continued in New York in 1979, where she helped organize a health fair. In 1980, she was among the fourth-year students Cornell University sent along with physicians and residents to Thailand to staff clinics after the Khmer Rouge were overthrown and there was an influx of Cambodian refugees. Mae found this experience broadened her knowledge of Asia.

Her yen for involvement in space exploration never left her. Mae wanted to apply for the astronaut program. She hadn't talked about it much, but one day she did in a group of people that included the boyfriend of a friend's sister.

"What do you want to go into space for?" he roared, the sheer force of his laughter bending him over. Mae let it pass, thinking he was a little strange.[13]

After she completed her medical studies at Cornell in 1981, Doctor Jemison performed her internship at the Los Angeles County-University of Southern California Medical Center. In July 1982, she became a general practitioner with the INA/Ross Loos Medical Group in Los Angeles for the rest of that year.

In January 1983, it was back to Africa with the Peace Corps—to Sierra Leone, a country named after the winds that roar in the mountains like lions. A land where runaway American slaves and those rescued from slave ships sought surcease. In Liberia, founded in 1822 as a place to send free blacks from the United States, the land of the Kru, the Vai, the Mandingoes. A place where only blacks can be citizens.

Doctor Jemison was the Area Peace Corps Medical Officer, and at age twenty-six, one of the youngest persons ever to hold that post. She managed the health care systems for U.S. Peace Corps and embassy staff. As such, she handled pharmaceutical and laboratory issues, developed manuals, and conducted research projects on a Hepatitis B. vaccine, schistosomiasis, and rabies—which killed one of her volunteers.

After returning to the United States in June 1985, Mae began work in October as a general practitioner with CIGNA Health Plans of California. In January 1986, she found herself mourning the explosion of *Challenger* and the death of the astronauts she, like the rest of the country, had so admired. When Mae finally went to work that morning, her visage was somber. Nobody in the office knew she'd applied for the astronaut program.

In 1987, the word came down from NASA. She'd been accepted. Then she shared her news with her CIGNA Health Care coworkers. They baked her a cake.[14] A childhood dream and fantasy was about to come true.

In August 1988, after training and evaluation, Jemison was proclaimed qualified for assignment as a mission specialist. It would be 1992 before she flew, however, because of delays linked to the *Challenger* accident.

It was worth the wait. She would be flying aboard the newest shuttle, *Endeavour,* on only its second flight as a replacement for *Challenger*. It would also be a milestone flight: the fiftieth shuttle mission; the first cooperative flight between the United States and Japan. A *Spacelab* scientific mission, they called it *Spacelab J,* the "J" denoting Japanese involvement. The National Space Development Agency of Japan contributed $43 million in experiments to the flight and another $47 million to NASA for the launch.[15]

For months, Mae Jemison shuttled between America and Japan on coordination trips, preparing for her coming role as a mission specialist involved with life sciences investigations in space. Information gathered on the mission was expected to form a research base for *Space Station Freedom*.[16]

As 11 September 1992 approached, media people buttonholed Jemison, the first African-American woman scheduled to go into space. She had always said that her dance and dramatic training helped her in what she did. It had given her the ability to control stage fright. Suddenly she was at center stage again. She said she had known she'd fly in space one day. She said she was proud to be the first black woman selected to travel in space and that she hoped others would soon follow. There were quotable quotes galore.

On the subject of positive images and the realization that blacks can excel at all times: "As far as being a role model, I think it is important that people have images, and I don't use the word role model sometimes because I think people, young black children, children of color, minorities, have certain images that we already see and those images may not be very positive—or the images may not be things we want people to get involved in and yet, that's the only image, perhaps the only thing they see of themselves!"[17]

If stage fright were ever an issue, it had completely disappeared. Jemison said she thought her presence on the coming flight was positive, that people should be able to see and understand that all around the world people have power, skills, and ability. It was a matter, she said archly, of realizing that "we have to face up and allow people to use that power, those skills, and those abilities. And I think this is a positive step toward that."[18]

Her time to sit on top of a controlled explosion drew closer. Was she afraid? Of course not. But:

I'm sober about possibilities and things that could go wrong. You have to digest that. One thing that strikes me, and that has struck me recently is that, I always knew this, but it's become more pressing. I've recently rethought about it and reevaluated my significance in the scheme of things. A lot of people have stock in what happens to me on this flight, or what happens to me, period. Some people [will] want to say [I] did really well, [and] that [that] proves one thing or another. Other people [will] want to detract, and say it didn't, and that means another thing to them.

But to Mae Jemison, about to leap into outer space, it was still a very personal thing. It was something she had always ached for. The hope for her was that people would look at the ultimate value of what she was about to do. She agonized over it and talked to her sister, Ada, the psychiatrist, about the issue.

"Ada," she asked, "what's the big deal?"

"Well, for many people," replied Ada, "it represents hope. Maybe for the first time, black women, who have traditionally been at the bottom rung of advancement in our society, are brought in. People see certain fields as male-oriented—for example, science, technology, business, sports. We're saying, 'Hey! We're gonna participate—and maybe [that'll] change [some] lives.'"

If Jemison ever doubted what becoming an astronaut meant to her people in America, she had only to remember the black man in his sixties who came up to her in Oakland.

"Mae," he said, "I just want to tell you that I've been working in the military, on airplanes even during World War II. I just want to tell you that I'm really proud to see you doing what you're doing, 'cause what you're doing is the kind of stuff I worked for."

She thanked him. And then he gave her a picture he'd had framed that featured the kings and queens of Africa.[19]

The crew gathered. The launch was scheduled for 9:23 A.M. EST the next day from Launchpad 39-A at the Kennedy Space Center. Robert L. "Hoot" Gibson was commander. Curtis L. Brown was pilot and Red Shift leader, with payload specialists Mark C. Lee and Mamoru Mohri. Jerome "Jay" Apt, mission specialist and Blue Shift leader, would work with mission specialists N. Jan Davis and Mae Jemison.[20]

Mae Jemison, a native of Decatur, Alabama, who called Chicago home, was about to make history.

THE AFRICAN-AMERICAN LADY ASTRONAUT
AND *ENDEAVOUR*

Basically, you have to understand and believe in yourself
and do what it is you know you are capable of
in spite of what anyone else may tell you.
—Astronaut Mae C. Jemison, M.D.,
Jet, *14 September 1992, 38*

Just after 9:00 A.M. EST at the Kennedy Space Center on 11 September 1992, attention was riveted on Launchpad 39-A and *Endeavour*, pointed toward the blue sky. The countdown tumbled to T-minus-two minutes and counting. The space shuttle main engines went to start positions, gimballing away to prevent contact with each other during the start transient. At T-minus-thirty-one seconds, the ground-control launch sequencer was "go" for automatic start as the orbiter's computers ran the launch.[21]

Showtime for Mae Jemison. The houselights dimmed; opening music teased her mind. The curtains rustled open and the lights came up. Helmeted and dressed in that big, orange space suit the astronauts wear, she was at center stage again, strapped into her seat on *Endeavour*'s middeck. Thoughts rushed through her mind. Her heart pounded. All those hours she'd spent training; all that study. So close to launch! She hoped the countdown didn't have to stop. Family, friends—where were they? What were they doing? For the most fleeting of seconds, the fact that she was about to be sitting on top of a controlled explosion zoomed through Mae's mind. But she knew about all the precautions; about the dedicated people she knew and how hard they worked to keep the program safe. So she left the thought alone.[22] There was no time to worry, she had a job to do.

At T-minus-sixteen seconds, the sound-suppression system activated. Three seconds later, the solid-rocket booster destruct system went live in case of a miscue. The countdown marched ahead; the main engines growled, muttered, and gimballed. *Endeavour* twanged. Liftoff! The roar was deafening. Explosive hold-down bolts fired, freeing *Endeavour* for flight.[23] Even though the shore birds had heard it all before, they opted for short, nervous flights of their own as the orange fire erupted into prepared trenches and smoke curlicued in monstrous abandon. The seven-member crew knew they were on their way.

A big smile creased Jemison's face from the sheer excitement. She was finally doing what she'd been preparing to do for a long, long time. To mark her time in space, she'd brought along things illustrative of her hopes and dreams. Things that helped sum up who she had become. An *Alvin Ailey Dance Troupe* poster, a symbol of her innate love of dance. A banner from the Mae C. Jemison Academy in Detroit, a school named after her that focuses on sciences and technology. A flag from the Organization of African Unity. Proclamations from the DuSable Museum of African-American History and from the Chicago public school system. And, according to *Jet* magazine, "she was bound to leave that pink and green *Alpha Kappa Alpha* flag up there in space," so that she could say, along with her sorority sisters, "AKA is *out* of this world!"[24] Some observers have noted that Jemison carried no memento touting her alma maters, Stanford and Cornell universities. In a December 1989 news release, the New York Hospital/Cornell Medical Center wondered aloud about the possibility. "Dr. Mae Jemison," it noted hopefully, "will fly into space aboard the shuttle. . . . She will be the first black woman to voyage into space. Let's see what reminder of her alma mater she will think of!"[25] Of course, she'd taken nothing this time. Her focus was on those things emanating from the culture and African-American society from which she sprang. Maybe on her next flight.

Endeavour went into the standard 184-mile orbit at an inclination that took it over all the islands of Japan. Changing into comfortable work clothes, the astronauts divided into two shifts. The Red Team (Curtis L. Brown, Mark C. Lee, and Mamoru Mohri) worked the "day shift," which began shortly after launch. They keyed primarily on the Japanese experiments, with Mohri doing most of them, other team members assisting.

Jemison's group, the Blue Team (Jerome Apt, N. Jan Davis, and Jemison) went to sleep shortly after launch. Their first "night shift" would begin about ten hours into the flight. An all-American team, their primary responsibility centered on the U.S. experiments, concentrating primarily on life sciences research. Scheduled to go on around the clock, these experiments consumed most of the waking hours of both teams working in the *Spacelab* module. Weightless in zero-G, the astronauts floated through a hatchway and into an 18.8-foot-long tunnel, then up into the module, a cylindrical conglomeration of experiments fitted into its walls in a space measuring thirty feet long by thirteen in diameter, its inner walls lined with scientific instruments.

Of forty-three main experiments, thirty-four were solely Japanese. Twenty-two of these concerned material sciences (i.e., crystal growth, fluid physics, materials processing, acceleration measurement), and twelve studied life sciences. The United States had nine experiments, seven of which were shared with the Japanese space agency. Two were in materials sciences and seven in life sciences (i.e., human health, cell development, radiation, and biological sample separation/growth).[26]

Waking up to go to work wasn't much different than on the ground, except for being weightless. The usual morning ablutions—brushing teeth and combing hair—were made more challenging by the movement of a wayward mirror determined to float away. On the way to work, the scenery was different. Jemison marveled at the sight of Chicago sliding by as *Endeavour* flew over the city. And there was the Kennedy Space Center, far below. Seeing the Nile "was a thrill." She longed to see West Africa, but every time she looked, it was shrouded in cloud cover.

Mohri, the Japanese astronaut, saw all the islands of Japan, including Hokkaido, where he used to work. There were satisfying moments by the galley, where food is prepared. Chopsticks worked for the crew. Mohri used a spoon.[27]

Jemison and Davis conducted lower-body negative-pressure tests, designed to determine how the body adjusts to microgravity using the process (counterpressure, using a cylindrical, inflatable fabric device that seals around the waist, thus adding pressure to the lower body, forcing body fluids back to the legs) as a countermeasure to help people readjust when they come back from outer space. Fluid therapy systems envisioned for use on space station *Freedom* were also tested. When in orbit, the lack of gravity creates problems for intravenous (IV) therapy. The system produced sterile water from on-board sources to formulate IV solutions for patient injection. The results appeared to be good. Up on the middeck, the orbiter crew performed crystal growth experiments, and tracked how the body utilizes food.

Jemison's big experiment was a study of the effects of weightlessness on the development of amphibian eggs fertilized in space. Essentially, female frogs were to be induced to shed eggs. Half of them were to be fertilized in a microgravity environment, the other half in a spinning centrifuge simulating earth's atmosphere. The objective was to see how microgravity affects early development of the tadpoles. Jemison was high on the experiment:

I was the main operator of the frog embryology experiment. I dealt with amphibian eggs—can you fertilize them and will they develop normally in space? What we've seen is that the eggs were fertilized and the tadpoles looked pretty good. It was *exciting* because that's a question that we didn't have any information on before![28]

She became a subject for an investigation called the Autogenic Feedback Training Experiment. Its objective was to prevent space sickness through what was called the Autogenic Feedback Training Vestibular Symptomatology Suit, which on a continuous basis measured Jemison's pulse, blood pressure, skin temperature, blood volume, skin conductivity, and respiration rate. Jemison's job was to use Auto Feedback Training (biofeedback) to alleviate the symptoms of space sickness.[29]

The SAREX experiment (astronauts talk to Ham radio operators using a hand-held transceiver) was up again. The astronauts talked to school children around the world. Over Japan, Mohri conducted "a series of space classrooms," explaining weightlessness and demonstrating parts of the experiments.

Extended by one day, the flight went a full eight days in orbit before it was time to go home.[30] Equipment was restowed. Systems were checked for normal landing operations. The outer bay doors were closed. The deorbit burn and the surrounding atmosphere turned red. The day was clear as they made their energy management turns. A chase plane escorted *Endeavour* in for its first landing at Kennedy Space Center. People on the ground finally saw the orbiter approach. So swiftly did it come, somebody noted that it looked like it was falling like a rock. "Wow!" someone shouted. At 175 knots, Curtis Brown lowered the landing gear and, for the first time as an experiment, he popped the drag chute before the shuttle's nose wheel touched the ground, thus "widening the envelope" of the landing system. Once they were down, the shadow of the chase plane above coursed like a ghost ship across the body of the orbiter as it rolled down the runway, parachute catching the wind.[31]

They went crazy for Mae Jemison in her hometown of Chicago. She was "their heroine." A six-day, city-wide celebration was hosted by the city, set to mesh with her thirty-sixth birthday. At Morgan Park High School, where Mae had graduated at sixteen, the place went wild with cheering as she entered the auditorium. She was visibly moved. *Ebony* magazine reported that "her voice was choked with emotion" as she said, "I have to tell you how wonderful, wonderful it is to see you. You don't know how much you do for me. You really don't."[32]

Then she told her audience about the days when she went to school there. About how it was and what she learned, things that helped her chase and capture a chemical engineering degree at Stanford University. She put out her caution lights about people who would have them "act or be a certain way." People who figure to limit a person because of their own "limited imagination." She knew. It had happened to her. There was the kindergarten teacher who corrected her when she said she wanted to be a scientist, suggesting that she really meant being a nurse. Or how about the misguided male principal who told her he planned to "have male teachers explain the NASA space camp program, because they were more knowledgeable about science."

Some folks said they didn't think she looked like an astronaut. Jemison's reply to those doubting Thomases was, "That's okay—'cause I am!" She really let down her hair at the University of Chicago when she did a little impromptu dance with the pom-pom girls.

Finally, she wanted everyone to know that she wasn't the only black astronaut. There were five active in the program, she told her listeners, with a sixth coming along as an astronaut candidate.

"It's exciting to be able to share my experiences and let people know that space exploration is not something that's totally detached from them," Jemison said.[33] It would be some time before the big bonfire celebrating her trip as the first black woman in space died out. Still, there will always remain at least a banked ember of that memory, because no other black woman in American history has done what she did. It was over and done. History. A statistic. A matter of record. Jemison knew it. She went "back to the pool" with the rest of the astronauts available for upcoming flight assignments. NASA would let her know when she would fly again.

There wasn't an awful lot of hullabaloo over the fact that Mae Carol Jemison, the first African-American woman astronaut, was about to go into space. Nothing like the media blitz NASA accorded Guy Bluford. There were no highly publicized "educational conferences," no chartered airplanes or buses bringing in hand-picked African Americans to witness her launch. No speeches were made by African-American astronauts about the purposes and goals of her mission.

The difference in NASA's approach probably resided in the progress made within the agency regarding the integration of its work force over the years. Fifteen years before, in 1977, Mae Jemison thoughtfully observed, "NASA had to push to make sure that they [brought] in those folks, and so they had to go out and recruit for them. They looked for them. And I don't think that [they've] looked for minorities since them."[34]

Having made the push, perhaps NASA's leadership no longer felt the need to look. Its "minority" plate was full and (until the *Challenger* accident) alive and well. Two of the early black astronauts went on to become highly respected shuttle commanders and pilots. Another consistently distinguished himself as an able mission specialist. With the selection of Daniel S. Goldin as NASA administrator, coming from TRW in the corporate world,[35] the futures of those African Americans already in NASA never seemed brighter.

In April 1992, astronaut Fred Gregory was appointed associate administrator, Office of Safety and Mission Quality. Astronaut Charles Bolden was appointed to the new position of assistant deputy administrator. It is worth noting that, under Goldin, these were not "window dressing" appointments, but carried, according to Joseph D. Atkinson, author of *The Real Stuff,* and long-time NASA official, the full weight of the authorities inherent in them. Atkinson added that, regardless of what some naysayers may suggest, NASA's decision to soft-pedal Jemison's flight was "never a case where [it was said]: 'Finally, there's a black female who's going to fly and we're going to push her down to the bottom of the ladder!'" Conversely, he noted, "it was more of a situation where, yes, we have a black female—she's going to be recognized as the other astronauts are recognized, and maybe where we did this Rah! Rah! Rah! for Bluford and some of the other blacks during the earlier years, perhaps we're at a point now where we can routinely do these things." NASA had finally come to the point where, "Whether you're black, blue, green, white, or yellow doesn't matter!"[36]

But there is a national black conscience in America that vividly remembers all those decades when that kind of attitude was *not* extant. Residing deep in the psyches of all African Americans, that conscience needs the opportunity to savor and cheer the accomplishments and successes of black people. It has to do with African-American excellence and recognition. The issue is black pride. A license to "shake a tailfeather"—as aficionados of yesterday's jive talk used to say. Some chafe when that opportunity isn't proffered. While that need certainly exists, equity should be present when weighing both points of view.

Atkinson explained that, "When you balance one thing against another [for example], as Mae's flight goes up, Charlie is being selected as the commander of a scheduled, joint United States and Russian shuttle shot—which means to say that the whole climate [within NASA] isn't bad."[37]

But Jemison isn't completely convinced of that. Reflecting on the observation that the astronaut exhibition at the Johnson Space Center does not address the contributions of African-American astronauts in its displays, she said

> I guess maybe the tone of society, the time of society, right now, people want to say, well, you're here and we don't want to make any big deal about it. However, things are not at such an extent, have not occurred, and things are not quote-unquote so equal, that everyone's treated the same way.[38]

So, it boils down to a strict judgment call as to whether more effort should have been made to promote Jemison's flight. NASA chose the more conservative route, resulting in one-liners regarding Jemison's "first-black-woman-in-space status" in the majority press, with somewhat more detailed "national conscience" coverage in the African-American press.

Which is why not a lot of Americans, including African Americans, even knew Jemison's name, let alone that she was actually going into space aboard Flight STS-47 on the U.S.'s newest shuttle, *Endeavour*. Some may have remembered her as she led the Martin Luther King parade up New York's Fifth Avenue in May 1991, in a jacket over a long dress, her "Grand Marshal" ribbon and sexy earrings, while the 719th Transportation Company of the 369th Battalion upstaged her as they triumphantly celebrated their return from the Persian Gulf War.[39]

Today, another black astronaut-scientist looks at the accomplishments of Bluford, Gregory, Bolden, McNair, and now Jemison. At how each and every one of them changed just a bit with every flight into "God's country," into that void where stars are born. Jemison knows it happened, but she doesn't quite know how to describe the impact on her of where she's been. When asked if going out there had changed her, she seemed tentative.

"Yes and no," she replied. She is, she continued, "the same person, in a large sense, that I was twenty years ago. I've changed some, of course . . . [but] going into space, if that doesn't change some perceptions, then you probably haven't done it right. You probably need to go back and figure out what it is you missed!"[40]

Space was quite a bit different from Africa. She had found it wonderful to be "in another culture; able to stretch your boundaries—able to be open and almost be like a child [finding] out how things affect you." She became a full-fledged child of planet Earth in Africa, learning

How [she] affected the world around [her]. How people look at things differently. [How] whole family structures are different in other societies. How much people can depend upon one another. Those are valuable lessons that you can take with you throughout life. They make you a little bit more tolerant. It makes you wiser in terms of knowing that situations and circumstances will change and outcomes and meanings are relative, whatever events are occurring and the cultural, social environment you are in.[41]

Now, like all the astronauts, she is learning to become a child of the universe, a thing most of us have to die to achieve.

Maybe *that* is what Mae Jemison began to detect when she noted the "calm" she felt; the knowledge somehow that "everything was right." She knows that everyone who goes up is somehow changed, and she waits expectantly for the full impact of what she has done to hit.

"I haven't had the time to sit back and reflect," said Jemison. "I'm sure that a year from now, I'll have more ideas about what it all meant. How it changes you depends on what you took up there with you."[42]

One can only wonder what exactly it was she "took up there" with her, since scarcely six months after her triumphant return to earth, Mae Jemison walked away from the astronaut program. All the taxpayer dollars spent in training, all the NASA expertise and staff time expended in her behalf, and all the adulation accorded her by young and old African Americans, so proud of her their buttons almost popped, couldn't put Mae Carol Jemison, the astronaut, back together again. Her astronaut game was over.

It seemed rather like an author who, having written one book, forever forsook the writing life. New horizons and ventures called her, epitomized by something she'd been doing since January 1993: teaching at Dartmouth College in New Hampshire, so that she might "Refocus her energies on teaching, health care, and science projects related to women and minorities. [Participate in a] project aimed at trying to improve health care in West Africa through satellite communications."[43]

And so, with what hardly seemed a backward glance, Mae Jemison shocked the space community and her admirers as she left a career millions might envy, noting that, "I leave with the honor of having been the first woman of color in space and with an appreciation of NASA—the organization that gave me the opportunity to make one of my dreams possible."[44]

There would be detractors, some noting that perhaps she was on a monstrous ego trip, hungry for fame, a moment in the sun, a place in the record books. That her announced goal of making a difference in the study of outer space was a chimera at best. She didn't have to wait long.

"You're going to be leaving and there won't be any other African-American women in the program," some prattled in her ear.

Simeon Booker, Washington bureau chief for *Jet* magazine, shared the following "confidential" bit of gossip with his readers:

The sudden resignation of Dr. Mae C. Jemison, the first Black and only minority woman astronaut, after her initial flight in space, has caused an abnormal share of speculation. Insiders hint that the brainy woman was dissatisfied and eventually will write a book about her experiences. Meanwhile, NASA now must spend hundreds of thousands of dollars to recruit and train another minority woman candidate, possibly Hispanic. . . .[45]

The same weekend Booker's column appeared, Jemison was speaking to faculty and students at Howard University in Washington, D.C. She sought to put an end to the speculation about her move, pointing out that from time to time, life situations change and the need exists to move on. She said that being an astronaut was "only part of [her] life." Having been an astronaut helped her define who she really was and, while proud to have served in that capacity, the decision to walk away wasn't an easy one.

It was a matter of determining whether she stayed in "a position forever" because it was right for her versus staying there because it was something others thought she ought to do. Then too, she reasoned, was the sum total of her life to be "only one opportunity" to be kept for life? Some folks listened to that logic and said, "You're making a mistake. What could you possibly do to top being an astronaut?" To which Mae responded

I had to look deep down inside and see what my life stood for. I have had many other challenges to face and other contributions to make to the world. From a different perspective, maybe I can be a better force for space exploration than just "human development."

As she began to construct her new reality, she seemed to think little of those who off-handedly noted that "she's simply in the process of reinventing Mae Jemison again!" It wasn't that complex to her. She simply was "taking on another of her incarnations," remembering an old saw she was taught as a child: "If you don't change directions, you're liable to end up where you're headed."[46]

Still, speculation was rampant. People wondered what happened up there aboard STS-47. If that was an issue, then only Jemison knows for sure. The world will have to wait for her book. History will certainly note, however, that she exercised her freedom of choice as an American and her own God-given free will. History will also record that in the autumn of 1992, the first American black woman ever to do so took a ride into space on the orbiter *Endeavour* and conducted an experiment with some tadpoles, among other things. Perhaps the greatest thing Jemison did as an astronaut was to plant the desire to be an astronaut in the minds and hearts of black girls still in middle schools somewhere in America.

CHAPTER 12

PERCEIVED REALITY

Bernard A. Harris, Jr., M.D.

"I still like movies about space; after all, what are movies except a way in which we act out a perceived reality? In some instances, what we envision actually becomes reality. Remember ray guns that used a powerful beam of light to paralyze alien space invaders? Today, those ray guns are known as laser weapons."[1]

That's Dr. Bernard Harris, astronaut, talking. It's his way of acknowledging his personal quest for scientific knowledge that began as far back as he can remember. Growing up, he savored the wonderful robot in *Lost in Space*. Movies in which "flying saucers looked like inverted pie plates." Heroes, like Buck Rogers and Flash Gordon, and Captain Kirk, Mr. Spock, and the crew of the starship *Enterprise*.

The very act of growing up had an aura of adventure about it, thanks to his mother, who found herself a single parent after a divorce when Bernard, his sister, Gillette, and brother, Dennis, were only tots. Worse yet, they lived not far from Houston's Fifth Ward, an area most people would call a ghetto without thinking twice. The vice, violence, and drugs. Lawlessness and desperation. A far cry from Temple, Texas, where Bernard was born on 26 June 1956 and where the family lived before his father left.

When he was about seven, Bernard's mother, Gussie Burgess, found work with the Bureau of Indian Affairs. She moved her family first to Arizona and then New Mexico, into the heart of the Navajo Indian Reservation. There they lived in a centralized complex that included dormitories adjacent to the junior and senior high schools. The Indian kids would come there in the fall and stay for the entire year. The Harrises lived in a housing complex for employees, where they were one of only two black families in the entire area. Bernard and Dennis were to get an instant and somewhat different twist on the idea of racism and what that meant:

> Not only were the blacks minorities out there, but the whites [were] also, because this whole complex was mostly Navajo Indians. The first few weeks were difficult for my brother and I. [The Indians] were themselves an oppressed people and my brother and I spent two or three weeks fighting them for calling us "nigger" in *their* language!

Even at seven, he could see that although many of the Indians were having harder times than they, the Indians found a strange satisfaction in "picking on us because we were different." That was how Bernard discovered that black folks tend to "always stand out" in a crowd and oftentimes become either intentional or unintentional targets. But after they got to know each other, Bernard recalled:

> We learned to deal with different types of people. . . . Not only were there whites there, there were Afro-Americans, other Indians born on the reservations and [various] types of them. There were [also] Mexican-Americans—and we all ended up playing together. I think [this] dramatically affected our lives in terms of how we perceived ourselves and related to the people around us.

That settled, the need to push into the desert surfaced, to see what new adventures were to be found out there. So, on weekends, this newly formed international band of small humanoids would gather ("guys with guys and girls with girls") and go exploring. This exploring thing was right down Bernard's alley. It was something he'd always wanted to do:

> So we grabbed our BB guns and slingshots (those of us who had them) and hiked up the mountains—unbeknownst to our parents, of course. There were black bear and bobcat and rattlesnakes all over the place that we ran into on occasion. And we dealt with it![2]

Many more creatures than he enumerated lived out there in the desert and mountainous foothills that could've threatened these small, intrepid adventurers. Proud pronghorn antelope. Mexican jaguars also prowled among the "creepy-crawlies." Poisonous Gila monsters lazed in the sun.[3] Pitting their derring-do, BB guns, and slingshots against the wild kingdom, they survived, allowing, as Bernard Harris likes to put it, "the environment [to permit] a certain creativity to grow in us, and I think it's still prevalent."[4]

He didn't know it at the time, but his adventure in the desert was only a step away from a lifelong interest in space exploration.

The Harrises returned to Texas, and Bernard attended Fort Sam Houston High School in San Antonio. There, his interest in space took center stage as he watched the *Apollo* lunar expeditions on television. He admired the astronauts as they performed during the late sixties and early seventies. He anxiously watched Neil Armstrong step down on the moon's surface and thought excitedly that was what he wanted to do. Fascinatedly watching a launch, his mind yelled, "God! I'd like that! I'd like that!"

While his interest in space didn't become an obsession, it took a premier place in his consciousness. He joined the school science club, the physics club, and any other thing that had anything at all to do with space or science fiction. He fell in love with the television series *Star Trek*. ("I probably was one of the earlier Trekkies.")

Something else was at work, too. Bernard had always noticed he had "a sort of giving side, that said I like dealing with people. Dealing with [them] on a personal level when they're hurt." By the time he reached high school, the feeling was like a shining beacon, pointing toward an ultimate decision about his life. After he graduated from Fort Sam Houston High School, the question of just what to do burned.[5]

*   *   *

The University of Houston was Bernard's next stop. There he earned
a bachelor's degree in biology while fighting an internal battle over
his goals. Music was also a passion. For years he'd played the saxophone with a group called *Purple Haze* (after Jimi Hendrix) and that
involvement became his chief employment during the summer months.
But that need to help people still had top billing on his personal marquee.
While playing in the band during football games, he hated to see someone
in the stands or on the field hurt because he didn't know what to do
for them.[6]

His desire to help other people won. In 1978, he enrolled in the Texas
Tech University School of Medicine. After receiving his medical diploma four years later, he went north to the Mayo Clinic to complete
a three-year residency in internal medicine.[7] While he was there he
rediscovered his interest in space:

> My first rotation was in Rheumatology with Dr. Joseph Combs,
> who was part of NASA's *Gemini* effort. When he talked about the
> obstacles they had overcome in sending the first man up in space,
> I was hooked. That's when I knew the combination of medicine
> and space was for me![8]

Bernard began to do research work on bone demineralization and
spinal cord injury with physicians Larry Riggs, Heinz Wahner, Mehrsheed
Sinaki, and Joe Melton. Two other physicians, Ed Rosenow and Pat
Palumbo, became his mentors. After his stint at the Mayo Clinic, Bernard
became a national research council fellow at NASA's Ames Research
Center in California. Near the end of this fellowship, in 1987, he decided
to apply for the astronaut training program.

Although Harris didn't make the first round of selections, NASA
hired him to work at the Johnson Space Center, where he helped determine
the medical requirements to survive in space and to build the necessary tools and facilities to put a clinic in space.

So far, so good—but he still yearned to become an astronaut. "I
knew it would just take time to do it. I simply made up my mind to
give it one more try."

In September 1989, Bernard was selected as one of 106 candidates
for interview and testing from a field of more than 2,500 applicants.
Today, the NASA selection process bears no resemblance to the one

the first astronauts underwent. It's not that the first astronauts' tests weren't rigorous, but now it's almost a science. The final interview phase extends over an entire week. Psychological evaluation. Intelligence testing. Personality tests. Seven hours of psychological examinations. Physiological testing, medical tests, eye examinations, X rays. On the last day, each candidate went before a twelve-member team responsible for making the final selections.

In January 1990, Harris was selected as an astronaut candidate by NASA. A year later, his training and evaluation completed, he was ready for assignment as a mission specialist on a shuttle crew.[9]

Looking back, Bernard acknowledged that part of it had been the men and women he'd gotten to know during his residency back at "the Mayo" who opened the door for him. They had called up the head of NASA and said: "Hey, we've got this guy interested in doing research in space. What should we do?" At that point, NASA sent him a list of programs, and that's when Bernard began working toward his ultimate goal.[10]

Now, he could sit back from time to time and mull over all of it, that last year before becoming a bona fide astronaut. The constant training. Land survival. Water survival, somersaulting from the orbiter hatchway mockup into the NASA swimming pool interminably. Parachuting. Ejection seat training. It was almost like medical school. A "whole bunch of smart guys sitting out there absorbing information." Astronomy. Oceanography. Orbital mechanics. Planetary science. Learning to fly a T-38 jet trainer.[11]

That was the "cat's meow!" Taking off in one just blows his mind clean into the next county:

Now, *that's* a kick! In commercial planes, you creep down the runway and take off in slow motion. In a T-38, you roll down about half the runway at a hundred and fifty miles per hour and the plane lifts eight feet off the ground. You pull in the gear and pick up airspeed to about 180—and you're still only eight to ten feet from the ground. At the end of the runway, you flick on the afterburners, your head snaps back, and you're gone—straight up— until you reach your approved altitude![12]

If you didn't know any better, you'd think this guy was a closet fighter pilot. That's the way they talk about flight and flying. But he's done other flying duties not quite so glamorous, such as serving as project manager for NASA's Exercise Countermeasures Project. There, he designed exercises targeted to offset loss of physical conditioning "that can result from extended time in space." Bernard tested the validity of the exercises aboard the "vomit comet," a KC-135 flying special parabolic flight paths in order to simulate thirty seconds of weightlessness.[13]

Such exercises are Dr. Harris's forte. Beyond the duties of a flight surgeon, he's spent three years studying the physiological and biomechanical effects of microgravity, developing exercises and equipment to offset the cardiovascular, muscular, neuromuscular, and skeletal deconditioning that happens in spaceflight. According to Harris:

> We are born in one gravity and in one gravity we develop. When we enter zero gravity, deconditioning occurs. The heart becomes smaller because it doesn't have to work as hard to pump blood through the body. The lack of gravity results in muscle atrophy and eventually in bone resorption. We've found that exercise can be used as a prescription to counter certain aspects of deconditioning. This is crucial if we expect astronauts to spend extended periods in space. We need to make sure they have the strength and the conditioning to carry out their mission—and to return home.[14]

Originally not scheduled to fly until 1992, the year flew by without his being assigned to a shuttle flight. While he waited for his name to be placed on a manifest, he continued to conduct research supporting the NASA Extended Duration Orbiter Program, in which astronauts stay sixteen to twenty-eight days in space and then come home. Those astronauts who stay that long in space (or longer) will be using the exercise vehicles and routines Harris helped devise and design. Equipment that uses resistance instead of weight to achieve the desired results. Treadmills for aerobics. A multifunctional device that can be used to row, run, or cycle. A weight-lifting device. Monitors measuring metabolic gases, heart rate and blood pressure.[15]

Then the word came down. Bernard Harris would be going along as a mission specialist on STS-55, scheduled to launch on 25 February 1993 aboard *Columbia,* the flagship of the shuttle fleet. It would be the second German *Spacelab* mission and the fifty-fourth shuttle flight, if all went according to plan.

Dubbed the D-2 Mission (for *Zweite Deutsche Spacelab*), it was an extension of the first German *Spacelab* flight, D-1, in October 1985.[16]

Early on, Bernard made several trips to the German space operations and training centers in Cologne and Oberpfaffenhofen. His training and orientation alternated between those centers and the Kennedy Space Center. In both locales, he trained and worked with his German counterparts, helping ensure that the integrated systems shipped from Bremen coincided with NASA storage and fit checks aboard the orbiter and were ready for installation during July-August 1992. At the end of a strictly business day, people would find it was nice to have the relaxed Bernard Harris around.

"Well, okay!" he announced at the end of a long routine, smiling widely.

"*Danke! Danke!*" enjoined the German instructor with great enthusiasm.

"Well—er—er—" Harris would begin, fishing his limited German vocabulary for an appropriate response. Nonplussed, he threw back his head and roared "*Si!*"—followed by an enormous laugh as the training room dissolved in laughter.[17]

The goals of the mission were ambitious. There would be over ninety experiments, fully one-third more than were aboard *Spacelab* D-1. The crew would work in two shifts around the clock as they completed investigations in the areas of fluid physics, materials sciences, life sciences, biological sciences, and astronomy. Experiments dovetailed with the earlier German D-1 mission by conducting similar tests or by using upgraded processing hardware, taking full advantage of all the technical advancements made since 1985. Most of the *Spacelab* D-2 experiments were designed to explore the behavior of humans and other living organisms and materials in microgravity. Others were to focus on the growth of semiconductor materials, and on protein crystal growth. There would be experiments monitoring the development of balance-sensing organs in tadpoles, to gain insights into the causes of space sickness. At the other end of the scale, the *Baroflex* experiment would investigate the "theory that lightheadedness and a reduction in blood pressures in astronauts upon standing after landing" may occur because the normal body system regulating blood pressure acts differently after experiencing a microgravity environment for an extended period of time. The object of the experiment was understanding the causes of the condition.[18]

Other experiments tracked the effects of weightlessness on body organs and their controlling mechanisms, on heart and blood circulation, and the functions of the lung. An interesting experiment in robotics (ROTEX) would operate in a closed workspace within a *Spacelab* module. Capable of having its robotic arms operated from both an on-board work station and a work station located on the ground, the experiment augurs future spaceflight, reducing the costs of space systems through the informed use of robotic systems in space.[19] Still other experiments would track the effects of radiation on living organisms, as other crew members performed both earth and space observations while recording their findings.[20]

After months of delay, *Spacelab* D-2 finally appeared ready for launch on 22 March 1993. The crew was more than ready: Col. Steven R. Nagel, mission commander; Col. Terence T. Hendricks, pilot; Col. Jerry L. Ross, payload commander; and mission specialists Bernard Harris and Lt. Col. Charles J. Precourt. The German members of the crew, Ulrich Walter and Hans W. Schlegel, were both payload specialists.

They'd tried this once before. The initial flight, scheduled for 25 February 1993 had been canceled because of an inoperative pump.

After the usual morning breakfast and journey to the launchpad, the crew settled in for blastoff. The countdown descended and the engines fired as the astronauts steeled themselves for the explosive ride into space. Months before, Bernard had considered the coming moment:

> Once they light the main engines, they can shut them down. . . . but once they light the solid rocket boosters—and that's what I'll be looking for—I'll be looking for the light of the SRB, knowing that everything is probably okay at this point. So I'll probably be very relieved that now we're going to finally clear this tower with our launch. I think, at another point I'll be very relieved is when we get rid of the SRBs. Once those SRBs are gone, I think the rest is just a moot point. . . .[21]

But, Bernard's perception of reality was flawed. CNN television cameras recorded ignition as the announcer began describing the early morning launch. Three seconds before liftoff, computers automatically stopped the launch and the engines died.

The breath caught in the throats of over two hundred family members come to the space center to watch the launch. Bernard's wife Sandra held their nine-month-old daughter Brooke Alexandria a bit tighter.

Staffers in the launch control center suddenly jumped into action. The computer had done its job and shut down the launch because of a problem human eyes had missed. Training and routine took over both inside and outside the orbiter. "The launch control people," Harris recalled, "did not miss a beat—it was almost like the countdown continued, it ran that smoothly." A pad abort had been declared a mere three seconds before liftoff. The astronauts felt the vibration of initial engine startup, punctuated by the master alarm as the engines shut down.[22]

Inside the orbiter, the crew may have felt momentary stress, but there was no panic. They'd been there before in training. The dry count, where they'd actually climbed into the vehicle to go through the launch, portions of which involved emergency scenarios, one of which was a pad abort. So they sat inside the gleaming orbiter and let other people do their jobs. Finally, the astronauts learned what had happened: one of the engines had not come fully up to speed and the computer had canceled the launch.

NASA support people advised worried families that the crew members were in no danger and would be fine. CNN news cameras went live at Launchpad 39-A several minutes later to show the astronauts hurriedly exiting the orbiter. The camera zoomed to a medium closeup shot just in time to catch Bernard Harris climbing out, a bit of concern etched on his face.

It was the first engine shutdown at the launchpad in eight years. Later investigation traced the problem to a stuck valve that kept the engine from coming up to speed.

The flight was rescheduled. Perhaps Harris thought about his wife and how she must be feeling now. She was aware of the risk. They'd talked about it. She'd told him that as long as he was happy being an astronaut, everything was fine. But he knew that she hadn't had the opportunity to go through a successful launch. There had been one postponement, and now a pad abort. He knew it would be nerve-racking for her, seeing him "sit on top of seven million pounds of thrust."

NASA tried to launch them again on 24 April 1993, only to experience another delay because of a balky inertial measurement unit, resulting in a two-day delay.

Bernard Harris and the rest of his crew moved with purpose in the predawn hours of 26 April 1993. They were up at 4:30, and by 5:00 A.M. were having breakfast together. Their German counterparts went for an early suit-up because of the amount of bioinstrumentation involved in their experiment assignments. The weather briefing was go for launch, although the forecast called for showers later in the day. Bernard suited up around 7:00 A.M. Later, the astrovan took the crew out to the launchpad and the orbiter. The crew felt new resolve. "I didn't want to come out of that vehicle again," Bernard recalled. "I wanted to go into space." The entire crew felt that way. They'd waited and suffered delay after long delay. Like Bernard, they too were ready to go.

Everyone strapped in. The countdown marched along to seven seconds before launch. Visions of the prior pad abort coursed through his mind as Bernard crossed his fingers.

Liftoff! He heard the giant engines growl up to speed. He could feel it. There was no master alarm this time. Within seconds, the solid-rocket boosters lit. Bernard and the crew knew they were going.

When he watched other launches, Bernard would hold his breath until the solids lit. Oddly, he couldn't recall if he'd done that this time. But he *was* breathing, marveling at the smoothness of the ride; accepting the rough edges of the turbulence and the awesome, thrusting power beneath him.

He'd switched seats with Jerry Ross, the payload commander, during the ascent and rode on the flight deck, able to watch the computers confirm that everything was working perfectly. Bernard looked out the windows. Things rushed by. He saw that they'd cleared the launchpad; could see that they'd done the prescribed roll maneuver, then headed out "in the direction we're supposed to go!" The rest of it was "just blue sky going to black sky." Main engine cut-off begat the weightless state and ultimate injection into orbit, 165 miles above the earth.

The crew had lots of postinsertion work to do, readying things for the myriad experiments. Bernard's shift was the first to sleep. Upon awakening, he noted things had begun to happen to their bodies that brought the medical doctor in Bernard alive. Their faces began puffing up, their sinuses closing down a bit. Swelling caused by fluids shifting from their legs into their trunk area. Their heads felt full, as if they all had colds.

These physiological changes were of particular importance to Bernard Harris. In addition to his responsibility to assist the German astronauts as they performed their experiments (Bernard was fully trained in all experiments except two), he also keyed on a special study in human physiology.

Part of an experiment he'd supported for inclusion on this flight, it was called "physical diagnosis in space," or "physical examination in space." The whole idea was to try to gather data on the immediate physiological changes in space using the medical examination as the initial forum. According to Bernard:

> The reasoning for this approach was the fact that, traditionally, this is the first thing that physicians use to diagnose their patients. From there, [they] decide what tests (and other things) are necessary. In our high-tech arena, we seem to have forgotten that [this] skill will be needed for future manned spaceflight. So we're going back, trying to gather that data. . . .

The hope, Bernard added, is to develop handbooks for future physicians. The knowledge will also help to direct future research. "As we do these exams and we find that a person changes in one area more than another, then we know that we have to concentrate our research in that area for a possible countermeasure, which will prevent that change from occurring, or devise a treatment to combat a particular disease."

Bernard conducted the first "medical conference in space" with researchers at the Mayo Clinic. Discussing the physical exam approach to "see if we can detect changes in the human physiology while in space," he shared with the Mayo doctors his findings that changes do in fact occur and that they can be detected through the medium of the physical exam alone. Swelling of the face; rales in the lungs (a physical description of moisture in the lungs, which could be linked to the shifting of fluids from the legs). All of these things seemed to clear up within a day or two, and it was obvious that the body easily adapted.

Bernard also noted that when the body was in a weightless state, the heart seemed to shift. It didn't "move out of the chest into the stomach or someplace else," he noted, but it did relocate within the chest.

Utilizing the usual medical examination approach to locate the "point of maximum impulse" (PMI) of the heart (placing the hand just under the left nipple, the usual site of PMI), Bernard verified its location on two of the crew prior to flight. Then, their heartbeat was easily palpable; the location of the heart certain. On orbit, the heartbeat and its impulse had disappeared from that location.

Four or five days into the flight, Bernard finally located the errant impulse

> on one individual right in the middle of the chest—not under the left nipple, but right under the sternum. You could feel it pulsating. It all makes sense when you stop to think about it. [Gravity] pulls on organs just like it pulls on your legs and everything else. And if you don't have that, then the natural tug from the ligaments [holding] the heart in place are going to pull in the direction they are strongest—toward the center of the chest.

Bernard was so busy working the experiments with the other specialists, there wasn't an awful lot of time for sightseeing. He did speak with his wife over SAREX and with some school children across the country. When he did get a moment to sightsee, he found himself on the flight deck, where it was possible to position himself to see the earth's curvature. "It was just fantastic," he recalled.

Most of all, Bernard was fascinated by the quality of the sunrises and sunsets. "You wouldn't believe the colors in the atmosphere," he asserted. "You can actually see the different layers of the atmosphere, and, as the sun shines through it, [you can see] the characteristic colors of those distinctive [atmospheric] layers."

As the sun came up, Bernard recalled, if there were any thunderstorms or clouds on the horizon, he could see the great leader clouds, thirty to forty thousand feet high, billowing up into the atmosphere, riding the towering thunderstorms.

He was amazed, too, at how swiftly the orbiter moved above the earth. It was, he remembered, "just incredible—you're over Australia—you turn your head to do something and ten minutes later, you're off the coast of California!"

After ten days in space, it was time to come home to a scheduled landing at the Kennedy Space Center. Their deorbit burn was set to start off the coast of Africa, but inclement weather forced a change to Edwards in California. "You'd think," Bernard marveled, "that when we were that far out [over the coast of Africa], that we could do one deorbit burn and land at Edwards, since we hadn't made it to the U.S. yet." But because of the speed at which they moved, it took another one and a half orbits to facilitate the proper energy management maneuvers for an Edwards landing, taking about forty minutes to an hour to accomplish.

Bernard had only one regret about the landing. He'd given the payload commander his seat back on the flight deck, so he missed the reentry spectacular. He couldn't see it from the middeck. All he could do was listen to the accolades from the flight-deck crew.

"Wow!"

"Marvelous!"

"This is fantastic!"

It had been a nighttime reentry burn. Those on the flight deck could see the sun rising on one side of the orbiter and the red plasma flow and glow the orbiter created as it plunged through the atmosphere on the other. Bernard pledged he'd be on the flight deck during the next reentry. He felt the slight buffeting as the orbiter negotiated the sound barrier. Burglar alarms sounded in California.

Sandra and his baby daughter were there to greet him on the ground. Little Brooke Alexandria "had a strange look in her eyes when she saw her father," Bernard recalled. After all, he'd been gone for more than three weeks. But she was in his arms again, so everything was all right.

Bernard Harris had been evolving a special message for young people—African-American youngsters in particular—as he spoke around the country. But now, since his journey into space, that message seemed right for expansion because it seemed more viable and urgent.

It was about young people who seemed lost, always wondering what they're going to do. It pained Bernard to consider the fact that some kids never discover the keys to success and accomplishment in life—that they never really try. So, today he tells them:

You know, we always hear that you never get anywhere unless you try, and I think it's really true. It's an old cliché. You never ever get anywhere if you don't set goals in your life. And so, I've had a chance to reflect on how I got here. I got here because I set a goal.

It was a little goal at first. Playing on the basketball team; the football team. He accomplished something. Then he said, "If I can do that, maybe I can do this." Then Bernard decided to play music for a while, to learn an instrument, then several instruments. Enlightenment soon followed: "Hey! Maybe I've got a talent in this area!" All of that led to something else. College. Medical school, and a truly stupendous awareness of his potential: "God! I made it through medical school! If I can do that, I can do anything!"

That was what led him to the astronaut corps.

"Maybe it is a cliché that the rich get richer," said Bernard, "but the rich get richer because they've already accomplished something. You're never going to do anything worthwhile until you make that step to acquire that goal—to accomplish whatever you set your mind to do."

It was no gravy train becoming an athlete, musician, doctor, and astronaut. Bernard Harris doesn't believe in gravy trains. He worries about young Americans, and African-Americans in particular, who "always look for the easy way out," not realizing that success isn't automatic. Success only comes with hard work.

Until his next flight and after, Bernard A. Harris, Jr., will be spreading the word.

EPILOGUE

With the promotion of Charles Bolden[1] and Fred Gregory to relatively high-powered positions at NASA headquarters in Washington, D.C. (some say they are the civilian equivalent of a three-star general), the number of African-American shuttle pilots and commanders sank to zero. Bluford, Harris, and, for a short while, Jemison—experts in the areas of payload and science—continued to serve as mission specialists. Important positions to be sure, but not the same as pilot or mission commander. The latter are truly high profile jobs. Often, the commander's is the only name mentioned by the media when a flight is pending. It is also an honor, vested with the special trust only NASA itself can confer. It's a little like being class valedictorian or graduating summa cum laude from a prestigious university. It's the top of the operational pecking order among astronauts, and not to have an African-American in either role seemed unnatural after all the years spent getting there.

The African-American presence, Gregory noted, is still felt, but it's different now. The important thing is there are, "as far as we can see, very few [blacks], if any, in the pipeline." It isn't that he and Bolden haven't tried to find, interest, and recruit young blacks for the astronaut program. In the eighties, for example, Gregory remembered trying to interest Air Force Academy cadets (especially those who "were ready to leave the service and go on to other pursuits"). He managed to get some of them into test pilot school. But almost always, a problem arose that prevented their getting through. It might be a medical problem the NASA flight surgeons would not waive, or simply an inexplicable lack of interest. Gregory lamented that:

Charlie and I have done an awful lot to try to encourage our folks to get into this career field. But, where all this stuff is starting is down in the second and third grade, with schools and communities and parents, and we look with [concern] and dismay at the

241

generations that are coming up. Looking at the drug culture and the drugs, we, I think, have almost admitted that we've lost a couple of generations.[2]

Washington, D.C., statistics seem to bear him out. Quoting Wendell Ludler, the president/CEO of the Young Astronaut Program, Gregory noted that in that city, four out of five black males (black *males,* not black youth) have had some kind of run-in with the law, and are either in jail, on parole, or have been arrested. Four out of five. The statistic is mortifying. Multiplied by every major city in the United States, it is a deep concern, and that is why Gregory and Bolden spend great chunks of time in addition to their other duties "down in elementary schools talking to kids, trying to give them something to aim for, other than making money selling drugs."[3]

So a significant percentage of young black minds are being short-circuited before they even reach a place where they can begin to reach for a goal as exotic as the stars. Some people, like Ludler, think they have been lost forever to the American mainstream.

That is only part of the explanation for the drop in black candidates for the astronaut program, however. There was a time, for example, when the armed services, especially the air force, were a prime source for astronaut candidates. The services still are—for young, qualified white males.[4] Oddly, it is no longer so for young, qualified black males.

So, where have all the black military pilots gone?

As NASA's Joseph D. Atkinson pointed out, "there are more pilots during a war, and there has been no war recently." Economics plays a hand, too. Many black pilots have been joining the major airlines—earning salaries the average astronaut can only dream of. "People think that astronauts must make loads of money. They don't. They're not rich," Atkinson added.[5]

Beyond that, the services themselves are caught up in the great drawdown in the wake of the end of the Cold War. Black officers do not seem to fare well. Budget cuts will continue to hit hard at officer candidate schools. With fewer pilot seats to fill, fewer academy graduates will be funneled into pilot training. ROTC programs are suffering.[6]

There is also what some critics call an "intangible bias"—that subtle discriminatory attitude that deters African Americans from aviation careers.

Kirk Spitzer of the Gannett News Service writes that black officers are "underrepresented in navy aviation, and frequently assigned to less prestigious jobs and hold relatively few commands." Spitzer goes on to quote an equal opportunity officer in the Pentagon as being cognizant that "there's nothing to crow about," and if the navy wants the black aviator numbers to get better, "we're going to have to do some things or it's not going to happen."[7]

Navy statistics regarding black officers and navy careers aren't heartwarming. According to Spitzer, navy statistics show that 15 percent of African-American pilots and 43.21 percent of African-American flight officers leave the navy within six to eleven years, compared with 7.9 percent of pilots and 9.6 percent of flight officers overall. Of ninety-three navy aviation squadrons, blacks command only three. Of all pilots in the navy (11,116), only 2 percent are black. Even more telling is the fact that there are more women pilots than African-American pilots even though (until 1993) women were barred from combat assignments.

"It's a system," John Reid, a retired helicopter pilot told Spitzer, "that shuts blacks out. The navy doesn't want blacks to fly jets. They don't want to share the glory."[8] Similar accusations have been levied against the marines and the air force.

The air force, too, is shrinking. According to Joe West, an *Air Force Times* staff writer, that service remains "still mostly young, white, and male." The Defense Personnel Manpower Center supported this contention in 1991 by pointing out that, of almost 20,000 pilots, only 224 were black. Of some 8,000 navigators, only 59 were black.[9] A defense official noted that "it is difficult for the services to compete with other services and civilian employers for African-American college graduates, who form the pool of potential aviation candidates."

The vanishing black military officer, especially pilots and navigators, is of supreme concern to veterans like Col. William Campbell, a retired former commander of the revered 99th Pursuit Squadron, the first Tuskegee Airmen fighter unit to see combat in World War II. Proud of their past and the strides made by NASA in including African Americans in its astronaut corps, the Airmen fear for the future as they see the traditional sources in the military drying up. Unless the services produce more black pilots, there will likely be few, if any, black shuttle pilots or commanders in the future.[10]

In the midseventies and later, the services and NASA had the answer. The country had heard then, as it is hearing now, all of the excuses why parity in officer pilot procurement and assignment could not be achieved. Yet minority attendance almost doubled at the Naval Academy, because the navy went out and found and then recruited minority members. In commenting on that phenomenon, the late Gen. Daniel "Chappie" James noted in a speech at the Air Command and Staff College that the navy offered a $50,000-plus education in return for five years of their lives. "You don't find too many, no matter what color they are, who are going to turn that down," James said.

James added that, given the racial tenor of the country, the best way to ensure minority involvement was to go out and talk to potential recruits in all areas of society. NASA itself bought into that concept, hence African-American involvement in a real way in the space program. As far as racial bias is concerned in America, not an awful lot has changed the hearts of the majority of citizens. Therefore, someplace, sometime, someone has to deal with the fact that "freedom must be repurchased with each succeeding generation," as the late General James observed. The services contribute to that by not having anyplace in their ranks for commanders who cannot be concerned about racism and demonstrate a commitment against it.[11]

In June 1990, Air Force Secretary Donald B. Rice wrote

> Quality people are critical to high-quality forces. History shows that the human dimension, the dimension of ready, well-trained forces, has been vital to success on the battlefield. People programs must remain at the top of our priority list.[12]

One might add that no part of any military "people program" is more important than maintaining a racial mix in the ranks that is representative of America itself. In short, as the Tuskegee Airmen tout, "parity, if you please."

Although critics sometimes malign affirmative action, it would seem it is precisely that idea that may solve the problem. As Christopher Jencks noted

> The controversy surrounding affirmative action illustrates liberals' inability to find a politically workable definition of equal op-

portunity. Without some kind of numerical targets, profit-oriented firms will often deny blacks jobs they deserve.

Of course, the armed forces are not, by tradition, profit oriented, but the tendency of their leaders is often to accomplish the same kind of *manipulation* of targets and quotas to ensure that whites get the jobs, even when qualified blacks are available. According to Jencks, "black activists and white liberals" have done the same number in reverse and, as he further points out, "both outcomes perpetuate racial conflict."[13]

If the military is to remain above reproach in this arena, then its command structure should have these matters under strict control. As a result, there will not only be African-American pilots in visible numbers, but astronaut candidates as well.

Few Americans today have a greater sense of their place in the universe than do astronauts who have been two or three hundred miles into space. Immediately obvious is a great sense of order and orderliness. A sense of divine control. Of our intrinsic smallness as human beings, and highly insignificant ones at that, in the grand scheme of things. There is a sense of peace, of a lack of boundaries, and of the relative smallness of oceans we once considered uncrossable. It is important that Americans, especially young Americans, listen to the things these privileged people have to say.

The world is changing rapidly. American school systems, for example, are slated for a major overhaul, one that will be based on the "technology of virtual reality," meaning that computers will allow students to "experience historical events as they are reenacted" before their eyes. They will go to far-off places, from "the top of Mount Everest to the moons of Jupiter." At MIT's Media Lab, students experiment with and experience total immersion in subject matter, signaling a "great leap in learning." High school diplomas will be a thing of the past. "Achievement goals" will take their place. Going to "college, a trade school, or [a] career will be based on individual attainment of these goals. By the fifth grade, the regular curriculum, as it now exists, will disappear." The name of the game will not simply be reading, writing, and arithmetic. Students will be required to demonstrate "a solid background in U.S. history and government." Competency tests will be the deciding factors for measuring success. "Homework will be fashionable."[14]

Clearly, running with gangs, dealing and using drugs, killing and robbing people, burgling, and other scams won't cut it for *any* American youngster in the twenty-first century, regardless of his or her skin color, if these goals are to be realized.

African-American parents of all economic and social strata must pause in their headlong flight into assimilation and competition to look the long way back at their children, who need their help more than ever. Each of the astronauts mentioned in this book knew deep *parental involvement* in his or her life. Even when in an ostensibly single-parent home, the extended family took over and *nourished, directed, counseled, and protected them from an unfair and often dangerous society.* If, as Ludler and Gregory suspect, black America has "lost a couple of generations," then that translates into the fact that, in far too many instances, African-American parents have lost many of the children they brought into this world. Without mental and physical support from their parents, children suffer, and then positive achievement becomes difficult, if not impossible.

Sylvester Monroe, writing in *Time* magazine, tells the story of Keri Wingo in Chicago, who wonders where his old Phillips High School went. Twenty-five years before, four thousand children walked its halls and it was the center of the black community. By 1992, enrollment had shrunk to a little over eleven hundred, and the school is merely "thought of" as a positive force. Times have indeed changed. Keri Wingo remembered that

> There was hope in our world. The civil rights movement was in high gear and most kids still dared to dream. And with hard work, determination, and a little help from a variety of successful Great Society programs, many of those dreams came true.[15]

Some of those programs were instrumental in helping the African-American astronauts achieve their goals. Those programs may or may not be available in the future. But there are still some sure-fire ways to achieve success within the American system, regardless of skin color or ethnic background. Those ways are over the same roads traveled by the African-American astronauts.

What are those roads?

Charles Bolden would say

Believe in yourself. Don't let anybody else determine what your
life is going to be. Pick some goal that's just slightly out of your
reach, then go for it. Be persistent and don't be afraid of failing.
Some of my best accomplishments, some of the things I'm hap-
piest with, have come after I've failed, picked myself up, and
tried again.[16]

In his soft, gentlemanly way, Guy Bluford would counsel African-
American youths to

Aim high [because] we [blacks] tend to aim too low. In my case,
I aimed too low. I didn't realize that. *Aim high!* There's an awful
lot of work [in] achieving a goal. My success primarily [was
achieved] through perseverance. [You don't have to be] smarter
than anybody else. Make [it] through determination. Set goals.
Be persistent. You can do anything you set your mind to. You've
got to decide that you want to put in the hard work and perspi-
ration to do it. Once you do that—you're on your way.[17]

If Ron McNair were still around, he'd probably talk about the need
to balance the self; to learn to be at one with society, nature, and the
universe. He did by learning and remaining proficient in karate. He
would say one has to learn how to be neither hard nor soft, but to be
both—like water. Water is soft, able to flow, and assume any shape.
If pressed down, it flees. In quantity, it can knock things down; kill,
even. Ron would probably talk a bit about the importance of duality
in the human psyche. The achievement of yin and yang: understanding that all things in the world are made of opposites working in harmony;
complementing each other.[18] He lived his life that way. Beyond that,
he might have said:

Identify the field in which you plan to endeavor as early as possible. Learn as much as you can. Don't be afraid to talk to people.
Write here—write there. Ask questions. Find out as much as you
can. People with self-doubt . . . believing that something is bigger than you are should know that it is not true. Everything is
complicated, but once prepared, you can conquer—like everybody else.[19]

Bernard Harris believes that "we are, as African Americans, responsible for ourselves despite what has happened in the past; despite what will happen to us in the future. If we want to project on what's going on right now, we have to own up to a responsibility for ourselves and our survival, or else we will not have a future." Mae Jemison believes that self-motivation is the way to go, because "I've *always* been motivated!" Furthermore, she said youngsters should realize that

> Everyone is *somebody*. That's the baseline and that's what they have to first of all understand. Understand that they are somebody, regardless of what society says. And they have to establish for themselves who it is they want to be and then work toward doing it. [They shouldn't] feel that they have to have somebody's permission or okay to go beyond certain bounds. The most important thing is to look inside your heart and feel if what you want to do is correct for you. I think that will always lead you true.

All of them strongly believe that young African Americans need to, as Harris pointed out, "get rid of this whole deal of 'I got to have money and I got to have money now—so I've got to do drugs and there's no way out. The Man's holding me down!'" The bottom line, they all would agree, is that *nobody is holding anybody down except the individual so stricken.*[20]

The road to the stars was full of potholes—bumpy and poorly marked for African Americans. Ed Dwight was detoured; Bob Lawrence accidentally killed. But in the end, Guy Bluford, Fred Gregory, Ron McNair, Charles Bolden, Mae Jemison, and Bernard Harris each experienced the joy of slipping the "surly bonds of earth" and floating weightless in space, awed by the bright, blue-green orb turning in the black void before them.

A millennium or two from now, perhaps some archaeologist will discover evidence of our civilization. Among the artifacts uncovered could be pieces of the space shuttle *Challenger,* buried deep in its deserted and sealed missile silo on what was Cape Canaveral Air Force Station. And, as the scientists ponder them, they may somehow feel the heart-wrenching agonies we shared on that sad day in January 1986, when we were given an important lesson to learn—if we were really paying attention.

The lost astronauts were a part of us all. They were peculiarly American—representative of our collective psyche. Our desire to reach the next frontier had created the challenge that brought them to that moment. Because of that, their deaths were intensely personal—all the more unbearable because our society had made some of them struggle harder than others to attain the goal that eluded them that day. Regardless how we, as individuals, thought of women, blacks, Asians, and white males in our society, we bled from all our pores and felt we, too, had been torn asunder, our fragments scattered to the wind long before our time.

An important fact emerged: We discovered we truly loved each other in spite of ourselves.

NOTES

INTRODUCTION

1. Tom Wolfe, *The Right Stuff* (New York: Farrar, Straus & Giroux, 1979), 206. See also Walter Cunningham, *The All-American Boys* (New York: Macmillan, 1977), 17.

2. Wolfe, *Right Stuff,* 19, 411.

3. Ibid.; Kenneth Gatland, *The Illustrated Encyclopedia of Space Technology: A Comprehensive History of Space Exploration* (New York: Salamander, 1981), 206; Chuck Yeager and Leo Janis, *Yeager: An Autobiography* (New York: Bantam, 1985), 265–72.

4. Joseph D. Atkinson and Jay M. Shafritz, *The Real Stuff: A History of NASA's Astronaut Recruitment Program* (New York: Praeger, 1985), 12.

5. Wolfe, *Right Stuff,* 413, 419–21.

6. Arthur M. Schlesinger, Jr., *Robert Kennedy and His Times* (New York: Ballantine, 1978), 309.

7. Arthur M. Schlesinger, Jr., draft memorandum to Robert F. Kennedy, "Report of Civil Rights Work in the Campaign," 1 August 1960, John F. Kennedy Library, Boston, Mass. (Hereafter cited as JFK Library.)

8. Arthur Chapin, memorandum to Sen. Henry M. Jackson, "Negro Vote," 22 July 1960, JFK Library.

9. Arthur Chapin, "Convention Report: How Negro Vote Can Decide 1960 Election," *Jet,* 11 August 1960, 12.

10. Edward J. Dwight, Jr., telephone interview with author, 30 October 1990. (Hereafter cited as EJD interview.)

11. Atkinson and Shafritz, *Real Stuff,* 98.

12. Ibid.

13. A. M. Sperber, *Murrow: His Life and Times* (New York: Freundlich, 1986), 657.

14. Ibid.

15. Charles L. Sanders, "The Troubles of 'Astronaut' Edward Dwight," *Ebony,* June 1965, 32.

16. EJD interview.

CHAPTER 1

1. Louie Robinson, "First Negro Astronaut Candidate," *Ebony*, July 1963, 71.

2. Ibid., 76.

3. Ibid., 80.

4. Ibid., 81.

5. Ibid., 75.

6. Ibid., 81.

7. Ibid., 76.

8. As quoted in *Black Stars in Orbit,* PBS Television, produced by William Miles.

9. Robinson, "First Candidate," 78.

10. Ibid.

11. Ibid.

12. Ibid.

13. Ibid., 74.

14. Barbara Lawrence, telephone interviews with author, 25 September 1991 and 22 October 1991. (Hereafter cited as BL interviews.)

15. Sanders, "Troubles," 34.

16. Ibid.

17. EJD interview.

18. Ibid.

19. "History of the Air Force Flight Test Center, Edwards AFB, Calif." 1 July–31 December 1963," Air Force Historical Records Center, Maxwell Air Force Base, Ala., 151.

20. EJD interview.

21. Robinson, "First Candidate," 75.

22. EJD interview. See also Benjamin O. Davis, Jr., *Benjamin O. Davis, Jr., American: An Autobiography* (Washington, D.C.: Smithsonian Institution, 1991), 21–50.

23. Wolfe, *Right Stuff,* 420.

24. EJD interview.

25. Curtis M. Graves, Ph.D., telephone interview with author, 23 October 1990. (Hereafter cited as CMG interview.)

26. Sanders, "Troubles," 30–31.

27. Senator Frank Carlson to Lawrence O'Brien, special assistant to the president, 21 March 1963, JFK Library.

28. Carl M. Nelson, USAF, draft memorandum for the Air Force Aide to the President, "Reply to Senator Frank Carlson Re: Captain Edward J. Dwight, Jr.," 2 April 1963, JFK Library.

29. Sanders, "Troubles."

30. Schlesinger, *Robert Kennedy,* 551.

31. Yeager and Janis, *Yeager.* Italics added to these quotes by author.

32. Wolfe, *Right Stuff.*

33. CMG interview.

34. Yeager and Janis, *Yeager.*

35. CMG interview.

36. Yeager and Janis, *Yeager.*

37. Ibid.

38. Initial Report, "Equality of Treatment and Opportunity for Negro Military Personnel Stationed Within the U.S.," The President's Committee on Equal Opportunity in the Armed Forces, 13 June 1963, Table I, "Statistics on Negro Commissioned Officers," JFK Library, 8.

39. Ibid.

40. Fred Ferris, "First Negro Designated Space-Flight Candidate," *Washington Post,* 31 March 1963, A-8.

41. James H. Browne to John F. Kennedy, 1 April 1963, JFK Library.

42. *The* (Washington, D.C.) *Sunday Star,* 31 March 1963.

43. Mr. and Mrs. Edward Dwight to John F. Kennedy, 4 April 1963, JFK Library.

44. *The Sunday Star,* 31 March 1963.

45. O'Brien to Carlson, 9 April 1963, JFK Library.

46. Wolfe, *Right Stuff.*

47. Mark S. Hoffman, ed., *The World Almanac and Book of Facts, 1991* (New York: Pharos, 1990), 173.

48. "The Man and The Moon: Moon's OK With Me," *Afro-American Newspapers,* Washington, D.C., 17 September 1963, magazine section.

49. "Urban League Cites Space Trainee," *New York Times,* 15 July 1963.

50. Frank White III, "The Sculptor Who Would Have Gone Into Space," *Ebony,* February 1984, 55.

51. Atkinson and Shafritz, *Real Stuff,* 104.

52. "The Man and The Moon."

53. Ibid.

54. Sanders, "Troubles."

55. Ibid.

56. Ibid., 35.

57. Cunningham, *All-American Boys,* 7.

58. EJD interview.

59. Ibid.

60. Yeager and Janis, *Yeager,* 270–71.

61. Ibid.

62. Atkinson and Shafritz, *Real Stuff.*

63. Yeager and Janis, *Yeager,* 271.

64. Sanders, "Troubles," 32.

65. Yeager and Janis, *Yeager.*

66. Sanders, "Troubles."

67. Ibid.

68. Ibid.

69. Yeager and Janis, *Yeager,* 271–72.

70. Ibid.

71. Ibid.

72. Atkinson and Shafritz, *Real Stuff,* 101. Emmett Hatch, one of two African-American fighter pilots whose flying talents Yeager admired, and who Yeager had hoped would apply for test pilot school and astronaut training, said he thought Yeager was responding to pressure to eliminate Dwight exerted by air force chief of staff Gen. Curtis LeMay. Hatch bases that assertion on conversations he had with Yeager. Hatch characterized Yeager as "a fair person who related to qualified, competent people, and who had no use for people who didn't measure up." (Interview with author, 2 July 1993.)

73. Yeager and Janis, *Yeager.*

74. CMG interview; Martin Caidin, telephone interviews with author, July–August 1991.

75. Manned Space Center (MSC) press release no. MSC-180-63, 18 October 1963, Lyndon B. Johnson Space Center Archives, Houston, Texas. (Hereafter cited as LBJ Center.)

76. Robert R. Gilruth, MSC director, to NASA headquarters, subject "Captain Edward J. Dwight, Jr., USAF," 26 April 1965, LBJ Center.

77. CMG interview.

78. "History of the Flight Test Center."

79. Sanders, "Troubles," 32.

80. Ibid., 34.

81. Ibid., 33.

82. Ibid.

83. Ibid.

84. E. Eric Lincoln, *The Negro Pilgrimage in America* (New York: Bantam, 1967), 153–54.

85. Ibid., 155.

86. "Negro Astronaut Trainee's Score Too Low, NASA Says," (Washington, D.C.) *Evening Star,* 3 June 1965.

87. "Bias in Astronaut Choice Denied," *New York Times,* 3 June 1965; "Negro Passed Over in Astronaut Choice," 3 June 1965.

88. "Negro Astronaut Takes Issue With Air Force," *Bakersfield Californian,* 4 June 1965.

89. *Washington Post,* 4 June 1965.

90. "Astronauts Testing Endurance After Successful Walk in Space: Our Guy in the Sky Has a Taste for Space," *Milwaukee Journal,* 4 June 1965, 1.

91. Ibid.

92. Atkinson and Shafritz, *Real Stuff,* 103.

93. Ibid., 103–04.

94. Walter A. Pennino to Cheryl Aaron, 11 June 1965, File AFP, LBJ Center.

95. A. S. Hodgson, draft letter to Honorable Robert N. C. Nix, 30 April 1965, LBJ Center.

96. Robert R. Gilruth to NASA headquarters, "Captain Edward J. Dwight, Jr., USAF," 26 April 1965, LBJ Center.

97. "Bias Denied."

98. "Astronauts Lose Selves Over Africa," *Baltimore Sun,* reprinted in *NASA Current News,* LBJ Center.

99. Ibid.

100. Captain Edward J. Dwight, Jr., to President Lyndon B. Johnson, 30 September 1965, LBJ Center.

101. Paul M. Popple, Referral to NASA Administrator, "Capt. Edw. J. Dwight, Jr., USAF, Reveals Intention to Leave Military," 4 October 1965, LBJ Center.

102. Memorandum, "Letter to President Johnson, September 30, 1965—Captain Edward J. Dwight, Jr., October 15, 1965," File AF, LBJ Center.

103. NASA response to Capt. Edward J. Dwight, Jr., re: Colonel Cooper Intentions, 27 October 1965, LBJ Center.

104. Robert F. Freitag to Donald K. Slayton, "A Note to Deke Slayton: Letter to White House from Captain Edward J. Dwight, Jr., USAF, Negro Candidate for Astronaut Training," 23 November 1965, LBJ Center.

105. Schlesinger, *Robert Kennedy,* 232, 307.

106. Thomas U. McElmurray, telephone interview with author, 11 October 1991.

107. Ibid.

108. Ibid.

109. Ibid.

110. Atkinson and Shafritz, *Real Stuff,* 101.

111. McElmurray interview.

112. EJD interview.

113. McElmurray interview.

114. Lieutenant Colonel John Whitehead, USAF (Ret.), interview with author, 6 October 1991.

115. White, "The Sculptor," 55–58.

116. Brigadier General Charles E. Yeager, interview with author, 24 September 1992.

117. EJD interview.

118. White, "The Sculptor."

119. Ibid., 58.

120. Wolfe, *Right Stuff,* 366.

121. EJD interview.

122. J. Alfred Phelps, *Chappie: America's First Black Four-Star General, The Life and Times of Daniel James, Jr.* (Novato, Calif.: Presidio, 1991), 204–05.

123. White, "The Sculptor."

124. Ibid.

125. Ibid.

126. EJD interview and Freedom of Information Act (FOIA) responses the author received from a number of federal agencies tend to confirm this viewpoint.

127. William Stewart, retired archivist for the National Archives, telephone interview with author, 15 October 1990.

128. EJD interview.

CHAPTER 2

1. James L. Stokesbury, *A Short History of Air Power* (New York: Morrow, 1978), 281; and USAF Accident Summary, 8 December 1967, private collection of Mrs. Barbara Lawrence, Chicago.

2. USAF Accident Summary, 8 December 1967; *Astronautics and Aeronautics,* 7 December 1967, 371; letter, USAF Mid-West Office of Information, 29 April 1969, private collection of Mrs. Barbara Lawrence.

3. Jack Broughton, *Going Downtown: The War Against Hanoi and Washington* (New York: Orion, 1988), 47.

4. "History of the Flight Test Center," 74. The X-15 was one of a series of experimental, rocket-propelled aircraft built in the 1940s and 1950s. It provided important data on the control of a winged vehicle at high speeds and high altitudes. The X-15 program involved three aircraft completing 199 flights from 1959 to 1968, including 83 above the 50-mile boundary between air and space.

5. "History of the Flight Test Center," 156–58.

6. Broughton, *Going Downtown,* 48–49. See Bill Gunston and Mike Spick, *Modern Air Combat* (New York: Crescent, 1983), 178–79, for a discussion of lift and aerodynamic impact, and 116 for an explanation of boundary air for low-speed lift. This was achieved in the F-104 with blown flaps, blasted engine air at the landing setting, and drooped leading edges.

7. USAF Accident Summary.

8. Gen. J. P. McConnell to Captain Robert H. Lawrence, 20 June 1967, private collection of Mrs. Barbara H. Lawrence.

9. BL interviews. The following material reflects Mrs. Lawrence's impressions and recollections of the events of that day and of her

relationship with her husband and is also derived from telephone interviews with the author.

10. "Tragic Death of Air Force Major Robert H. Lawrence, Jr.," *The Congressional Record*, H16746, 12 December 1967.

11. Ibid.

12. BL interviews.

13. President Johnson to Barbara Lawrence, 14 December 1967, LBJ Library, Austin, Texas; "Memorial Scholarship Fund Established for Lawrence: First Negro Astronaut Killed in Air Crash," Bradley University *Hilltopics 57* (December 1967).

14. David Flores, "To an Astronaut: Last Rites for Maj. Robert Lawrence Honor Brilliant Career of Pilot-Scientist," *Ebony*, January 1968, 91.

15. Ibid., 94.

16. Ibid.

17. Ibid.

18. Ibid., 95.

19. Ibid.

20. JW interview.

21. Reverend Ben Richardson, "The Measure of a Man," eulogy delivered at the funeral of Maj. Robert H. Lawrence, Jr., USAF. Private collection of Mrs. Barbara Lawrence.

22. Blake Powers, "Space Personality: Robert Lawrence," *Space World*, December 1983, 21.

23. Bradley *Hilltopics*.

24. Flores, "To an Astronaut."

25. Manned Spaceflight Management Council, "Summary of Agreements and Actions," 12 September 1973, Box 1 (1973–1978), LBJ Center.

26. Ibid.

27. Atkinson and Shafritz, *Real Stuff*, 105.

28. Memorandum, "Minutes of NASA EO Meeting," 16 April 1974, and "EEO Quarterly Report to Chris Kraft," 22 March 1976, Box 1 (1973–1978), LBJ Center.

29. Ibid.

30. Ibid.

31. Ibid.

32. Nichelle Nichols in Miles, *Black Stars in Orbit*. The remainder

of this section describing Nichols's work with NASA is derived from that PBS documentary.

33. Nigel MacKnight, *Shuttle 2* (Osceola, Wis.: Motorbooks, 1986), 7–16.

34. Hoffman, *World Almanac,* 174.

35. "Postscripts," *Washington Post,* 19 December 1977.

36. "NASA Announces Selection of 35 Shuttle Astronauts," *Washington Post,* 17 January 1978.

37. James A. Michener, *Space* (New York: Random House, 1982), 359–64. The remainder of this segment is derived from this source.

38. "Careers Behind the Launchpad," *Black Enterprise,* February 1983, 59.

39. Carlow Byars, "Prospective Astronauts Visit Space Center," *Houston Chronicle,* 1 February 1978.

40. "New Black NASA Pilots Say Money is Well Spent," *Jet,* 2 February 1978.

41. "U.S. Women Astronauts May Orbit Within 3 Years," *Washington Star,* 17 January 1978, A5.

42. MacKnight, *Shuttle 2,* 18–22; David Shayler, *Shuttle Challenger* (New York: Prentice Hall, 1987), 8.

43. Shayler, *Shuttle Challenger,* 7–8.

44. Colonel Charles F. Bolden, Jr., USMC, astronaut, interviews with author, 16 July 1991 and 1992, LBJ Center. (Hereafter cited as CFB interviews.)

45. Stephen J. Lynton, "Frederick Gregory; Frederick Hauck," *Washington Post,* January 1978.

46. Charles Moritz, ed., *Current Biography Yearbook, 1984* (New York: Wilson, 1985), 29–32.

47. CFB interviews.

48. Miles, *Black Stars in Orbit.*

49. Colonel Guion S. Bluford, Jr., USAF, astronaut–mission specialist, interviews with author, 16 July 1991 and 23 September 1992, LBJ Center. (Hereafter cited as GSB interviews.)

50. Ibid.

51. MacKnight, *Shuttle 2,* 13–17.

52. Dixon P. Otto, *On Orbit: Bringing On the Space Shuttle* (Athens, Ohio: Main Stage Productions, 1986), 18–41.

CHAPTER 3

1. Dixon, *On Orbit,* 42; Shayler, *Shuttle Challenger,* 30.
2. GSB interviews; Shayler, *Shuttle Challenger,* 30–31.
3. Hannibal Guidice, author, sociologist, futurist, interview with author, 20 December 1991; Shayler, *Shuttle Challenger,* 30.
4. CMG interview.
5. Moritz, *Current Biography,* 30.
6. Ibid., 30–31.
7. GSB interviews.
8. Walter J. Boyne, *Phantom in Combat* (Washington, D.C.: Smithsonian Institution, 1985), 64.
9. GSB interviews. The remainder of this section is derived from these interviews.
10. CMG interview.
11. Shayler, *Shuttle Challenger,* 30; MacKnight, *Shuttle 2,* 26–33.
12. CMG interview.
13. Associated Press, "Shuttle—Sally Ride," message number 36, AP-WX-08-30-83, 1115 EDT. Courtesy NASA Archives, Washington, D.C.
14. CMG interview.
15. Shayler, *Shuttle Challenger.*
16. Jim Haskins and Kathleen Benson, *Space Challenger: The Story of Guion Bluford* (Minneapolis: Carolrhoda, 1984), 7.
17. CMG interview; Walter Leavy, "Lt. Col. Guion S. Bluford, Jr., Takes A Historic Step Into Outer Space," *Ebony,* November 1989, 169–70.
18. Haskins and Benson, S*pace Challenger,* 7; Otto, *On Orbit,* 44.
19. GSB interviews; Moritz, *Current Biography,* 31.
20. Leavy, "Bluford."
21. Haskins and Benson, *Space Challenger.*
22. Ibid.; MacKnight, *Shuttle 2,* 45.
23. Leavy, "Bluford," 163.
24. Associated Press, AP-WX-08-30-83, 1115 EDT.
25. GSB interviews.
26. Otto, *On Orbit,* 44.
27. GSB interviews.
28. John and Nancy Dewaard, *History of NASA: America's Voyage to The Stars* (New York: Exeter, 1984), 164–65.

29. GSB interviews.

30. MacKnight, *Shuttle 2*, 57–58.

31. Otto, *On Orbit*, 43–44.

32. Leavy, "Bluford," 162–70.

33. GSB interviews.

34. Ibid.; Otto, *On Orbit*, 44.

35. Ibid.

36. Shayler, *Shuttle Challenger*, 30–31; Sharon Begley, "NASA's Nighttime Spectacular," *Newsweek*, 5 September 1983, 69.

37. Moritz, *Current Biography*, 32.

38. Miles, *Black Stars in Orbit*.

39. CMG interview.

40. Moritz, *Current Biography*.

41. Gerald C. Lubanau, "He Changed a Lot of Things," *Newsweek*, 29 August 1983, 16.

42. Moritz, *Current Biography*.

43. Shayler, *Shuttle Challenger*.

CHAPTER 4

1. Dudley Clendinen, "Seven Lives/The Last Crew of the Challenger—Two Paths to the Stars: Turnings and Triumphs," *New York Times*, 9 February 1986.

2. Ibid.

3. Miles, *Black Stars in Orbit*.

4. Dr. Thomas Sandin, telephone interview with author, June 1991 and 2 September 1991. (Hereafter cited as TS interviews.)

5. Clendinen.

6. TS interview.

7. Steve Curwood, "Black Astronaut Speaks Out," *Boston Globe*, 29 April 1984, A-33.

8. TS interviews; Donald Edwards, telephone interviews with author, 29 February 1992 and September 1992. (Hereafter cited as DE interviews) Also see Clendinen and Curwood.

9. Curwood, "Black Astronaut."

10. Jay Buchanan, "Alumnus Astronaut Ron McNair Profiled in Magazine." *The Black Collegian*, December 1980/January 1981.

11. Clendinen, "Seven Lives"; Cheryl McNair, telephone interview with author, 24 November 1992. (Hereafter cited as CM interview.)

12. Constance Neyer, "Challenger Victim Recalled Fondly in City," *Hartford* (Conn.) *Courant*, 28 January 1987; Kim S. Hirsch, "To Many, McNair Was Friend and Hero," *New Haven* (Conn.) *Register*, 25 January 1987.

13. Clendinen, "Seven Lives"; CM interview.

14. Program, *Dedication Ceremonies. The Ronald E. McNair Building*, Massachusetts Institute of Technology, 5 December 1986.

15. Scott Shane, "Astronaut Sees Dreams Begin to Take Flight," *Greensboro* (N.C.) *Daily News and Record*, 22 November 1980.

16. Ibid.; TS interviews.

17. Clendinen, "Seven Lives"; CM interview. Also see Buchanan.

18. Bernadette Hearne, "Astronaut Loves Challenges," *Greensboro* (N.C.) *News and Record*, 22 January 1984, C-1, C-4.

19. Buchanan, "Is There a Future?"

20. Shane, "Astronaut Sees Dream."

21. Otto, *On Orbit*, 47–48.

22. Mae C. Jemison, M.D., telephone interviews with author, 30 January 1992 and 16 June 1992. (Hereafter cited as MCJ interviews.)

23. Otto, *On Orbit*, 53.

24. Hearne, "Astronaut Loves Challenges."

25. Buchanan, "Is There a Future?"

26. Curwood, "Black Astronaut," A-34.

27. NASA Video: *STS-11: Mission 41B*, LBJ Center.

28. Ibid.

29. Shayler, *Shuttle Challenger*, 32.

30. Ibid., 10.

31. NASA Video Resource Tape; Otto, *On Orbit*, 54.

32. Shayler, *Shuttle Challenger*, 12.

33. Ibid.

34. NASA Video; Otto, *On Orbit*, 54.

35. Ibid.

36. Miles, *Black Stars in Orbit*.

37. NASA Video.

38. Shayler, *Shuttle Challenger*, 13; Otto, *On Orbit*, 56.

39. Otto, *On Orbit*.

40. Miles, *Black Stars in Orbit*.

41. Shayler, *Shuttle Challenger,* 32.

42. Clendinen, "Seven Lives."

43. TS interviews.

44. Ibid.; Curwood, "Black Astronaut," A-33.

45. Tom Sandin, draft: "Presentation of Ron McNair at North Carolina A&T State University," 24 April 1984. Professor Sandin's private collection.

46. *MIT Dedication Program,* 5 December 1986.

47. CM Interview.

CHAPTER 5

1. Frederick D. Gregory, interviews with author, LBJ Center, 16 July 1991 and 30 April 1992. (Hereafter cited as FG interviews.)

2. Matthew Brennan, ed., *Hunter Killer Squadron* (Novato, Calif.: Presidio, 1990), 16; 23–24.

3. FG interviews.

4. Ibid.

5. Ibid.

6. Ibid. The remainder of this description of his youth is derived from those interviews.

7. John A. Garraty, ed., *Dictionary of American Biography, Supplement 4, 1946–1950* (New York: Scribners, 1974), 242–43.

8. "Police Power," *Time,* 16 August 1954, 82.

9. "Time of the Schools," *Time,* 27 September 1954, 60.

10. FG interviews. The rest of this section is derived from those interviews.

11. George Torres, *Space Shuttle: A Quantum Leap* (Novato, Calif.: Presidio, 1986), 68–69.

12. Ibid., 58–65.

13. Shayler, *Shuttle Challenger,* 45.

14. Ibid., 40.

15. *MIT Dedication Program,* 5 December 1986.

16. Shayler, *Shuttle Challenger;* STS-51B, *Post-Flight, Press Conference* NASA Videotape, JCS 866, LBJ Center.

17. "STS-44 Becomes a Shortened Duration Mission," *Countdown,* February 1992, 10; Shayler, *Shuttle Challenger,* 40.

18. FG interviews.

19. Shayler, *Shuttle Challenger,* 40; "STS-44 Becomes," 10.

20. STS-51B, *Post-Flight Video.*

21. FG interviews.

22. STS-51B, *Post-Flight Video.*

23. Otto, *On Orbit.*

24. John Blaha, "Space and People: An Astronaut's Story," *Countdown,* June 1992, 12–14.

25. FG interviews.

26. Blaha, "Space and People," 14.

27. FG interviews.

28. Otto, *On Orbit;* Oliver J. Lee, "Aurora Borealis," in *The World Book Encyclopedia,* vol. 1 (Chicago: Field Enterprises, 1963), 747–48.

29. FG interviews.

30. Ibid.

31. "Le Colonel Frederick Gregory Ravi de Son Séjour Malgache," *Midi Société,* 28 June 1990; "L'Astronaute Américain Frederick Gregory à Madagascar, *Madagascar,* undated; "L'Astronaute Américain Face à la Presse," *Tribune R.D.M.-USA,* undated. Courtesy USIA Office of Public Liaison.

32. Otto, *On Orbit;* Shayler, *Shuttle Challenger.*

33. Otto, *On Orbit,* 84.

34. Ibid.; STS-51B *Post-Flight Video.*

35. Otto, *On Orbit,* 86, 89, 92, 96.

36. Shayler, *Shuttle Challenger.*

37. Otto, *On Orbit,* 105.

CHAPTER 6

1. Albert Schlstedt, Jr., "Black Astronaut Overcame Self-Doubt; Found He Had 'Right Stuff,' " *The* (Baltimore) *Sun,* 12 August 1983, 9.

2. Deborah Kent, *America the Beautiful: South Carolina* (Chicago: Children's Press, 1990), 7–23; *The World Book Encyclopedia,* vol. 18 (Chicago: World Book, Inc., 1989), 649.

3. CFB interviews. The remainder of this description of his youth is based on these interviews.

4. Retired Judge Bennett, in a telephone interview with the author on 21 April 1993, remembered the incident clearly: "Couldn't find anyone in South Carolina to give Charlie an appointment, so I went to Hubert Humphrey"—Johnson's vice president. Bennett thinks Humphrey may have contacted Congressman Dawson in Bolden's behalf.

5. Graydon DeCamp, Paul Ilyinska, et al., *The Blue and Gold: The Annapolis Story* (New York: Arco, 1974), frontispiece, 4.

6. Ibid., 5–9.

7. CFB interviews.

8. DeCamp, Ilyinska, et al., *Blue and Gold,* 12–13.

9. Ibid., 28.

10. Colonel John Riley Love, USMC (Ret.), telephone interview with author, August 1992.

11. Annapolis Yearbook, 2d Battalion, 11th Company, 1968. Xeroxed pages courtesy Kelly Merrell, U.S. Naval Academy.

12. CFB interviews.

13. DeCamp, Ilyinska, et al., *Blue and Gold,* 122.

14. John de St. Jorre, Anthony Edgewater, et al., *The Marines* (New York: Doubleday, 1986), 68.

15. CFB interviews.

16. John Trotti, *Phantom Over Vietnam* (Novato, Calif.: Presidio, 1984), 205.

17. CFB interviews.

18. Oretha D. Swartz, *Service Etiquette,* 4th ed. (Annapolis, Md.: Naval Institute Press, 1988), 343–44.

19. CFB interviews.

20. "Biographical Data," Col. Charles F. Bolden, Jr., USMC, LBJ Center.

21. Gordon Swanborough and Peter A. Bowers, eds., *United States Navy Aircraft Since 1911,* 3d ed. (Annapolis, Md.: Naval Institute Press, 1968), 268–72.

22. CFB interviews; Stephen Coonts, *Flight of the Intruder* (Annapolis, Md.: Naval Institute Press, 1986), 220–40.

23. "Biographical Data," Charles Bolden, LBJ Center.

24. CFB interviews.

25. CMG interview.

26. CFB interviews.

27. Ibid.

28. Otto, *On Orbit,* 105.

29. CFB interviews.

30. Otto, *On Orbit.*

31. CFB interviews.

32. NASA Videotape, STS-61C, *Post-Flight Press Conference,* JCS 897, LBJ Center.

33. CFB interviews.

34. Otto, *On Orbit,* 106.

35. CFB interviews.

36. Ibid.

CHAPTER 7

1. John Noble Wilford, "Waking Up to a Nightmare as Technology Turns Killer," *Sacramento Bee,* 29 January 1986.

2. Shayler, *Shuttle Challenger,* 46.

3. Ibid.

4. "Challenger Liftoff Set for Today," *Sacramento Bee,* 28 January 1986, A-4.

5. Ibid.

6. Ibid.

7. Miles, *Black Stars in Orbit.*

8. Otto, *On Orbit,* 108; Bruce Desilva, "Teacher Saw Opportunity Not Danger in Flight," *Sacramento Bee,* 29 January 1986.

9. Shayler, *Shuttle Challenger,* 47.

10. Otto, *On Orbit,* 108.

11. China Altman, "Touring Band Witnessed Explosion," *MIT Tech Talk,* 12 February 1986.

12. GSB interviews.

13. CFB interviews.

14. MCJ interviews.

15. FG interviews.

16. Shayler, *Shuttle Challenger,* 46–49; MacKnight, *Shuttle 2,* 92–99.

17. Altman, "Touring Band."

18. Otto, *On Orbit,* 111.
19. FG interviews.
20. Miles, *Black Stars in Orbit.*
21. CFB interviews; CM interview.
22. Altman, "Touring Band."

CHAPTER 8

1. David Wiegand, "McNair Had Ties to City," *Cambridge* (Mass.) *Chronicle,* 30 January 1986.
2. Program, *Memorial Services for Dr. Ronald C. McNair,* Wesley United Methodist Church, Lake City, S.C.; manuscript of text, "Celebration of Life and Legacy of Dr. Ron McNair," Rev. Jesse Jackson. Courtesy Dr. S. J. Ahrens, Department of Physics, North Carolina A&T State University.
3. DE interviews.
4. Mark Glover, "Teachers Lose One of Theirs: McAuliffe Presence Had Schools Tuned In," *Sacramento Bee,* 29 January 1986, A-6.
5. Perie Longo, telephone interview with author, 15 October 1992 and California-Poets-in-the-Schools 1988 Poetry Anthology, *Under the Bride of Silence.*
6. Ibid.
7. Remarks by Dr. Paul E. Gray, "McNair Is Remembered," *MIT Tech Talk,* 26 February 1986, 8.
8. DE interviews.
9. Shayler, *Shuttle Challenger.*
10. Robert C. DiIorio, "Program Set for McNair Building Dedication," *MIT Tech Talk,* 19 November 1986, 1, 6.
11. MIT *Dedication Program,* 5 December 1986; Robert C. DiIorio, "Tributes Mark McNair Building Dedication," *MIT Tech Talk,* 10 December 1986, 1, 7.
12. Ibid.
13. Neyer, "Challenger Victim."
14. Weigand, "McNair Had Ties."
15. Neyer, "Challenger Victim."

CHAPTER 9

1. Leo Rennert, "We Mourn Seven Heroes: Space Program Will Continue, Reagan Says," *Sacramento Bee,* 29 January 1986, A-5.
2. "Reagans to Attend Texas Rites," *Sacramento Bee,* 30 January 1986.
3. MacKnight, *Shuttle 2,* 97.
4. GSB interviews.
5. CFB interviews.
6. FG interviews.
7. MCJ interviews.
8. Shayler, *Shuttle Challenger,* 52–53.
9. Ibid.
10. FG interviews.
11. CFB interviews.
12. GSB interviews.
13. Shayler, *Shuttle Challenger,* 53.
14. Ibid.
15. MCJ interviews.
16. Ibid.
17. Otto, *On Orbit,* 112.
18. MacKnight, *Shuttle 2,* 106–07.
19. Valerie K. Sorosiak to the author, 16 October 1992.
20. Teri DePriest, City of Jackson/Davis Planetarium to Dr. Thomas Sandin, 20 November 1986, private collection of Dr. Sandin.

CHAPTER 10

1. Hoffman, *World Almanac,* 175.
2. "Biographical Data," Frederick D. Gregory, USAF, LBJ Center.
3. MacKnight, *Shuttle 2,* 111; Torres, *Space Shuttle,* 113.
4. Torres, *Space Shuttle,* 4–9; CFB interviews.
5. CFB interviews.
6. NASA Videotape, STS-31, *Post-Flight Briefing,* LBJ Center.
7. Torres, *Space Shuttle,* 7–9.
8. Dianne William Hayes, "Astronaut Talks About Heavens to Star-Struck Students," *Anne Arundel County* (Md.) *Sun,* Annapolis, 12 June 1990; Bart Jansen, "Astronaut's Down-to-Earth Advice: Academy Grad

Tells Children to Buckle Down, Focus on the Future," *The Capital,* Annapolis, Md., 12 June 1990.

9. NASA Videotape, STS-44, *Post-Flight Conference Highlights,* 31 December 1991, LBJ Center; Dixon P. Otto, "STS-44 Becomes a Shortened-Duration Mission," *Countdown,* February 1992, 3.

10. Otto, "STS-44." The remaining discussion of this mission is derived from this source unless otherwise noted.

11. FG interviews.

12. Otto, "STS-44," 20–21.

13. "ATLAS-1 Explores the Atmosphere," *Countdown,* June 1992, 5.

14. CFB interviews.

15. "ATLAS-1," 6–7.

16. Ibid., 9.

17. Ibid.

18. Ibid., 2.

19. Blaha, "Space and People."

20. Bluford, "Biographical Data."

21. MCJ interviews.

CHAPTER 11

1. "Biographical Data," Mae C. Jemison, M.D., LBJ Center.

2. MCJ interviews. The remainder of this description of her youth is derived from this source.

3. Ibid.

4. Ibid.; press release, "Astronaut Jemison Finds Use for Dance, Drama Courses as Well as Her Science Education," Stanford University News Service, 12 September 1990.

5. MCJ interviews; "Jemison Says Teacher Tried to Persuade Her Not to Pursue Science," *Jet,* 16 November 1992, 36. The remainder of this segment is derived from these sources.

6. MCJ interviews.

7. Ibid.

8. Robert Ardrey, *African Genesis: A Personal Investigation Into the Animal Origins and Nature of Man* (New York: Dell, 1961), 361.

9. MCJ interviews.

10. Ardrey, *African Genesis,* 362–63.

11. MCJ interviews.

12. Ardrey, *African Genesis,* 361.

13. MCJ interviews.

14. "Dr. Mae Jemison Becomes First Black Woman in Space," *Jet,* 14 September 1992, 34–35.

15. "Spacelab-J Makes It 50 Flights," *Countdown,* September 1992, 27.

16. Ibid.

17. MCJ interviews.

18. Ibid.

19. Ibid.

20. "Spacelab-J."

21. "Spacelab-J"; "The Countdown Flowchart: STS Mission Profiles," *Countdown,* 1 January 1992, 10–11.

22. Karima A. Haynes, "Mae Jemison—Coming In from Outer Space," *Ebony,* December 1992, 121.

23. "Mission Profiles," 11.

24. Simeon Booker, "Ticker Tape, U.S.A.," *Jet,* 12 October 1992, 10; MCJ interviews.

25. Diana S. Goldin and Jonathan Weil, "Astronaut Ellen Baker and Cornell Medical College Zoom Out of This World," Office of Public Affairs, *The New York Hospital/Cornell Medical Center News Release,* 17 October 1989; MCJ interviews.

26. "Spacelab-J," 28.

27. NASA Videotape, STS-47, *Post-Flight Conference,* JCS 1278, LBJ Center Media Service Branch.

28. STS-47, *Post-Flight Conference,* JCS 1278; "Spacelab-J," 32.

29. MCJ interviews.

30. "Spacelab-J," 27.

31. STS-47, *Post-Flight Conference,* JCS 1278.

32. Haynes, "Mae Jemison," 120–23.

33. Ibid.

34. MCJ interviews.

35. "Space Capsules," *Countdown,* July 1992, 22.

36. Joseph D. Atkinson, Ph.D., telephone interview with author, 15 November 1992.

37. Ibid.

38. MCJ interviews.

39. Richard Steier, "It's 'Mae Day' as Marchers Honor Dr. King," *New York Post,* 20 May 1991.

40. Haynes, "Mae Jemison."

41. MCJ interviews.

42. Ibid.

43. "Astronaut Turns to New Horizons," *Sacramento Bee,* 7 March 1993, A-2.

44. As quoted ibid.

45. Booker, "Ticker Tape," 11.

46. "Mae Jemison Speaking at Howard University," Videotape from C-Span, 12 April 1993, copy in author's collection.

CHAPTER 12

1. Maria Hockema, "Bound for the Heavens," *The Mayo Alumnus,* undated, 16. Courtesy Texas Tech University, Lubbock, Texas.

2. Bernard A. Harris, M.D., interview with author, 16 July 1991, LBJ Center. (Hereafter cited as BAH interview.)

3. Russell C. Ewing, ed., "Arizona: The Grand Canyon State," *The World Book Encyclopedia,* vol. 1 (Chicago: Field Enterprises, 1963), 556.

4. Hockema, "Bound."

5. BAH interview; Hockema, "Bound," 18.

6. Ibid.

7. Biographical Data, Bernard A. Harris, Jr., M.D., LBJ Center, August 1990.

8. Hockema, "Bound," 19.

9. Ibid., 20.

10. BAH interview.

11. Hockema, "Bound," 21.

12. Ibid.

13. Ibid.

14. Ibid., 21–22.

15. Ibid.

16. NASA Press Kit, "Space Shuttle Mission STS-55: *Zweite Deutsche Spacelab Mission*," February 1993, 3.

17. NASA Publication NW-017/2-93, "STS-55 The Second German

Spacelab Mission," Flight Crew Operations, Johnson Space Center, February 1993, 1.

18. NASA Videotape, STS-55, *Crew Profiles*, VJSC1305A, LBJ Center.

19. NASA Press Kit, "Space Shuttle," 4.

20. Ibid., 25–26.

21. BAH interview.

22. Ibid. The remainder of this chapter is derived from this source and a special interview conducted 13 May 1993.

EPILOGUE

1. Charles Bolden, as of this writing, had been reassigned to the LBJ Space Center to participate in the training and planning associated with performing the duties of commander of the first Soviet-American space mission, scheduled for late 1993.

2. FG interviews.

3. Ibid.

4. Joe West, "Shrinking Air Force Still Mostly Young, White, Male," *Air Force Times,* 23 November 1992, 7.

5. Joseph D. Atkinson, interview with author, 15 November 1992. But the pay *is* substantial. Michael Ryan ("So You Want to Be an Astronaut," *Parade*, 14 February 1993, 7–8) pegs the annual salaries as ranging between $46,210 and $83,502, plus civil service protections, fringe benefits, and optional working conditions—not to mention a chance to see the world.

6. Colonel William Campbell, USAF (Ret.), telephone interview with author 14 November 1992. (Hereafter cited as WC interview.)

7. Kirk Spitzer, "Few Blacks Get Top Flying Jobs in Navy: Critics See Low Morale, 'Intangible' Bias," *Sacramento Bee,* 19 October 1992.

8. Ibid.

9. *Defense Personnel Manpower Center,* "Black Officer Distribution—Pilot and Navigator by Year vs. Total Officer Distribution—Pilot and Navigator by Year," Copy courtesy Capt. Edward Woodward, USAF (Ret.).

10. WC interview.

11. Phelps, *Chappie*, 280–81.

12. Donald B. Rice, secretary of the air force, "The Air Force and U.S. National Security: Global Reach—Global Power," June 1990. Copy courtesy Capt. Edward Woodward, USAF (Ret.).

13. Christopher Jencks, *Rethinking Social Policy: Race, Poverty, and the Underclass* (Cambridge, Mass.: Harvard University, 1992), 13, 67–68.

14. Michael D. Limonick, "Tomorrow's Lessons: Learn or Perish," *Time*, Fall 1992 (Special), 59–60.

15. Sylvester Monroe, "Breaking Out, Then and Now," *Time*, 5 October 1992, 59–60.

16. CFB interviews.

17. GSB interviews.

18. Susan Ribner and Dr. Richard Chin, *The Martial Arts* (New York: Harper and Row, 1978), 38.

19. Buchanan, *MIT Tech Talk*, 17 December 1980.

20. BAH interview; Miles, *Black Stars in Orbit;* MCJ interviews.

SELECTED BIBLIOGRAPHY

Books

Ardrey, Robert. *African Genesis: A Personal Investigation Into the Animal Origins and Nature of Man.* New York: Dell, 1961.

Atkinson, Joseph D., and Jay M. Shafritz, et al. *The Real Stuff: A History of NASA's Astronaut Recruitment Program.* New York: Praeger, 1985.

Boyne, Walter J. *Phantom in Combat.* Washington: Smithsonian Institute, 1985.

Brennan, Matthew. *Hunter Killer Squadron.* Novato, Calif.: Presidio, 1990.

Broughton, Jack. *Going Downtown: The War Against Hanoi and Washington.* New York: Orion, 1988.

Coonts, Stephen. *Flight of the Intruder.* Annapolis, Md.: U.S. Naval Institute, 1986.

Cunningham, Walter. *The All-American Boys.* New York: Macmillan, 1977.

Davis, Benjamin O., Jr., *Benjamin O. Davis, Jr., American: An Autobiography.* Washington, D.C.: Smithsonian Institution, 1991.

De St. Jorre, John, Anthony Edgewater, et al. *The Marines.* New York: Doubleday, 1986.

DeCamp, Graydon, and Paul Ilyinska, et al. *The Blue and Gold: The Annapolis Story.* New York: Arco, 1974.

Dewaard, John and Nancy. *History of NASA: America's Voyage to the Stars.* New York: Exeter, 1984.

Garraty, John A., ed. *Dictionary of American Biography, Supplement 4, 1946–1950.* New York: Scribners, 1974.

Gatland, Kenneth. *The Illustrated Encyclopedia of Space Technology: A Comprehensive History of Space Exploration.* New York: Salamander, 1981.

Gillcrist, Paul T. *Feet Wet: Reflections of a Carrier Pilot.* Novato, Calif.: Presidio, 1990.

Gunston, Bill, and Mike Spick. *Modern Air Combat.* New York: Crescent, 1983.

Haskins, Jim, and Kathleen Benson. *Space Challenger: The Story of Guion Bluford.* Minneapolis: Carolrhoda, 1984.

Hoffman, Mark S., ed. *The World Almanac and Book of Facts, 1991.* New York: Pharos, 1990.

Jencks, Christopher. *Rethinking Social Policy: Race, Poverty, and the Underclass.* Cambridge, Mass.: Harvard University, 1992.

Kent, Deborah. *America the Beautiful: South Carolina.* Chicago: Children's Press, 1990.

Lincoln, E. Eric. *The Negro Pilgrimage in America.* New York: Bantam, 1967.

MacKnight, Nigel. *Shuttle 2.* Osceola, Wis.: Motorbooks, 1986.

McNamara, Robert S. *The Essence of Security: Reflections in Office.* New York: Harper and Row, 1968.

Michener, James A. *Space.* New York: Random House, 1982.

Moritz, Charles, ed. *Current Biography Yearbook, 1984.* New York: Wilson, 1985.

Otto, Dixon P. *On Orbit: Bringing On the Space Shuttle.* Athens, Ohio: Main Stage Productions, 1986.

Phelps, J. Alfred. *Chappie: America's First Black Four-Star General, The Life and Times of Daniel James, Jr.* Novato, Calif.: Presidio, 1991.

Ribner, Susan, and Dr. Richard Chin. *The Martial Arts.* New York: Harper and Row, 1978.

Schlesinger, Arthur M., Jr. *Robert Kennedy and His Times.* New York: Ballantine, 1978.

Shayler, David. *Shuttle Challenger.* New York: Prentice Hall, 1987.

Sperber, A. M. *Murrow: His Life and Times.* New York: Freundlich, 1986.

Stokesbury, James L. *A Short History of Air Power.* New York: Morrow, 1978.

Swanborough, Gordon, and Peter A. Bowers. *United States Navy Aircraft Since 1911.* 3d ed. Annapolis, Md.: U.S. Naval Institute, 1968.

Swartz, Oretha D. *Service Etiquette.* 4th ed. Annapolis, Md.: U.S. Naval Institute, 1988.

Torres, George. *Space Shuttle: A Quantum Leap.* Novato, Calif.: Presidio, 1986.
Trotti, John. *Phantom Over Vietnam.* Novato, Calif.: Presidio, 1984.
Wolfe, Tom. *The Right Stuff.* New York: Farrar, Straus & Giroux, 1979.
Yeager, Chuck, and Leo Janis. *Yeager: An Autobiography.* New York: Bantam, 1985.

Periodicals and Documentaries

Blaha, John. "Space and People: An Astronaut's Story." *Countdown,* June 1992, 12–14.
Buchanan, Jay. "Alumnus Astronaut Ron McNair Profiled in Magazine." *The Black Collegian,* December 1980/January 1981.
Byars, Carlow. "Prospective Astronauts Visit Space Center." *Houston Chronicle,* 1 February 1978.
———. "NASA Announces Selection of 35 Shuttle Astronauts." *Washington Post,* 17 January 1978.
———. "Careers Behind the Launchpad." *Black Enterprise,* February 1983, 59.
———. "New Black NASA Pilots Say Money Is Well Spent." *Jet,* February 1978.
———. "U.S. Women Astronauts May Orbit Within 3 Years." *Washington Star,* 17 January 1978, A-5.
Clendinen, Dudley. "Seven Lives/The Last Crew of the Challenger—Two Paths to the Stars: Turnings and Triumphs." *New York Times,* 9 February 1986.
Curwood, Steve. "Black Astronaut Speaks Out." *Boston Globe,* 29 April 1984, A-33, A-34.
Ferris, Fred. "First Negro Designated Space-Flight Candidate." *Washington Post,* 31 March 1963, A-8.
———. "The Man and the Moon: Moon's OK With Me." *Afro-American Newspapers,* 17 September 1963.
———. "Urban League Cites Space Trainee." *New York Times,* 15 July 1963.
Flores, David. "To an American Astronaut: Last Rites for Maj. Robert

Lawrence Honor Brilliant Career of Pilot-Scientist." *Ebony,* January 1968, 90–95.

Hearne, Bernadette. "Astronaut Loves Challenges." *Greensboro* (N.C.) *News and Record,* 22 January 1984, C-1, C-4.

Hirsch, Kim S. "To Many, McNair Was Friend and Hero." *New Haven* (Conn.) *Register,* 25 January 1987.

Leavy, Walter. "Lt. Col. Guion S. Bluford, Jr., Takes a Historic Step into Outer Space." *Ebony,* November 1989, 162–70.

Limonick, Michael D. "Tomorrow's Lessons: Learn or Perish." *Time,* Fall 1992.

Lubanau, Gerald C. "He Changed a Lot of Things." *Newsweek,* 28 August 1983, 16.

Lynton, Stephen J. "Frederick Gregory; Frederick Hauck." *Washington Post,* January 1978.

Miles, William. *Black Stars in Orbit.* PBS documentary.

Mitchell, Emily. "Do the Poor Deserve Poor Schools?" *Time,* 14 October 1991, 60.

Monroe, Sylvester. "Breaking Out, Then and Now." *Time,* 5 October 1992.

Neyer, Constance. "Challenger Victim Recalled Fondly in City." *Hartford* (Conn.) *Courant,* 28 January 1987.

Obatala, J. K. "We Need to Correct a Space Age Injustice: America Can Still Have a Black Astronaut." *Los Angeles Times,* 21 March 1974, Part II, 7.

Powers, Blake. "Space Personality: Robert Lawrence." *Space World,* December 1983, 21.

Robinson, Louie. "First Negro Astronaut Candidate." *Ebony,* July 1963, 71–87.

———. "Negro Trainee Elated Over Space Role." *The* (Washington, D.C.) *Sunday Star,* 31 March 1963.

———. "John H. Glenn." *The World Book Encyclopedia,* vol. III (1962): 214d.

Sanders, Charles L. "The Troubles of 'Astronaut' Edward Dwight." *Ebony,* June 1965, 30–34.

———. "Negro Astronaut Trainee's Score Too Low, NASA Says." *The* (Washington, D.C.) *Evening Star,* 3 June 1965.

———. "Bias in Astronaut Choice Denied." *New York Times,* 3 June 1965.

———. "Negro Passed Over in Astronaut Choice." *Los Angeles Times,* 3 June 1965.

———. "Negro Astronaut Takes Issue With Air Force." *Bakersfield Californian,* 4 June 1965.

———. "Astronauts Lose Selves Over Africa." *NASA Current News,* Johnson Space Center, Texas.

Seymour, Gene. "Another Carved His Place in History." *Philadelphia Daily News,* 30 August 1983, 14.

Shane, Scott. "Astronaut Sees Dreams Begin to Take Flight," *Greensboro (N.C.) Daily News,* 22 November 1980.

Sharbutt, Jay. "Bigotry in Space." *Philadelphia Daily News,* 22 February 1990, 46.

Spitzer, Kirk. "Few Blacks Get Top Flying Jobs in Navy: Critics See Low Morale, 'Intangible' Bias," *Sacramento Bee,* 19 October 1992.

West, Joe. "Shrinking Air Force Still Mostly Young, White, Male." *Air Force Times,* 23 November 1992.

White, Frank III. "The Sculptor Who Would Have Gone Into Space." *Ebony,* February 1984, 55–58.

Government Documents

The Congressional Record. House H16746, 12 December 1967.

"History of the Air Force Flight Test Center, Edwards Air Force Base, Calif. 1 January–30 June 1961." K286.69–37. Air Force Historical Records Center, Maxwell Air Force Base, Ala. (Hereafter cited as AFHRC.

———. 1 July–31 December 1961. K286.69–37. AFHRC.

———. 1 January–30 June 1962. K286.69–38. AFHRC.

———. 1 July–31 December 1962. K286.69–38. AFHRC.

———. 1 January–30 June 1963. K286.69–39. AFHRC.

———. 1 July–31 December 1963. K286.69–39. AFHRC.

Initial Report, The President's Committee on Equal Opportunity in the Armed Forces: "Equality of Treatment and Opportunity for Negro Military Personnel Stationed Within the United States," 13 June 1963. John F. Kennedy Library, Boston, Mass.

USAF Accident Summary, 8 December 1967. Private collection of Mrs. Barbara Lawrence, Chicago.

Interviews

Atkinson, Joseph D., Ph.D., 15 November 1992.
Bennett, Judge L. Howard, 21 April 1993.
Bluford, Col. Guion S., Jr., USAF, 16 July 1991, 23 September 1992.
Bolden, Col. Charles F., Jr., USMC, 16 July 1991, 1992.
Campbell, Col. William, USAF, 14 November 1992.
Dwight, Edward J., Jr., 1990, 1991, 1992.
Dyer, Bernard, M.D., September 1991.
Edwards, Donald, Ph.D., 7 September 1991, 29 February 1992.
Graves, Curtis M., Ph.D., 23 October 1990, ET SEQ.
Gregory, Col. Frederick D., Jr., USAF, 16 July 1991, 30 April 1992.
Guidice, Hannibal, 20 December 1991.
Harris, Bernard A., M.D., 16 July 1991, 13 May 1993.
Hatch, Emmett, 2 July 1993.
Jemison, Mae C., M.D., 30 January 1992, 16 June 1992.
Lawrence, Mrs. Barbara, 25 September 1991, 22 October 1991.
Longo, Perie, 15 October 1992.
Love, Col. John Riley, USMC (Ret.), August 1992.
Macon, Frank, 1991.
McElmurray, Col. Thomas U., USAF (Ret.), 11 October 1991.
McNair, Cheryl, 24 November 1992.
Miles, William, September 1991.
Minorbrook, Scott H., 23 October 1991.
Sandin, Thomas, Ph.D., 2 September 1991, 13 September 1991.
Schweiker, Richard E., September 1991.
Shivers, Clarence, 1 October 1991.
Stewart, William, 15 October 1990, 2 May 1991.
Torres, George, June 1991.
Whitehead, Lt. Col. John "Mr. Death," USAF (Ret.), 8 September 1991,
    6 October 1991.
Yeager, Brig. Gen. Charles E., USAF (Ret.), 4 September 1992.

Letters

Ahrens, Stuart T., Ph.D., 7 August 1991, 3 September 1991.
Bluford, Col. Guion S., Jr., USAF, 26 August 1991, 2 December 1992.

Bolden, Col. Charles F., undated.
Brooks, Catherine Wood, 20 May 1991.
Dyer, Valerie, 1 June 1992.
Fort, Edward B., Ph.D., 9 July 1991.
Gumm, Cheryl, 18 October 1991.
Harris, Bernard A., M.D., 3 March 1992.
Haskins, Capt. Michael D., USN, 23 July 1991.
Lamb, Lawrence E., M.D., 10 November 1990.
Lawrence, Barbara, 27 September 1991.
Lee, Barbara A., 6 January 1992.
Manners, Myrna, 14 January 1992.
McDonald, W. M., 10 May 1991.
Merrell, Lt. (jg) Kelly L., USN, 23 July 1991, 20 August 1991.
Moore, Jeanne, 13 May 1991.
Morgan, James, 5 May 1992.
Mudd, Roger, 23 August 1991.
Payne, John, 10 January 1991.
Porter, Maura, 10 April 1991.
Prince, Carolyn W., 22 May 1991.
Rinkus, John J., 22 May 1991.
Rooney, Emily, 21 October 1992.
Saegasser, Lee, 31 December 1990.
Schneider, JoAnn, 18 November 1991.
Schwartz, Barbara, 16 January 1991, 1 March 1991, 10 June 1991.
Schweiker, Richard S., 4 October 1991.
Somerville, Vonda K., 23 May 1991.
Sorosiak, Valerie K., 16 October 1992.
Spinks, Barry L., 2 April 1992.
Stafford, Lt. Gen. Thomas P., 13 June 1991.
Underwood, Enos, 30 October 1991.
Wilson, John, 22 July 1991.

INDEX

Aaron, Cheryl, 32
Abrahamson, Gen. James A., 54, 58
Ace Moving Company, 76
Aerospace Research Pilot School (ARPS), 14
Africa, 210–12, 222–23, 239
African Medical Research and Education Foundation, 210
Aircraft types: A-1 SPAD, 125; A-6 *Intruder,* 145, 154–55; B-57, 5; C-130, 154; F-4C *Phantom,* 80; F9F *Cougar,* 154; F-104D *Starfighter,* 47–49; H-43F, 123–25; KC-135, 232; MiG, 155; P-39, 1; T-33, 21; T-34, 154; T-38, 74, 113, 231; SCA 737, 64; X-1, 64; X-15, 48
Air Force: Academy, 132–33, 203; chief lawyer of, 21; Command and Staff College, 244; Flight Test Center, 6; Institute of Technology, 90; Systems Command, 25
AK-47, 125, 156
Allen, Bob, 176
Allen, Joseph P., 76
Ames Research Center, 74, 230
Amherst University, 132
Anderson, C. Alfred, 85
Andrews Air Force Base, Md., 124
Annapolis. *See* U.S. Naval Academy.
Apollo-Saturn system, 72, 229
Apt, Jerome, 215, 217

Archer, Barbara, 129–30.
Arizona State University, 35
Armstrong, Neil A., 110, 184
ARPS Class IV, 25, 45, 47–48
Astronaut High School, 167
Atkinson, Joseph D., 221, 241
Atlantis, 191; and STS-44 mission, 195–200; and STS-45 mission, 200–03
Atmospheric Laboratory for Applications in Science (AT-LAS), 201–02
Attles, Rev. Dr. LeRoy, 106, 173, 178
aurora australis, 140–41
Austin, Lela M., 103
Australia, 161

Bakersfield Californian, 31
Baltimore Sun, 36
Baroflex experiment, 233
Bean, Alan, 63
Beethoven School, 206
Bennett, Judge L. Howard, 148
Bermuda, 107
Black Caucus, 97
Black Muslims, 10
Blaha, John, 191, 203
Bluford, Col. Guion S., Jr.: and first spaceflight, 77–78, 84–89, 91–96; assessment of *Challenger* accident by, 197; assessment of skills of as mission specialist, 203; childhood of, 79–80;

283